THE FIELD GUIDE FOR
SINGLE PARENTS

Praise for *The Field Guide for Single Parents*

"Hankin presents a comprehensive guide that offers workable solutions for pressing issues facing single parents . . . Hankin taps into the largely unspoken and ignored aspects of single parenting . . . [The] narrative voice is straightforward and no-nonsense, while still offering a sense of warmth and support that will likely come as a welcome relief to readers who are currently struggling . . . personal anecdotes strewn throughout are, notably, not merely success stories of children thriving in a one-parent household, and they, along with Hankin's considerate counsel, ultimately create a realistic and hopeful portrait of possibilities.

—*Kirkus Reviews*

"Pat Hankin's *The Field Guide for Single Parents* is the book I wish I'd had a decade ago... Hankin's writing style is clear, practical, and conversational, and reads like a chat with a knowledgeable, caring friend with lots of experience. . . . Hankin has a mature perspective that's grounded and necessary. . . . This guide effectively combines actionable suggestions with a tone that respects the reader's intelligence and experience, making it a reliable resource for those seeking constructive support. . . . Very highly recommended."

—*Jamie Michele for Readers' Favorite*

Hankin, a business consultant and single parent, and Ames, a family therapist, debut with an ambitious guide to single-parenting. The authors incorporate tips from their personal experiences (as when Hankin shares a chore chart she used with her daughter), and crowd-sourced advice from single-parent Reddit users, who offer insights on topics like letting dates sleep over and balancing child-rearing with college classes. Hankin counsels solo parents on paying for childcare, noting that lesser-known options . . . may be available, as well as on taking smart steps to secure their family's financial futures.

Those raising children alone face many trade-offs, she acknowledges; for example, tackling tasks with DIY methods like mending clothes instead of hiring help can save money but result in lost time. . . . When it comes to relationship management, Hankin notes single parents often struggle to find friendships in a couples-oriented world and advocates for using social media to find meetups to join. While Hankin doesn't linger long on any one subject, she gives readers plenty of ideas for forming their own single-parenting blueprints.

This will be a boon to readers looking for new approaches to solo parenting.

—*Publishers Weekly*

THE **FIELD GUIDE** FOR

SINGLE PARENTS

Practical Tips to Gain Control of Your Life

PAT HANKIN

with contributions from Jessica Ames, LICSW

Published by
Bold Bound Media LLC
CONCORD, MASSACHUSETTS
singleparentguides.com

ISBNs: 979-8-9927693-0-2 (Paperback)
         979-8-9927693-1-9 (Hardback)
         979-8-9927693-3-3 (Ebook)

Printed in the United States of America

for Charlotte

About the design of this book

This book has been designed for maximum accessibility for all readers. The chapter titles are set in Avenir, subheads in Roboto, and text in Palatino. Insets and special features are set in san serif fonts for obvious differentiation from the running text.

All the material in this book is left aligned to facilitate continuous reading. The overall font size, line spacing, and margins are larger to accommodate note taking as well as increase ease of reading. Sentences and paragraphs have been kept short in order to keep the reader moving smoothly through the text.

The intention of this book is to be comprehensive and useful, not appear intimidating. You can either progress from cover to cover or skip to the sections most useful to you.

The ebook version is completely customizable to your preferred settings and offers a multilevel table of contents as well as active hyperlinks to referenced websites.

Contents

Part 4. Relationships with Kids, Peers, and Potential Partners

Why and How to Use This Book

PARENTING BOOKS LINE SHELVES IN LIBRARIES and bookstores. If they don't presume the presence of a second adult, they sidestep the issue. None address single parenting and its unique challenges. Single parenting means you're on your own, whether you are a single parent by choice or by chance.

This book is for single parents and those who support them. It focuses on factors that contribute to single parents' well-being because this, in turn, affects their parenting. Managing well-being is the most effective way for single parents to help their children's security.

And the fact is that there are a lot of us—19 million by the 2023 American Community Survey Census data. We vary in age, gender, income, and education levels. Our reasons for being single parents run the gamut from being divorced, abandoned, or widowed to choosing to go solo. We incur the same costs as two-parent families, yet our hours available to earn and parent are cut in half. We pay a "single-parent tax."

My daughter is now finished with college. With life's ups and downs, and my fears of incorrectly parenting, she's made it to adulthood successfully. She has awesome friends, an education, and skills for independence.

I couldn't have written this book while in the throes of daily single parenting. I had to put some distance between those days and me. I had to step back and see what went well and what I could have done differently.

Still, this book would have been invaluable to me when I started on my journey of single parenting two decades ago.

I also seem to have survived single parenting intact. I am now retired from working in banks, where I spent my career while independently raising my daughter without any outside support. I learned a lot and now hope to pass on beneficial lessons to others. During the hands-on parenting journey, I also moderated an online community of 470,000 single parents.

Many academic publications I have read on the topic of single parenting acknowledge two problems that are intertwined: internal vulnerability and external stress. This book works to help with those two problems in ways experienced by single parents.

If you've ever wanted someone to stand shoulder to shoulder with you through tough times, this guidebook is it. With this *Field Guide for Single Parents*, I've heeded the expression "write the book you want to read."

> *"When I read articles about parenting struggles, the most common suggestion is to speak to your spouse, coparent, or partner, and that isn't the most helpful advice to those without any of those people."*
> —Reddit single-parent community member

Goals of *The Field Guide for Single Parents*

Despite our being a significant demographic, the media and greater society still don't know what to do with us. Should we be praised, criticized, pitied, blamed, or ignored?

This book, written by a single parent for single parents, answers that question. It will:

- Give you skills to design your own best life by using knowledge from others who have been there.

- Let you know you are not alone.

- Share stories of resilience.

- Address issues that no one wants to talk about.

- Source the crowd's wisdom for recommendations for single-parent problems.

- Bust myths about single parents.

- Demonstrate that single-parent families of all economic levels can achieve goals and live well (or at least less stressfully).

We'll achieve these goals by sharing:

Stories. Humans, as natural storytellers, learn best with context.

Lessons learned. I like to think I raised my child well and gave her a magical childhood. But I also have enough distance from it to have collected a list of things I would have done differently. You have the benefit of those lessons learned here in this book.

Strategies. Everyone's situation is different. However, some approaches to problems can be universal, and those are the strategies I share here.

Other parents' voices. Throughout this book, I'll be quoting members of the online community of single parents that I was fortunate enough to help moderate for many years.

How to Use This Book

Our circumstances may vary widely, but single parents have four major needs in common: self-compassion (which includes a team of helpers for you and your children), more time, enough money, and healthy relationships with our kids and our peers.

Those four imperatives serve as the organizing principle for the book as a whole. Like being a single parent, this book starts and ends with you.

- **Part 1** focuses on keeping yourself healthy and (relatively) sane.

- **Part 2** addresses the single parent's biggest challenge: creating and managing time.

- **Part 3** is all about money: how to get it, spend it wisely, and, yes, save it.

- **Part 4** is about your relationships: with your kids, your family and friends, potential romantic partners, and, ultimately, yourself.

And because I know just how time starved you always are, I've chunked this book out to provide helpful advice and resources in fifteen-minute increments.

Fact based for decision-making, this book covers crucial topics from work and childcare to relationships, vacations, and finances. Each chapter is meant to stand alone, but I think you will get more out of it if you read it through first and then refer back to it as needed.

As a guidebook, it points out optional routes, must-see sites, and even a few reviews. I hope you find it a helpful companion on your journey through single parenthood.

PART 1

Keeping Yourself Healthy
(and Relatively Sane)

CHAPTER 1

The Tao of Single Parenting

Less Is More

The "Fifteen-Minute Parent": A Gift for Single Parents

Adults Ask for Help

Put a Floor Under It

Respite Comes in Lots of Ways

One Need at a Time

The Right Team Is Everything

Choose Your People Wisely

I DEVELOPED THESE FIVE PRINCIPALS of single parenting through years of good and bad decisions and a lot of research with our brethren of fellow singletons.

1. Go easy on yourself (and others for that matter).
   We're all imperfect. Keep trying.

2. Abandon perfection.

3. Acquire data.

4. Achieve big changes through small steps.

5. Listen without jumping to a solution.

Common challenges endure among all parents, but the single parent faces these alone with the full financial and emotional weight of the decision. Single parents don't have anyone in their life to take for granted. Not financially, emotionally, or physically.

Some may have an engaged coparent who can share a burden. Some may be lucky *not* to have a coparent who screws things up. I am not here to debate the exceptions. I want to let you know that this book is for single parents and is a representation of a partner who will stand with you.

LESS IS MORE

In the 1950s, a British pediatrician coined the term "good enough mother." The pediatrician and psychoanalyst noticed in his work that a child could benefit when their parent made "manageable" mistakes. Children can learn to live in an imperfect world. The goal of parenting is not to live perfectly; it's to be human.

This idea refers to mistakes *after infancy*, such as:

- Times we don't respond right away

- Times we don't give them our undivided attention

- Times we feed them dinner, and they don't want to eat

- Times we make them share toys when they don't want to

Being "good enough" prepares children to function in a society that will frustrate and disappoint them regularly. A good rule of thumb is to let yourself finish what you are doing before responding to them. At whatever age. It teaches children that parents (as well as others) have lives, too. In small ways, every day, it teaches children that the world doesn't revolve around them.

THE "FIFTEEN-MINUTE PARENT": A GIFT FOR SINGLE PARENTS

If there are "fifteen-minute managers" and "fifteen-minute cooks," we can have "fifteen-minute parents." In all seriousness, the approach acknowledges our major deficits of time and resources. It allows us to feel successful as parents without a massive amount of time commitments. I read so many posts online from parents feeling guilty about the amount of time they can actively play with a young child. This mainstream theory gets you off the hook.

We could even go with the "five-minute parent," learning to fuel your child and yourself with short interactions (multiple times per day). This is an extension of the parent-child interactive therapy concept. Whether you have five minutes or fifteen, invite your child to lead a conversation. You can reflect back to them or describe their actions or thoughts with enthusiasm. A child at every age wants to feel heard, and this is a simple technique that plays well with time-starved single parents. (Jessica Ames, LICSW)

ADULTS ASK FOR HELP

The struggle is real for single parents. The always-on, complicated juggling act; social bias; and challenges with time and money make it understandable that some days feel dark.

Asking for help is a good thing, even if it is a vent on social media. Perhaps you relate to one or more of these online posts:

"Going through a divorce and custody parenting plan. I have days that I'm emotionally exhausted."

"I've had no support since my son's been born; I have depression and anxiety."

Getting and keeping perspective through the experience of others will help keep the inner critic at bay and let you survive another day. Holding onto the tiny victories ("the car turned on and so did the lights") can refill your energy tank.

That's why, *selectively*, social media can be a source of useful advice and resources. Those who have "been there" have helpful suggestions. From a Reddit single-parent community user:

> *"Getting some time and a break makes a huge difference in my mood, and it's easy to fall into depression when I haven't had it for a while. Having a pause to breathe, even if it's a little while, really helps my mental health. . . . You might be surprised if you reach out to anyone [to help]. . . . Hire a sitter for some time. If it's not in your budget, many local churches have free programs."*

PUT A FLOOR UNDER IT

Medication, therapy, meditation, and finding community. On their own or in combination, these four actions provide a floor to support you.

Neuroscience has made tremendous strides in the last decade. We have more information than ever on how the brain works and what can get in the way. In the face of this, we've developed tremendous therapies—both verbal and pharmaceutical—to help push away barriers in moving toward our goals.

Single parents have cited medication as supporting them to implement healthy changes in their life. No one can take care of a child if their brains are misfiring and causing serious depression. But I understand resistance to a dependency on chemical solutions and do know of some who treat conditions such as attention deficit hyperactivity disorder (ADHD) with strict exercise and diet. Some add coaching to the mix. Or talk therapy. A later section in this book discusses therapy in more detail.

How My Mom Showed Me the Value of Asking for Help

My mom has never shied from asking for help, especially from people even more knowledgeable on the subject than her. Feeling sick? Call the doctor's office, they will know better. Feeling confused on a math problem? Ask a peer tutor. Cat acting out of control? Ask a cat behavioral expert what they think. They've already done all the hard work for you in learning the problems and solutions.

It wasn't until I experienced shopping with friends' parents that I realized it could be so . . . time-consuming. I'll never forget wandering the endless store aisles while my friend's mom hunted down a singular item. "How silly," I remember thinking out loud to my friend, "when it would be so simple just to ask for help." My friend was baffled, yet the concept was so familiar to me. It was then I realized the countless hours my mom had gained for us by simply putting her pride aside

"I do know what worked for me, and that was getting into therapy. I am on state insurance, and if you call [the insurance company], they can give you a list of places that accept your insurance and get set up with a therapist . . . I wish I would have done it sooner."
—Reddit single-parent community member

Meditation as a means of calming anxiety and creating emotional support has been around for millennia. Focusing the mind on a narrow word, thought, or function lets one interrupt swirling thoughts and worries. It clears a path. I know several single parents who find this technique enormously helpful for their anxiety. It has never clicked for me. I can't sit still that long, but for others, it is life-changing.

and asking an employee for assistance. Some hours, she explained, that could be better spent with family or earning capital.

Those hours cut to minutes stuck with me. In college, when peers would pull their hair out over seemingly unsolvable problems for days, I reduced stress by asking for help when I was stuck or would rebalance my class deliverables by petitioning for extensions when too many deadlines loomed simultaneously. "Professors (and managers) are willing to work with you to smooth out your workload. They just don't want to be asked at the last minute. Show them you are proactively managing your life," mom would say. The time I gained was put back into my work for better understandings of subject concepts versus wasting time on stress.

Whether stuck on a math problem or suffering from mental health issues, take my mom's advice: ask for help.

—Charlotte

The message here is that you have alternatives to establish support for yourself and to take back your life.

> "Mindful **meditation** helped in the beginning; it took a while to get into the groove, but it was the first step for me."
> —Reddit single-parent community member

View help as a step in making a good life for your children. Asking for it should not be a source of humiliation or shame: It's about finding a better future. In fact, the only thing that can reflect badly on you is if you do nothing to help yourself.

*"When things are too hard, I look for help. Women's shelters, churches, moms' groups, rec centers, libraries, etc. **It is so many people's dreams to help people.** Find them!"*
—Reddit single-parent community member

DIFFERENT PATHS TO PEACE

India did not gravitate to talk therapy. She found the process and commentary tone-deaf to her situation. Instead, she discovered meditation and attends classes and retreats for her "floor." When I interviewed her for this book, she was on her way to a local weekend retreat.

Her story also supports the theory that "visioning" is a useful mechanism. She did get the perfect house with a child. Just not the perfect partner.

RESPITE COMES IN LOTS OF WAYS

This may clear your head and provide you with perspective to help yourself. In my own single mother's lowest moments, she couldn't get out of bed. An aunt came to stay for a week and took care of my siblings and me. I remember it as a turning point. Another member points out the same:

"CPS [Child Protective Services] isn't just for turning your kids over. They may be able to offer respite or point you in the direction of services/support. Ideally, they want to keep families together. No shame in calling to chat."
—Reddit single-parent community member

What single parents need is space to breathe and think, which is hard to come by when there is always something to be done and few ways to pass off responsibilities. This was particularly acute for me with full-time work and no coparent or family. I was blessed with a few friends who could pitch in once in a while. I remember each of those moments. Which brings me to another piece of advice.

ONE NEED AT A TIME

"I try to focus on getting through one tiny moment at a time and not overthinking about the future; otherwise, I get scared and overwhelmed." —Reddit single-parent community member

Later on in this book we get more sophisticated about goal-setting and practical ways to achieve goals. The shortcut answer at this point is to start with small steps. Every motivational book, speaker, or podcast will tell you to start small. Look up the phone number. Put the phone number by the computer. Make a call. Each a day apart. Every. Single. Person. Will tell you this. That's good. Small actions are about all we can handle with our lives.

Start with one of the basic needs like housing or food. Take small steps. Once you nail those you can move up the hierarchy of needs. If housing, food, and childcare are secure, you can move off the base of the triangle and work on your income to build feelings of safety. And so on.

THE RIGHT TEAM IS EVERYTHING

Short and sweet: You have to build your support system. While this is good advice for every adult, it's critical for single parents and lifesaving for solo parents. If you are having a tough day or need to resolve a parenting issue, a friendly voice on your team makes all the difference.

Recently, I was stranded at home with a bad back, and the cat started exhibiting signs of serious illness. Since it was Saturday, my local vet was closed until Monday. I couldn't get her to the vet, anyway, and my usual suspects to help weren't available. In a spark of genius, I called my previous vet, who had retired to Florida. He called me right back and talked me through the issues and what to watch for. I held it together until that Monday when I would feel well enough to drive. That vet had been the right team member.

Beyond friends and family, you need to start building your team of people in the most important areas of your life: health, education, legal, and financial (see chapters 4–8 for more on this).

These relationships are everything. They will stand with you in conflict, help manage your family's health, guide decisions when problems arise, and serve as objective grown-ups who can stand with you.

Some of these suggestions—such as having a lawyer—may feel far-fetched, but sooner or later, you will need one or several. You will need a lawyer for buying a house, drawing up a will and estate plan, and, sadly, maybe for litigation.

The quality of your relationship with these team members matters. Relationships get built over time. Research has correlated good health outcomes with the length of a doctor relationship, for example. I have had the same dentist since college, primary care physician since I was thirty, and plumber for twenty years. Those long-term relationships have been comforting and tinged with consistent honesty. When you find someone who works, stick with them—but if the relationship slides backward, move on.

It's OK to change your long-term relationships. While it makes sense to find someone deep into their legal career, as you age you may want someone closer to your kids' age to help later on. A dentist who has developed tremors (an occupational hazard) may be a sign they will retire soon, and you need to start looking around.

I've changed my family attorney twice, used three retirement plan companies, and hired multiple electricians. I kept my hairdresser for years until she got judgmental about my teen's choice of hairstyle and wardrobe.

I moved on. My daughter's first pediatrician couldn't remember her name or health after ten years of being a patient. I felt something was "off" and transferred to another doctor in the practice.

Don't stick with your parents' team. I have had to fire every one of my parents' team members for their outdated and, frankly, lazy approach to the relationship. Choose someone who cares about you.

CHOOSE YOUR PEOPLE WISELY

A commonplace saying is that we are the average of our five closest friends. Modern social network theory expands that to friends of friends. We pick up good health habits or bad financial habits from those we associate with the most. The same applies to personal growth.

As single parents, we can't be too choosy about friends, since we are limited to those who will accept us. However, if you look at your inner circle and see chaos, it may make you feel better about yourself in comparison, but it doesn't give you much chance to grow.

But if you look to your five (or twenty-five) people and see traits you admire, such as healthy relationships, gratifying careers, financial stability, or good parenting, then you have a support group you can learn from.

View expanding your social circle as practice to emerge from your past and experience different types of people.

You might try reaching out online or in person to other single parents, building a community of mutual support. Until you do, take some strength from one online single mom's words:

"There are saner people to be around, ways to improve sleep, and fun things to do. I know, sounds like fake news, doesn't it?"
—Reddit single-parent community member

CHAPTER 2

The Art of Well-Being in the Face of Stress

Managing Stress

Preempt Preventable Stress

Keep It Movin'

STRESS IS RIGHT UP THERE WITH DEATH and taxes as an unavoidable fact of life. But how you identify it, manage it, preempt it, and move through it—I hope to help you with these processes in this chapter.

MANAGING STRESS

Sometimes a look back lets us see forward. A client once posted a work memo that she found from the 1980s. The old typewriter font surprisingly comforts me, and the message—**WARNING: CONTENTS MAY EXPLODE UNDER PRESSURE!**—is as urgent today as it was forty years ago. I will break down the advice in this chapter because it is valuable.

"Take action to manage stress before it manages you," the internal memo implores.

STRESS
WARNING: CONTENTS MAY EXPLODE UNDER PRESSURE

PRIME Employee Assistance Program

If, under stress, you feel like throwing the typewriter (or boss) out of the window, what can you do to relieve the situation? We all handle or mishandle stress in our own way. How to channel stress toward achievement, integrate life's difficulties into challenges and opportunities -- these are essentials of happy, vibrant living. Perhaps some of these suggestions will be appropriate for you.

1. Confide in someone whom you can trust. Talking often relieves the strain. Others may help you to see what you can do about a problem because they aren't as emotionally involved as you are.

2. Get away from a problem for awhile. You may find when you come back to it that you have gained renewed strength to face it.

3. Own up to your fears. Everyone has fears. By confronting the fact that you are afraid of something, you may be able to deal with it better.

4. Compromise with other people. If you yield, others will too, and the result will be a relief from tension and a feeling of satisfaction.

5. Do something for someone else. You will feel better about yourself and will give yourself a respite from your personal problems.

6. Don't brush off a problem by telling yourself, "I'll snap out of it," or "It's them, not me." Bring the problem out in the open, and you will be more likely to rid yourself of it.

7. Realize that people who feel let down by the shortcomings of those around them are really let down about themselves. So, don't criticize others. Get off their backs and you will wind up off your own.

8. Give others a break. Competition is contagious, but so is cooperation. When you become a little less inflexible toward another person's desires, you very often make it easier for yourself. If others no longer feel that you are a threat to them, they become much less of a threat to you.

9. Go out and greet the world instead of sulking at home.

10. Take some time out to have fun. Find pleasure and build it into your schedule. Relaxation absorbs pressure like a sponge absorbs water

11. Remember that pressure is wound-up energy. If you know how to deal with it, you can use it to your advantage.

12. Be compassionate toward others and toward yourself. It is part of the challenge of learning to live -- not problem-free, but rather amid problems with grace.

It goes on to offer old-timey advice that is equally relevant to our modern day:

"Confide in someone you trust." Note that it doesn't say to complain. It's "confide." Be circumspect. Those closest to you are most likely to keep your confidence.

"Get away from the problem for a while." Do something to interrupt the trajectory of anxiety. A walk with your child can change your scenery and refocus your attention. Catch yourself if you go out to dinner with a friend and end up talking about your kids. Not really getting away, is it? More like irony. Also, avoid "futurizing," where we all become soothsayers and predict a scary future. (Funny how our prognostications are rarely optimistic.) Here's a lesson: the future can be rosy, too.

"Compromise with other people." Everything is negotiable. If it doesn't cause a cascade of negative consequences, let your ex-partner change their schedule once in a while, making sure you are flexible in exchange for something you need. If your employer can't afford more salary, think of nonsalary benefits that can function as "in kind." One potential employer couldn't pay me a sign-on bonus, so I negotiated for relocation expense reimbursement, something they could approve. You might ask for time off or flexible hours.

Make a list of things other people *can* do and see if any of those items can substitute for what *you* need. Ask for what you'll need in exchange for the compromise *in the moment*. Don't keep score and hope the other person will remember.

"Do something for someone else." We can update that to "commit to small acts of kindness." A friend 1,300 miles away was going through the worst hard time. I searched through a pile of random greeting cards in my paper organizer. A bunch sat, unloved because of their juvenile designs, like a jumping frog and the quote "Wish I Could Just Hop On Over." I marked them up with relevant sentiments and mailed them, a card every week for months. (Have a book of stamps around, by the way.) This was a small way to show I cared and was thinking of my friend during the difficult time.

"Don't brush off the problem." The first step to finding a solution is acknowledging the problem. "Yes, I am worried about my child's requests and the costs. What are some options I have?" Once you face the issue, it will be easier to break it down into manageable steps.

"Don't criticize others." Assume that most people are already self-critical. Chances are, telling someone what they are doing wrong is not news. It's just going to make them feel worse. Releasing stress by giving it to someone else is a short-term solution and is not likely to build relationships.

"Give others a break. Competition is contagious but so is cooperation." The world doesn't work perfectly, people aren't perfect, and "good enough" is a perfect description of a "good parent." The meals are simple but nutritious? That's good enough. Another adult minding your child is a safe person? That's good enough.

"Go out and greet the world instead of sulking at home." News alert! Pity parties elevate stress. If you want time out to lick your wounds, schedule it. Put it on your calendar. "From 5–6 p.m. on my commute home, I'll feel sorry for myself." But at 6 p.m., it stops. Then you won't feel deprived or let the negative thoughts take over your psyche.

"Take some time out to have fun." The *in*operative word here is "time," something single parents have in the negative column. It's less about a rip-roaring night out with your mates at a bar and more about "Now for Something Completely Different" (with apologies to Monty Python). My colleague Manila crafts jewelry to "turn off her analytical brain." I make kitschy crafts that I can then send to friends going through hard times. Like "get away from the problem for a while," time out interrupts the stress trajectory. Here's where your scratch paper comes in for list-making. Write out a list of fun stuff and keep it on hand when the occasion arises.

"Remember that stress is wound-up energy. You can use it to your advantage if you know how to deal with it." In modern jargon, act the way you feel and visualize having a store of energy to unleash on a project, task, or activity. Tackle the weekly chores, take the kids for a walk, or cook up a storm. Turn stress to your advantage.

LAYING EXPECTATIONS

I lay supine on the physical therapist's treatment table while the seven-foot-tall man pulled on my left leg in an attempt to provide some relief from the bone-on-bone grinding in my left hip. A problem since college days, I had plenty of opportunity to learn from physical therapists over the years. Most of the guys were athletes, having experienced high-stakes, win-or-lose stresses. I gave it a shot. "Gaston," I queried to the giant, "you were a baseball pitcher. At such a young age, how did you deal with the fear of failure? After all, all eyes are on the pitcher for those games."

He thought, but not for too long. "I used to get really upset when I would place a ball perfectly and others made errors," he said. "A friend's dad was a sports psychologist. He put things in perspective. He told me, 'Once you put the ball in play, expect three things to go wrong.' That changed my view of the situation, taking away stress in the process."

We didn't talk for a minute or so while I chewed on the impact of that lesson. "That's a very Zen outlook," I replied.

Gurus are everywhere. Even on the treatment table.

"Be compassionate toward others and toward yourself. It is part of the challenge of learning to live—not problem free but amid problems with grace." Everyone makes mistakes. Don't beat yourself up, and don't be so hard on others. Instead, forgive the trespass and cut everyone some slack. Move on. And if anyone apologizes to you, accept it. Don't smugly declare moral victory. It's about getting along, not being right.

PREEMPT PREVENTABLE STRESS

Layoffs, pandemics, sick babysitters: These are the stressors that we can do little to prepare for. But there are other foreseeable and recurring challenges—such as running out of food, gifts for an upcoming birthday, or deciding what to wear—that you can proactively prevent.

Best of all, you don't have to be super organized to do it. In fact, prepurchased gifts or mass-produced baked goods are for those who are *not* well organized. Because you have gifts on hand, you don't have to remember to reciprocate. Nor do you have to know when disaster is going to strike. You just need to know that something somewhere is going to happen and prepare for it. This can feel like time (and money) in the bank.

Easy Ways to Prevent Stress

Here are some ideas for how to fend off those preventable stressors.

Get Rid of Stuff

Less crap = less energy to manage. Excess toys, unwanted gifts, extra clothes, or (my thing) books. It all takes time and energy to manage.

Let Go of "Perfect"

While raising my daughter, I never did anything as well as I would have liked. My home wasn't "designed," but it was generally neat enough for inner calm. A daycare may not engage as I would, but if my daughter enjoyed it, then "good enough." If a member of my support team did what I paid them for, then that was "good enough."

REDUNDANT SYSTEMS

This is a cause for a lot of eye-rolling from my daughter. Maybe it was my Red Cross training or years of living in disaster zones, but I developed a network of "just-in-case" systems to support me. I will do anything to avoid stress. I have put in place a way to get through the "uh-ohs" to minimize fallout when things don't go as planned.

Sometimes it's a redundancy like canned foods in the panty or a distributed function like mechanics to fix your car. Modern business systems employ duplicates and distributed systems in computer systems. In fact, they are mimicking nature, which uses both to survive and evolve. We have two strands of DNA. We have muscles that compensate when another is injured.

Buy the Obvious Ahead of Time

Extras on hand avoid the last-minute "I need to bring a birthday gift" panic. We had a "present box" of gifts picked up in advance when my daughter was young and attending many birthday parties.

A bad weather forecast immediately creates panic buying. I've never understood this. I lived in Florida. We knew a tropical storm would happen, just not when. In weather-related situations, milk and bread are the first to go. Instead of facing the prospect of empty supermarket shelves, freeze a loaf of bread and a carton of milk (yes, it's OK).

CREATE A CAPSULE WARDROBE

A capsule wardrobe is generally six to ten pieces that can make up a variety of outfits in rotation. The strategy assumes you use clothes in the same color family. If so, here is a system for getting a month's worth of outfits for work from nine pieces of essential clothing in one color family.

Start with these nine pieces each season: two blazers/sweaters, three tops, and four bottoms (skirts/slacks/jeans, etc.). I live in a four-season climate and did this with clothes I had on hand. My black blazer goes with bottoms in the gray, black, and denim categories. Many browns or navy blues go as well with the top as the accent color. This is a good activity when you have an hour one evening and want to see "what goes with what."

You establish a clothing rotation that won't repeat the combinations for a month. It reduces stress to have this preplanned and eliminates one less morning task. Here are the combinations:

Blazer #	1	1	1	1	1	1	1	1	1	1	1	1	2	2	2	2	2	2	2	2	2	2	2	2
Top/shirt #	1	1	1	1	2	2	2	2	3	3	3	3	1	1	1	1	2	2	2	2	3	3	3	3
Bottoms #	1	2	3	4	1	2	3	4	1	2	3	4	1	2	3	4	1	2	3	4	1	2	3	4

No combination is repeated for twenty-four days. Try it for a season and see. Assign each piece of clothing one of the numbers above. You can write it on the clothing tag with a permanent marker. With the combination chart above, you can tape it to the inside of your closet and have a stress-free day of pulling out articles of clothing that match the code above.

—Amy Dacyczn

KEEP IT MOVIN'

Single parents could all use more time, money, and support. But if we want to solve this problem, we can focus on taking tiny steps forward.

I attended a charity breakfast benefiting a homeless coalition. The keynote speaker was Dr. Maya Angelou. But it was the opening speaker whose message has stayed with me all these years later. Given by a formerly homeless single mother, her mantra to get through tough times exhorted the audience to "keep it movin'." As she recounted her journey to, through, and out of homelessness, this self-talk would motivate her to keep putting one foot in front of the other.

Here are some suggestions to "keep it movin'":

Start small. Make a cup of tea.

Enjoy teeny, well-timed treats. I like the studies suggesting that pairing small immediate rewards with a task work well.

Find your inner motivation. Write out your values and look at *why* you are doing something. If those values include a chaos-free home, then be OK with letting things drop. Kids don't need baths every day. Get them to help with chores. Don't fold clean clothes—put them in a hamper and let others take it from there. (Today's plastic clothes don't wrinkle much, at any rate.) Don't focus on *should*, focus on *might*. What you decide at this point is up to you.

Look for collaboration. Phone a friend for brainstorming or help. A relative confided in me that she was worried about becoming a hoarder. A few months later, I went and helped her organize her home.

Give yourself a break. I admit to difficulty with this one. I am my own worst critic. Maybe you are, too. Shut down the negative voice in the back of your head by reminding yourself of your awesomeness as someone who manages it all. Don't say anything to yourself you wouldn't say to someone else.

Take stock of what is going right. The lights went on when you flicked the switch. No dunning notices arrived today. Your child passed the midterm. The process is simple, and it takes practice. I'm working on it, too.

Know you are not alone. The idea of all of us trying and failing and trying again carries me to the end of a project (and to the end of this topic). Years ago, I was trying to quit smoking and kept failing. The support group counselor told me that the point was that I got up and tried again. I finally quit.

If you have stayed with me here, then maybe you have found some motivation in these ways to keep moving forward, one step at a time.

CHAPTER 3

Childcare

CONSIDER ALL THE QUALITIES YOU WANT in a childcare provider: trustworthy, convenient, kind, safe, and affordable, for example.

Before the Internet, people relied on word of mouth to find childcare. This is still the best option, as it comes with help and endorsements from people you know. But reviews can now be found online to help narrow your search.

For me, convenience was key. If childcare wasn't in my home, it had to be accessible by walking or on the transit line. This allowed me to consider a broader range of babysitters to pick up my child from the care center or after-school program since they wouldn't need a car.

PAYING FOR CHILDCARE

Even the most income constrained of us can afford some of the available opportunities where our children are well looked after while we work or reset.

Employer Cost Sharing

Some more forward-thinking employers (or those most desperate for labor) collaborate with national childcare organizations like Bright Horizons for on-site care. Affordability depends on how much the employer chooses to subsidize the program.

Flexible Spending Accounts

This is a way to pay for childcare with pretax dollars. You contribute money from your salary and reimburse yourself from the account. The reimbursement form is a pain. If you are in a 10 percent federal tax bracket, it represents about a 10 percent savings. If you are below the federal tax minimum, then this has $0 savings. You can decide if this is worth your time.

Child Support

It's a benefit to have childcare negotiated into child support agreements. Negotiate contributions from the other partner to match the real cost of care, not only for third-party caregiver time but also your time. If the other parent is income restricted for monetary child support, consider substituting in-kind support with increased time with the child. The child will benefit from increased time from a noncustodial parent. It also can help you increase your own income by having this childcare. Also, one parent's employer may have a better childcare benefit than the other. Make sure to consider that with your settlement.

Barter

Rent out a spare room in exchange for childcare. Have a clear agreement up front as to the time and days required. I tried it once but, being a "softy," had trouble enforcing the agreement.

Exchange Childcare with Another Family

I see this recommended frequently. Easier said than done. I am not dismissing it, but my community wasn't strong enough for it to be a genuinely two-way exchange. Any change in my schedule needed advance notice, and last-minute changes by the other party occurred too often. If your schedule is flexible, this could be a viable option.

Sliding Scale Subsidies

The Y, Boys & Girls Clubs, and community-sponsored programs charge on a sliding scale according to your income for their after-school programs. The one in my town had a shuttle bus that picked the kids up from the elementary schools, so the handoff was seamless.

211.org

Look up online or call "211," the clearing house for private and government programs. Children and youth services include childcare, after-school programs, educational assistance, summer camps, and tutoring.

Vouchers

Many state programs offer vouchers for childcare. These are income based. Contact your local Department of Human Services office. You may qualify for daycare assistance.

COMMUNITY-SPONSORED CHILDCARE

Some of the suggestions below are occasional, such as "Mother's" Day Out or a local sitter. Often, they can be parlayed into a regular schedule like every Tuesday, for example. Some, like daycare, require longer-term contracts. (I don't deal with overnight care here. Most single parents I know relied on family. Not having any, I had to go with the kindness of friends with same-age children. The vagaries of travel schedules, like on-time flights, made it impossible for me to hire help for overnight travel.)

Mother's (Parent's) Day Out Programs

Local churches offer these, usually Tuesdays and Thursdays from 9 a.m. to 2 p.m., and costs run about $125–150 per month. Most churches do not teach doctrine in these programs; they are typically just to support the community.

Benevolent Clubs

Boys & Girls Clubs of America and Y's provide after-school care. These nonprofit organizations have as their mission to provide safe places for children. If they provide pickup from the school, then it might work. Try it five times before you commit. A lot depends on the locale and chemistry with other kids. Take your child's lead.

Public Library

Check the programs offered by the children's department. Sometimes, for a structured program, they will let you leave the child while you browse. Park yourself in section 337 if that library uses the Dewey Decimal system and thumb through books on money and time management.

School Aftercare Program

The one attached to my daughter's school had a waiting list. We started two days a week and eventually moved to four days, even in middle school. On the off days, I employed some wonderful college sitters for the afternoons. They would pick my daughter up from school, walk home, have a snack, do homework, and then play.

After-school Enrichment Programs

I never found one I thought was worth the money charged. Worse, the artsy ones attached to the elementary school would have afternoon show-and-tells. Not wanting my child to be the only one whose parent didn't show, I had to take time off to attend. That being said, you may have better luck than I did.

After-school Activities

Sitting in school all day is exhausting. It is incredibly exhausting if a child struggles to maintain focus. Kids need to let off steam afterward. Scouting is an excellent outlet *if* meetings are held in the same building after school. Girl Scouts does this. (I am unsure if Boy Scouts have changed their traditions of meeting in churches and in the evenings.) My daughter belonged through high school and attained the Gold Award (Girl Scouts' highest honor) for her project on Lyme disease. The demonstration of commitment factored heavily into her college admissions acceptances to some competitive schools. Her college entrance essay, "I Have a Secret," based on her scouting experience, caught schools' attention.

School-Sponsored Sports/Clubs

This is another seamless transfer from school to supervised activity. The kids can move from their last class to the club meeting or the gym. I had college sitters by this age, and their time would start when they picked up my child from the after-school activity. By high school, there is a "late bus" that takes kids home following school activities.

COLLEGE-AFFILIATED CHILDCARE OPTIONS

Later in this chapter, I talk about what's available to parents who are also students. But even nonstudents can often take advantage of college-affiliated childcare resources.

Childcare Facilities at a Local College

For example, Tufts University has the Elliot-Pearson School of Child Development and runs a center for about eighty children. These slots fill up very quickly, so apply years early if you think you might want to enroll your child in the program.

Student Sitters

Every college and university has a job board for students.

ACTIVITY-RELATED CHILDCARE

Sports, arts, science: these and other activity-based programs have the dual benefit of fueling your child's interests and providing childcare while you work.

Y Memberships

Most Ys offer sports classes and summer day camps. These are generally on a sliding income scale and may have subsidized childcare.

THE SITTER WHO RESCUED MY DAUGHTER

Sarah came to our family as a graduate student from the Boston University Graduate School of Education. It was at the beginning of second grade. My daughter would get homework (yeah, don't start me on this topic) and was utterly lost. Sarah would pick her up from school and spend the afternoon with her.

She approached me with her theory that there was a learning disability at work. I explained my gut feeling that my daughter had the genetic gift of dyslexia. Schools don't usually test until third grade, but I was going to pull the rip cord on that early and have her evaluated privately. Sarah concurred and told me about a highly sought-after summer reading program at The Carroll School, about fifteen miles away. I raced to enroll my daughter and took out a second mortgage on my home to pay for it. (I was too late to apply for a grant.) The Carroll School is one of a handful of private schools specifically for children diagnosed with learning difficulties in reading and writing, such as dyslexia.

After one summer session there, my daughter learned to read, gained confidence, and was off to the races in her learning journey.

Thank you, Sarah.

Summer Camps

The least expensive day camps are those run by your city or town. The most expensive are privately run. Sleepaway camps with the Y or Scouts come highly rated for legacy and cost. I am not sure cost is a good determining factor for how well your child will adapt or learn independence. By kindergarten, my daughter would want to go with a friend, which may inform your decision on the summer activity.

For middle schoolers, my town offered a unique environmental science camp experience. None of my daughter's friends was interested in pulling invasive weeds, canoeing, or hiking for a week, so she went alone. I promised she could leave if she didn't like it after a week. She stayed three years. By the time high school rolled around, camps were a patchwork of sports camps and overnights. By junior year, she had a job and coached part time.

PRIVATE RESOURCES

Daycare centers and after-school programs can be difficult to get into and/ or inconvenient in their hours and locations. In those cases—and to augment those resources—it's great to have a private network of friends, family, and hired help.

Family Members

Generally, this is the cheapest and least stressful solution. Make sure to express gratitude.

Friends

Clarify whether they are offering free care, be grateful, and consider this as occasional help.

Mother's Helpers

The term may have gone out of favor, but I believe the concept is still valid. Traditionally, before a tween was old enough to be left alone to care for a child, they would hire out in the neighborhood as a childminder. The difference between these kids and high school babysitters is that you generally have to be around them. It does, though, give you uninterrupted time to go through your inbox, pay bills, read, or do anything else. You still have to pay, but it's less than a high school or older sitter. Plus, you'll be helping out another parent by giving their kid a job out of the house.

High School Students

The holy grail of occasional sitters. Offer great snacks and pay above the going rate. Make sure to leave explicit instructions on everything from food preferences to how to operate the TV. If you will be very late, give them a place to sleep.

College Students

I advertised on college job boards and had a dozen of the most wonderful sitters. Later, they also served as tutors, helping guide homework. Note that these students are generally only available on an academic calendar basis.

Au Pair

This can be a convenient option if you have a free room and an extra car. However, you must be willing to spend time mentoring your young guest worker. Remember, they are in a strange country for the first time.

Nannies

When my daughter was an infant and in preschool, daycare schedules did not mesh with my commuting schedule and work hours. Preschool was only half a day. I couldn't fight to get my daughter ready for daycare by 7:00 a.m. and then reverse in the evening. Instead, I used in-home help for my infant and preschool daughter. This was not the best option in my experience. I was reliant on one person whereas a daycare setting would diversify the caregivers' needs.

THE STUDENT PARENT

I talk frequently in this book about the value of acquiring new skills and credentials, and the good news is that childcare is generally available from institutions of higher education. It allows you to pursue a GED, college degree, certificate program, or vocational education. Childcare is most available at public colleges and universities, but many private ones also offer options. Sometimes, they have an onsite facility staffed by a child development department or vouchers through the state education department.

To learn about what options are available, make your first stop the admissions office, followed by the childcare department. The financial aid office should also be on your itinerary since they could choose to increase your loans to help cover childcare costs. Note: live phone calls or in-person visits are far more effective than email.

Foundation grants are another potential funding source. For example, if you live in California or Minnesota, Raise the Barr Foundation provides grants for BIPOC student parents. Lumina Foundation makes grants directly to community colleges, and you can see its grantees on their website, LuminaFoundation.org.

RESOURCES WHEN YOU BRING THE KIDS WITH YOU

Sometimes a respite of even an hour can make all the difference. And if you can get that break while doing something that nourishes you, so much the better.

Houses of Worship and Their Related Activities

Even if you are not religious, this represents an hour to hand over your children to trusted individuals, allowing time for reflection and meditation. If you don't have an established community, go shopping for a house of worship. Make a list of those that might be nearby or interest you. Whether it is Tot Shabbot, Khalsa School, Sunday School, or a mediation center, look around. Tell the kids you are going "church shopping" with them and try a few out. The first two churches I tried didn't mesh with us, so I moved on and landed at a university-affiliated, nondenominational church.

Adult Gyms

Some gyms offer free childcare while their members work out, and others charge a fee. It doesn't have to be "enriching." It just needs to be safe.

MIND THE GAP

When setting up childcare, keep in mind that many centers close for vacation periods around major holidays and the last few weeks of August.

CHAPTER 4

Legal Help

EVERYONE NEEDS A MALCOLM

I met Malcolm, Esq., while trying to track down some basic healthcare proxy forms for Louisiana. (Louisiana is the one state not covered in the cheapy online legal form sites.) He had a private practice out of his home and handled just about any basic legal need. He is decades younger than me, so he'll be able to continue addressing my daughter's needs as she gets older and life gets more complicated.

I've handed him bill disputes, landlord problems, legal research, and lease reviews. It is helpful to have someone to turn things over to when I get overwhelmed or feel outgunned by another party or system.

When building your team of support, be on the lookout for a general practice attorney who hopefully doesn't have much overhead (such as a fancy office or a team of specialists) built into his or her costs.

ONLINE LEGAL SERVICES

If your legal need is straightforward, it doesn't always have to involve a lawyer and $400/hour. Using an online service like Nolo.com or LegalZoom.com can cover many perfunctory legal needs.

Consumer Reports conducted a review of documents online for simple needs and concurred that online templates are better than nothing or DIY. If you are lending money to a friend, renting a room, or establishing a healthcare proxy, go online first. If you don't have a large number of assets needing protection, many of the forms on these websites will serve perfectly well for a fraction of the cost.

Of course, it's different if you need a review of a document that someone gives you or if you have a complicated issue. For example, both my daughter and I rented housing during the pandemic. I had both leases reviewed by a general practice attorney. One was "good enough" and cost me $200. The other needed substantial revision and cost twice that.

The quickie legal websites do provide education on issues, and you can decide after reading if you want to talk to a practicing attorney.

Here is a sample list of issues on Nolo.com:

- Accidents and injuries
- Starting and running your business
- Consumer protection
- Debt and credit repair
- Divorce and child custody
- Employment/human resources
- Gig economy
- Landlord-tenant
- Living together and marriage
- Real estate
- Small claims and lawsuits
- Wills and trusts
- Powers of attorney

FREE LEGAL HELP

While document templates are often adequate for standard contracts and procedures, there are occasions when you need to talk to an expert human being. If you don't have (or can't afford) a Malcolm, consider taking advantage of Legal Aid.

My locale abounds with law schools and therefore has multiple Legal Aid societies consisting of volunteer law students. Students get real-life experience, and the public gets free legal help. These free legal service organizations go by many names but do a search for "legal aid society" in your area and you should be presented with multiple options. In addition, many high-powered law firms require their lawyers to provide a certain amount of free legal services each year. This work is called "pro bono"— for the public good—and has a long tradition in this country.

In most cases, these services should suffice for your situation. You don't need Perry Mason to protect you in housing court, but you should have someone on your team.

CRIMINAL LAW

It is *never* a good idea to deal with the criminal legal and enforcement system on your own. Even a third-year law student is better than nothing.

DIVORCE

Since this is a guide for single parents, chances are that many of you have been in or are in the process of getting divorced.

I live in a state where the division of assets and support is calculated primarily by formula. Searching your state's website will give you the basics for divorce and support. Despite standardization, countless couples engage in a fight to the death over divorce terms. I once asked a renowned divorce mediator why people spend so much time and money fighting for a predetermined outcome. His response took me aback.

"Because they are hurt."

Those four words line up to express the most profound emotions of parties about to engage in battle. It's about more than the money or custody.

EIGHT GUIDING PRINCIPLES FOR THOSE CONTEMPLATING OR ALREADY ENGAGED IN SPLITTING UP

1. Prepare for a Lower Standard of Living

When I asked why this is usually the case, that mediator explained, "Because even before splitting up, the money was all spoken for."

This makes sense. Most people spend up to their earned income. Their lifestyle reflects the presence of two adults earning and caregiving. That needs to be split in half to create two households now, each with only one adult present. Income divided by two equals one half.

Emotionally, this cost is high, both for you and the children. The late advice columnist Ann Landers's mantra still holds. "Will you be better off without [your partner]?" Evaluate the situation with a cold eye and make the decision with the full knowledge that changes may have to be made in your lifestyle.

2. Expect Disappointment

If your partner disappointed you in marriage, then most likely they will disappoint you after divorce proceedings begin. Don't expect a divorce to bring out the best in your soon-to-be-former partner.

3. Don't Hide Assets

It's illegal and unethical. You will get caught, and judges hate cheats.

4. Get Professional Advice *Before* Deciding on Your Course

A colleague once confided to me about her marital difficulties. Her husband had found someone else and wanted a divorce. I gave her the phone number of that aforementioned mediator, recommending her husband call about mediation. One phone call with an objective expert ended that guy's fantasies. They spent the money on counseling instead.

Speaking of mediation, I am far more in favor of this than litigation.

5. Even if Divorce Is Mutual, Don't DIY

There are some financial and legal aspects of this that can come back to bite you decades later. That includes Social Security and pensions. Both require an expert review.

6. Pay Attention with an Eye to the Future

Understand the long-term impact on Social Security and pensions. The day for eligibility will be here before you know it. A friend executed a mutual divorce, using an attorney friend to draw up and file the papers. The divorce was finalized after nine years and nine months of being married. Had she waited three months, she could have drawn on her husband's Social Security when he turned sixty-two and she was sixty, since he was two years older than her. She could have drawn on his schedule until she reached full retirement age at sixty-seven and then converted to her higher earnings record. This mistake cost her about $100,000.

A pension (aka defined benefit plan) is less obvious and more complex.

Besides pensions, spend some time on insurance. If one spouse has an employer who provides insurance, flexible spending accounts, childcare benefits, Health Savings Accounts, and so forth, take a close look at that benefits package. Also, walk through a scenario if that spouse leaves the job. What happens then?

7. Alimony/Maintenance Isn't Just for Men

In a social twist, I've seen significant divorce settlements paid by women. In the case of one woman, her husband stopped working ten years into the marriage, so she made most of the family money and had to pay him a portion of her earnings when they divorced.

8. Don't Attempt to Imitate a Friend's Experience

Each situation is different. Many people don't understand the implications until many years later. If you hear stories, remember that people's experiences come through their lens and are refracted by personal experience. By all means, run some of these "stories" by an expert, but don't expect a mirror result.

CHILD SUPPORT ENFORCEMENT

A single parent faced with a nonpaying one creates major stress in everyone's life. "Chasing the Check" becomes a full-time job, creating huge amounts of resentment and embittering a parent who lives with chronic disappointment. It sucks up valuable time that could be better spent raising children and pursuing career aspirations.

There is an advocate for this problem, and it is the state. They take, very seriously, the obligations of parents to pay for the raising of their child and are willing to bring the full force of their child support enforcement laws on your behalf. This can include establishing paternity in pursuit of child support and enforcement of court agreements and judgments.

Of course, if you are the recipient of state aid such as TANF (Temporary Assistance for Needy Families, i.e., welfare), you are required to disclose the child support agreement. Federal laws require states to be reimbursed for monies paid out from the public coffers before passing through any funds collected to the custodial parent. Any past-due amounts collected from a nonpaying parent will go first to reimburse the state for TANF payments. Anything left is sent to the recipient.

If you are having difficulty receiving your agreed-upon support from the noncustodial parent, call your state office for child support. In my state, the child support enforcement division is in the Department of Revenue. The division has powers to attach salaries as well as other means that single parents don't have on their own. Do your research online. If you want to feel represented, you could look at family law practices or Legal Aid, but it won't cost anything to call the state, fill in some forms, and get a process for enforcement started. If that is what you want.

The wheels of justice grind slowly. Sometimes a single threatening letter will get the nonpaying parent to comply. Other times, it kerchunks through the legal system, and you are susceptible to roller-coaster emotions. Every roadblock brings up frustration and anger at having to go through this process. It is maddening, I hear you.

It's lonely and hard to battle for your child's rights. A child doesn't want to know what a deadbeat the other parent is. Your workmates have their own problems. Friends are good for a listen but not an onslaught of venting. Support groups, online forums, distraction, and goal-oriented focus can productively relieve some of your stress.

But don't deprive yourself of the right to worry. Schedule a period of time to think about the problem. Give yourself an hour on the calendar and say, "I'll worry about child support payments from 5–6 p.m. on Friday." That way, you aren't ignoring your feelings; you're just containing them.

The legal enforcement process is just that. A process. Let it take its course and focus your limited energy on positive actions such as getting a better job or establishing positive relationships. If you can afford an attorney or find an active Legal Aid advocate, find a way to "hand over" the emotional stress to your professional.

OTHER WAYS OF GETTING YOUR OWED SUPPORT

Further on in the parenting section, I discuss using in-kind types of support when a nonpaying parent isn't able to make good on their obligations. Draconian measures employed by the state as a result of policy can have a deleterious effect on everyone. The state's legal powers can extend to suspending driver's licenses and other penalties. Then who benefits if the parent can't work?

Layer that with the insignificant amounts being pursued and it makes one wonder if it is worth it. One option to consider when faced with a nonpaying parent is to negotiate with them for in-kind support while they are getting their act together. Studies show children benefit from knowing both parents, so maybe ask for increased childcare time from the other party. That has significant value to you. Other ways to make them feel more connected are to accept items like foodstuff, meals, or diapers. These substitutions may actually contribute more than a designated support amount.

CHAPTER 5

Educators

Tune In to Teachers

Support Your Teachers

TUNE IN TO TEACHERS

Teachers represent tremendous support for single parents. Get to know your child's teacher. Attend the conferences. Go to classrooms. Use volunteer days from work to help out at your child's school. Above all, let teachers get to know you as a person, not just the parent of their student. Many negative stereotypes surround single parenting. This can be countered by letting someone know who you are.

Teachers have cued me into peer conflicts, anxiety-driven behavior, and academic development. They've recommended possible actions to take and pointed out my daughter's talents and strengths. Some have been positive male role models; some held the line on discipline and instilled confidence. Yes, I met a few jerks, but given the multiple number of educators involved in your child's life in any one year, their impact will be mitigated.

Educators are humans. Everyone wants to feel valued. Your positive presence will be a breath of fresh air. My daughter had a second-grade teacher generally thought to be a tough cookie. I loved her. She was smart, witty, and no-nonsense but believed in her students, and they learned well.

If you are not an educator yourself, it's hard to understand the system. As a businessperson, I was gobsmacked by the amount of reporting and paperwork required by school districts. If your child uses any special services, the volume of reporting increases tenfold. While it is terrific that we are moving to "customized" teaching, it needs to be followed up with support from the community and the school district. My suggestion? Choose a school district where the educators are well paid and have a strong union.

SUPPORT YOUR TEACHERS

Teaching is a very difficult job. Teachers don't go into it for the money, so their love for the profession deserves recognition. Above all, show appreciation for those who have your children 186 days of the year. I've gifted concert tickets that I couldn't use, given Girl Scout cookies, and made nominations for district awards. Teachers are a blessing for single parents, and showing gratitude is a great way to pay it forward.

Even with the presence of a strong union and well-funded schools, there is never enough money to go around. Rapid advances in technology mean your home computers are usually newer than what the schools use. It's a fight for every dollar. So, support where you can.

Additionally, the schools were first on my list when I had extras. I'll get swag from clients on a frequent basis. The school is my first stop for donations. Some have been as pedestrian as pens with company logos and others more exotic like Mexican dinners for thirty with all the fixings. When I get to clearing out my stash, my first stops are the first-grade classrooms. Apparently, empty coffee cans and oatmeal cylinders are in high demand.

Teachers are in your tribe. Give the benefit of the doubt and remember them in your thoughts. It doesn't have to cost much. Just your attention.

CHAPTER 6

The "Medicals,"
AKA Your Care Team

Maintenance Medicals: Pediatricians, Primary Care Doctors, Specialists, and More

Go Partner Shopping, Not Diagnosis Shopping

How to Get the Best from Your Care Team

Dealing with Insensitivity and Judgers

CONTINUITY—HAVING A LONG-TERM RELATIONSHIP with the healthcare professionals in your life—is invaluable. The better they know you and your family, the more effectively you can work together.

Your care team might include pediatricians, specialists, dentists, nurses, physicians, nurse practitioners, mental health workers such as social workers, psychologists, and psychiatrists (who we'll address in the next chapter), pharmacists, or therapists (occupational, speech, etc).

As much as patients bemoan the fragmented state of our care system, the practitioners are people, too. They want the same as anyone—to be treated with respect and appreciation.

Act the way you want to feel, even if not at that moment. If you want to feel a supportive team alongside you, then behave like that team. It is incredible how much people respond to being appreciated and someone acting that way.

MAINTENANCE MEDICALS: PEDIATRICIANS, PRIMARY CARE DOCTORS, SPECIALISTS, AND MORE

At the time of this writing, primary care doctors have been in short supply. Some small shifts on who we view as the right care team for ourselves and our children can make lemonade here.

If you have been reading this book avidly, you are now a master of "good enough." We no longer have to have the doctor perform the most basic medical tasks. Doctors' offices should include a nurse along with nurse practitioners/physician assistants. The latter can examine and, in some states, write a prescription. They have protocols to move issues up the hierarchy of healthcare practitioners. They must take a licensing exam before they can practice professionally.

Nurses

Nursing is focused on the patient's overall health and wellness and providing basic treatment as necessary. Usually, the nurses in a doctor's office are a good place to start with questions over the phone.

Registered nurses (RNs) act as primary caregivers to patients. They complete the intake functions and can administer medications. They execute on a physician's orders. Many specialize in an area such as family medicine, surgery, and so forth.

Nurse practitioners (NPs) have advanced degrees and take on more complex assignments such as conducting routine and detailed examinations, ordering diagnostic tests for patients, and prescribing medicine to patients.

Doctors

MD stands for a medical doctor. These are the ones you are probably most familiar with. They do four years of medical school and then a residency during which they train under more experienced doctors.

DO stands for doctor of osteopathy. While this designation has always had some degree of demand, its popularity has soared in recent years. About one-quarter of all doctors are DOs. They have the same training as MDs and sit the same exams. The difference is that DOs must also take training in an osteopathic manipulative technique (OMT). DOs learn about how the bones, nerves, and muscles work together and influence people's health. The osteopathic manipulative technique focuses on methods used to relieve back pain, neck pain, strained muscles, and other conditions.

Physician assistants (PAs) follow the physicians' health model of being diseased focused. They can diagnose and treat a wide array of medical concerns, prescribe medicine, and may even perform surgery. They have less autonomy than a doctor, working directly under their protocols.

Specialists are what the term implies. These are doctors who have mastered a specific area of the body through additional training. When a condition warrants additional expertise, the doctor, nurse practitioner, or physician assistant will send you to a specialist. Every part of the body has a specialist field, but one field I want to direct you to specifically is age related.

Adolescent medicine is one of only three age-related specialties (the others being neonatal and geriatrics). Adolescent health is a pediatrics subspecialty, and its specialists are (mostly) pediatricians who enjoy working with teens and young adults so much they want to specialize in that age group. When my friend Nina became a pediatrician, she was one of the few who specifically took on adolescents. Now it has become a named specialty and not a moment too soon. You may consider this for your own children when they reach that age.

GO PARTNER SHOPPING, NOT DIAGNOSIS SHOPPING

Physical, emotional, developmental, and behavioral diagnoses are sometimes educated guesses by "the medicals" based on experience and triangulating data. They don't have a lock on knowledge and may even disagree with trending issues with patients. Chronic Lyme disease, chronic fatigue syndrome, and fibromyalgia are three that come to mind. For years the medical establishment didn't have defined parameters that gave them treatment protocols. These along with some other conditions were classified as "otherwise not specified" diagnoses.

You may encounter professional bias based on outdated information or personal filters from certain individuals. I've heard from the single-parent online community about untoward comments. One that comes to mind, particularly, was with regard to a hyperactive child's behavior. Personally, I have been presumed to be a "stereotypical" helicopter single parent, which is oxymoronic to me. When is all that overfocusing supposed to happen?

I am not advocating for shopping around for a diagnosis that you want. I support giving someone a chance, but continue your search if the situation doesn't improve. In short: single parents, "trust your gut."

THE SOAPBOX

Single parents battle negative stereotypes based on long-disproven research. I want to take those thirty-year-old studies and publicly put them in a "wastebasket" myself. Studies concluding children of single parents have worse outcomes rely on aggregated data that, when split apart, **show the same or better outcome for most of the subgroups of all families**. The one group that suffered the most in terms of risk was those operating below poverty levels. Even then, the risk factors did not differ between single- or duo-parent families. Extreme poverty and its social inequities should be looked at more than family composition.

HOW TO GET THE BEST FROM YOUR CARE TEAM

Small actions and paying attention can have a measurable effect on your healthcare experience. These tips can help streamline the experience and sidestep frustration with our fragmented healthcare system.

Walk away when your needs don't line up with a care provider.

Pay Attention to Your Onboarding Experience

You can tell a lot about a medical practice by your first encounter.

- Do they respond quickly to a message? You shouldn't have to chase.

- Is the scheduler courteous or curt?

- How hard is it to get an appointment?

- Are they generally on time?

- Can they respond by email or through a secure messaging system? Some don't like to put things in writing. Move on. You shouldn't have to work so hard to communicate.

- Do their electronic messages feel natural or stilted? Do they use proper email etiquette or short one-word answers? If the latter, move on. Some older practitioners can't get the hang of electronic communications, but anyone younger than sixty-five should be fluent in email.

- Will they file with your insurance? If not, move on.

Allow exceptions for great providers. One member of our care crew is age seventy-plus, won't file the insurance himself (but will give me the forms to do so), and doesn't email. However, he is a TikTok celebrity. Go figure.

Avoid "Doorknob Moments"

These are when patients are on the way out the door and have "one more thing." Instead, write down your questions ahead of time. If possible, email them through their messaging system with a note saying this is what you would like to discuss during your visit. Doctors are scheduled in fifteen-minute increments. Help their schedule, don't ruin it.

Give Feedback

Most medical practices send surveys after the visit. I've noticed that much of my feedback has been considered, particularly around scheduling and telehealth visits. Keep in mind that your practitioner will see the result and can probably guess who wrote what. Unless you plan to quit the practice, couch your comments in terms of questions and helpful suggestions.

Note: save negative feedback for an in-person visit, alerting your team member that you want a few minutes to discuss a particular experience in person.

SPEAK UP ABOUT INSECURITIES

"If you [or your child] needs to go to the dentist and are embarrassed that you have not maintained your dental care, ask to have an office visit with the dental hygienist first. Explain your anxiety and embarrassment. Explain your fear that if the doctor shames you, you may not come back. You may even ask that they note in your chart that you do not respond well to lecturing. Most medical providers truly do want you to continue getting medical care and will take the opportunity to be sensitive if you ensure they are informed of your needs."

—K.C. Davis, *How to Keep House While Drowning*

Expect Reciprocity

They take your money and your time, and you can expect to be treated well. If not, move on. I've worked hard to assemble my family's care team. Some have been members since I graduated college. Most will have to be replaced in the next few years as they roll into retirement, but the continuity has been wonderful.

DEALING WITH INSENSITIVITY AND JUDGERS

Ignoring ignoramuses is usually good guidance, but in the case of the medicals, it won't serve you. To achieve the best outcome, you need advice customized to your situation. A perfect example is only discharging you to an adult after sedation. As single parents, this is a particular problem.

Hand the problem back to the medical team when planning your procedure. This needs to be explained to the doctor, nurse, physician assistant, dentist, or whomever is coordinating your procedure. Don't accept one response I got, which was "we usually release patients to a spouse." You can check with Social Services at the center where you will be treated. Their job is to help with navigating assistance needs. They make the rules, so they can find a solution. Don't let it make you feel bad.

Elsewhere, I've discussed the single-parent negative bias in the medical and therapeutic fields based on now-discredited studies. Additionally, it's a natural tendency to base your view of the world on your personal experience. Did the medicals hear about "welfare queens" forty years ago? Then that may be their foundation. Did they listen to a friend gripe about an ex-wife bleeding him dry for support? There's another bedrock image. Did they meet a helicopter mother who happened to be single? Well then, now the doctor is an expert on neurotic single parents.

You're under no obligation to educate the medical staff in front of you. I am fine with you ignoring this. But don't get indignant or defensive. You want something from this badly informed medical person. However, ignore generalizing or sweeping presumptions they make, stand your ground, smile, and reply with one of the following statements:

"That's not my experience, so let's assume that [whatever he/she is saying] isn't universally true. Where do we go to get the best outcome for the problem at hand?"

"Oh, did you read the 2019 book that debunked those myths ginned up by Ronald Reagan?" (Cite facts to debunk the assumption.)

"Why don't I date? Why? Do you have someone for me to meet?"

"Can you tell me more about why you think I don't have different needs as a single parent?"

"I'm curious. What makes you say that?" (That's the kicker!)

Asking someone to explain themselves might have the effect of people really thinking about their presumptions. We don't have to educate the world, but it might make it easier for your next encounter.

CHAPTER 7

Therapists

Finding the Right Help for Yourself

Finding the Right Help for Your Child

Affording the Time

Affording the Cost

SOMETIMES YOU NEED TO SHARE YOUR feelings and struggles with someone who won't judge, who will be supportive, but who will also be unafraid to point out when your responses and behavior are working against your goals. A good therapist can do that and more, helping you to formulate strategies to both cope with what is going on in your life and formulate strategies to change it.

FINDING THE RIGHT HELP FOR YOURSELF

Establishing "Fit"

You need to make sure a therapist is a good "fit" for you in terms of background, approach, experience, demeanor, and more. The website PsychologyToday.com has a resource page with sample questions to ask a therapist when screening for compatibility, and Strugglecare.com lists five questions to ask a potential therapist in a phone interview.

INTERVIEW QUESTIONS FOR A NEW THERAPIST

What kind of experience do you have working with [your specific needs]? You want someone experienced working with your problem.

What kind of license do you have? Do not see a therapist who is not licensed. A "certification" in some form of therapy is not a license.

What type of therapy do you provide? Read up on the various types like cognitive behavioral therapy and dialectical behavior therapy to see if these are mainstream approaches. Avoid the fringe and crackpots.

What days/times do you see clients? It has to work for you.

What are the fees for therapy? Is insurance accepted? Do you file the insurance paperwork? If they don't, this could be a deal-breaker. It would create another task for you to secure the paperwork from the therapist and file it yourself.

How are cancellations or missed appointments handled? I live in New England. Weather trumps all appointments. Some therapists will switch to online sessions in case you can't make it in.

Do you have after-hours availability for crises? This really varies so expect a wide variety of responses. It's good to know how they handle off-hours crises with patients. Most don't have off-hours support, so it is "gravy" if you find one that does.

How long have you been providing therapy? Are you still under supervision? You really do want someone who has experience with your issue.

Red Flags

If you experience any of the following while in therapy, question the fit.

Single-Parent Bias

I live in the Boston Metro Area. You can't swing a dead cat here without hitting a therapist. Here are some of the real-life statements I've heard multiple times from meeting people who are therapists:

"So, 'Mom,' why don't you date?"

"Single parents overfocus on their kids and give them anxiety."

You may want to find someone with fewer stereotypes.

Being Forever Agreeable

The first five therapy sessions are about getting to know each other. It's part of the trust-building. But eventually, a therapist should be willing to challenge you and help you reframe how you look at a situation.

I have a friend with multiple counselors. She seeks validation from all of them and dumps them if they don't provide it. Most of these are "coaches." Life coaches, dating coaches, spiritual coaches.

Getting a Name

Your primary care doctor can provide you with a referral, and your insurance company can also provide names. If you have an Employee Assistance Plan at your workplace, it can be a good resource for therapy and for names of therapists. Alternatively, go online to PsychologyToday.com and put in your search criteria.

Many therapists will offer a free fifteen-minute phone consultation. Once you get some names or matches, pick three, and contact each one to get a sense of their communication skills and your chemistry. Use the same vetting questions for any recommendation. Then choose the one you are most comfortable with.

Making It Easy

Besides questions about personality fit, here are some administrative questions to help narrow the list of potential candidates.

Can They Communicate Well Electronically?

A competent therapist should be able to put together a timely and professional letter in an email or have staff who can. You may also ask if they text. I have witnessed the new generation of therapists using it.

Is It Easy to Schedule Your First Session?

If they make you work too hard to schedule sessions, then find another one (assuming that there's not a therapist shortage in your area, in which case *all* will be booking weeks out). Similarly, steer clear if they seem to always be "on vacation."

Do They Take Insurance and Process Claims?

Who needs another task? In this electronic age, they should be able to process insurance. Many don't want/can't do the administration function of running a practice. Too bad. We don't like it either. Insurance is a way of life.

If you are willing to pay out of pocket, hope you get an insurance form from the practitioner, and can remember to file it to get reimbursed, then you *might* consider doing it that way.

FINDING THE RIGHT HELP FOR YOUR CHILD

Looking for a child's therapist can be more involved than seeking one for yourself. You need to match issues with practitioners and may even have to try to interview a few before settling on one that feels right.

At the time of this writing, we are coming out from years of "psychological malnutrition" from the pandemic. This is a sense that nothing you are doing matters; you only feel overwhelmed. The effect of the pandemic on children is starting to be evident. Some are getting over it quickly while others will take time to recover. Particularly teens.

Adolescents have always experienced anxiety about their place in the world and wanting to fit in. Society's response has been to socialize them through school, camp, sports, and jobs. Then the world stopped in March 2020 due to the COVID-19 crisis, exasperating anxiety.

Here's an example. You are concerned about your child's behavior. He's withdrawn or disruptive. His grades are sliding, or she refuses to even go to school. Nothing makes them happy, and every interaction is a battle. You are concerned and want to bring in reinforcements. *But how to find the right help?*

Old-time parenting books might suggest waiting it out and seeing if they outgrow it. Sometimes they do. However, those books weren't dealing with twenty-four-hour news cycles, school shootings, self-harming behavior, or social media, which is minimally positive for kids. It might be time to bring in a therapist.

This can't revolve around self-blame for having a single-parent family. Yes, maybe it is harder to hold boundaries because of the stress of having to do it all or the trauma of a former partner, but you are also battling social ills beyond your control. School is a big part of their day, unlimited screen time bleeds over boundaries, and undiagnosed learning disabilities are masked by emotional frustrations.

What you can control is your response and, hopefully, help both you and your child find skills to manage in the face of it. You can bring in reinforcements.

Getting a Referral for Your Child

Doctor

You could start with your pediatrician. As I mention elsewhere, their time and training on behavior topics is limited, but if you belong to a large medical group, they could have colocated therapists, which would make the introduction feel familiar to your child.

School

Get input from the school social worker, psychologist, or special education teacher. If your child doesn't use services, then ask for a classroom observation. Sometimes it is difficult to untangle a problem if a behavior is masking another problem such as a learning disability. Boys can act out, and girls can withdraw. So much can be done with learning differences now, and the neuroscience around them has made tremendous strides in the past decade.

INITIATING A SCHOOL EVALUATION

A parent may request an evaluation to look into a child's strengths and challenges. It is best to put the request in writing. It can be as simple as an email to a teacher or school administrator (e.g., principal).—Jessica Ames, LICSW

If your child attends a private school that does not have licensed special educators, take your concern to your local public school district and ask to speak with the special education department. They should be able to advise you on a course of action.

Insurance Provider

Another resource is your insurance company, which can refer you to local practitioners who take your insurance (a must). Look on the back of your insurance card and call the number for behavioral health. It is sometimes different than the main member services number. Similarly, if your employer has an Employee Assistance Plan, calling them will also give you approved names that will take your insurance.

Friends

Closer to home, you can talk with your friend network, especially those forthcoming with concerns about their own children.

Once you get a few names from the mentioned resources, you can go to the PsychologyToday.com site online. You may be able to read profiles attached to these names. They should cover the type of therapy used, their interests, and, of course, insurance.

Narrow your list to three possibilities and schedule a call or visit. Each should provide you with a no-charge fifteen-minute consultation to assess fit.

Interviewing Potential Therapists

It's important to meet in person with a therapist on your own before deciding on their fit. You can do this in person (recommended) or online and meet for fifteen minutes or so for a free consultation. If they ask for a credit card before this meeting, you might ask why since you haven't signed on with them yet.

Ask about confidentiality. If the child is under eighteen, by law the code of confidentiality doesn't apply between parent and child, but some degree of privacy will enhance the therapist/child relationship. Ask the therapist what is helpful for them to keep confidential. While you may feel the need to know all, you could also think of this as a blessing that you now have a partner for the care of your child and can hand over stress. You don't have to know everything.

However, any child therapist should volunteer periodic check-in times with the parent.

Trust your gut and your child's if a therapist is the right one for them. It won't be doing anyone any good if you don't like them.

PARENT COACHING

Some therapists offer parent coaching with parents and also one-on-one sessions with the child. Parent coaching may consist of educating you about different parenting approaches, working on concrete behavior plans to support your child, and being a listening ear. If you do joint sessions, make sure there are clear boundaries so your child doesn't feel you're taking over. You also want to make sure the child feels they have enough privacy. —Jessica Ames, LICSW

AFFORDING THE TIME

Use Telehealth

If you can't afford the time to see a therapist, go the telehealth route. The first stop can be your health insurance company. They will have a list of therapists in their network approved to provide telehealth. If you are a student, the university health insurance plan will also generally have a list of providers using telehealth.

"Twofer" Options Beyond the Couch

Darron Anderson, LCSW, the author of *Daddy's Green Book*, offers fatherhood counseling in North Carolina. He works with dads helping to improve parenting skills by offering types of therapy that don't involve just sitting and talking. He may offer a gym session, a pickup ball game, or a group session.

AFFORDING THE COST

Most, if not all, medical insurance plans cover mental health treatment. It is also known as "behavioral health" in insurance jargon. Don't let "jargon" be an obstacle. If, when looking at your insurance benefits, you don't understand the terms, call that insurance company. Or phone a friend. You can even do searches on government websites and your insurance company's website to find therapists or practices that take your insurance plan.

Free (or Nearly Free) Online Counseling

Sometimes you just need someone to talk to. Other places for connection are:

- **Websites and apps.** One mental health resource is 7 Cups, which provides free counseling and listening services to those in need. The site (and its corresponding app) is based around an instant messaging model where you can either volunteer as a listener or message confidentially with a volunteer. The site does have a premium version where you can chat with licensed therapists, but it's designed to be an initial step for those seeking help. Note: Generally, it's a good idea to do some sleuthing on online therapy apps. You can check out reviews, but these aren't always reliable. New apps are coming out all the time so you can check a few out.

- **Groups.** For every problem, there is a group. Some help with those experiencing addictions—alcohol, drugs, cigarettes, sex, and so forth. Some help their families. Others work with codependencies or abusive situations. Online search is your best friend here. My friend, who I'll call Athena, attends Al-Anon for family members of alcoholics. She adopted their mantra for joining a group: "Go five times. If you don't like it, go five more times." Hospitals, private and public, also run groups. Some are for a sufferer, and others are for their parents. Looking on the websites of both local general and specialty hospitals will show community programs. Some even have parenting programs.

- **Advocate communities.** Sometimes support groups form around a particular condition. The autism community is strong, and Massachusetts fomented the Association for Autism and Neurodiversity (AANE), which supports individuals, families, and professionals with these profiles. The organization provides support groups and events on a broad range of topics. You can locate groups though alliances and common cause networks. Some are created though groups of like-minded people while others might be sponsored by healthcare providers. It helps to look around.

More Places to Check for Low-Cost Therapy

- Schools of social work and graduate psychology sometimes offer community programs for behavioral health.

- Local family service leagues offer parenting groups as well as family services.

- Community health centers are also useful for both cost and families and often take most insurance plans.

PART 2

Time: How to Make More when You Have None

CHAPTER 8

Time Management for Single Parents

Teaching Time Management to Children

Learning Time Management as an Adult

If Life Feels Out of Control, Do Less

Establish Your Priorities and Schedule Family Needs
Around Those

Choose Activities in Service of Your Goals

AS A PARENT AND POSSIBLY AN EMPLOYEE, time may well be your scarcest resource. In the next few chapters, I'm going to offer a lot of practical suggestions about how to create it and save it. But I want to start with some general principles of time management—for you and your children—that are particularly relevant to single-parent families.

TEACHING TIME MANAGEMENT TO CHILDREN

Ah, the prekindergarten days. Things are less complicated because as parents, we control the schedule. Enter the era of after-school activities, and all hell breaks loose. Time is an unnatural concept, and if your child is a right-brained, nonlinear thinker, this takes a longer development time. My successful, middle-aged, dyslexic brother never did get a sense of time.

ANOTHER SOAPBOX MOMENT

Teaching how to tell time also needs to be accompanied by teaching time management. I've seen many talented junior colleagues fall victim to paralyzing frustration accompanied with anxiety over deadlines. The anxiety has deep roots in the education system.

We all have competing demands on our time. Our responsibility is to manage those expectations. Often, I would sit with an employee to look over their workload and schedule. Together we would determine how much might be accomplished in a specified time or see what could be rescheduled or reallocated, perhaps to another resource. This happened regularly, or at least should happen regularly.

Teachers and professors will at times claim that due dates are immutable when that's actually rarely the case. If today's educational institutions want to train tomorrow's workers, the culture needs to be changed to "realistic expectations" versus "deadlines." We would all be better served if schools and employers taught schedule management through collaboration with the parties having expectations of our time. Otherwise, we'll continue to generate a stressed-out generation.

Until the world changes, we'll have to manage that challenge ourselves.

A visual method for creating a schedule will help your children take eventual responsibility for managing their time. Thankfully, technology has apps for that. By using a common calendar through Google Calendar or another program, both parents can see a child's schedule and, if granted, each other's availability.

Print out calendars and fill them in with appointments. Encourage your children to color code these. You can even go as far as to add in the family schedule of routines. The more they work with events and time, the faster they will learn its meaning. Children will learn they can't finish breakfast at home at 8:00 a.m. and be in their classroom by 8:01 a.m.

Be Patient

Time management is a learned skill and takes practice and brain development. Some children are taught to read by using finger paints to draw letters. This is kinesthetic learning. It cements lessons by using a different part of the brain. In the same vein, physical "calendaring" helps to work with time.

I remember the day my daughter caught on to the concept of time. It was a "Miracle Worker" moment when it all sunk in. Previous to that moment, calendaring was a fun coloring activity. Then, all of a sudden, the pride of mastery took over and she would avidly fill in calendars. She still does it to this day, in living color.

LEARNING TIME MANAGEMENT AS AN ADULT

Teaching time management is an industry unto itself. Hundreds of time gurus promote a method, each extolling their system's superiority. Type "time management" into a browser search box and get 10 million hits. If you are a visual person, look at a few images on Pinterest. If any appeal to you, explore them further. I support any system that maintains sanity.

Time management systems primarily revolve around four major concepts:

1. Visualize the end game (end of the day, end of a project, etc.)

2. Understand your prime energy time of day

3. Be realistic about what can get accomplished in the day

4. Break a task into smaller components and space those out

IF LIFE FEELS OUT OF CONTROL, DO LESS

I've never landed on a miraculous strategy to invent more time. Instead, my guiding principle for single parents is "do less." Before you start chuckling, here are some areas where I let things go.

- I don't have a spotless house, but it is generally neat.

- My cooking wouldn't be on *Top Chef*, but it is healthy and quick.

- I wear a simple hairstyle that doesn't require me to curl or straighten my hair before work.

- I don't get manicures; I can't afford them or sit still that long anyway.

- I didn't clean my daughter's room for her; instead, she had escalating amounts of tasks, deemed age-appropriate, to keep her space clean.

Dirty clothes in hamper (age 2+)	Toys and books in bin (age 2+)	Take clean clothes to room (3+)
Pull comforter over bed (3+)	Backpack to/from car (3+)	Make the bed (6+)
Empty wastebasket (6+)	Do own laundry (10+)	Dust furniture and vacuum (6+)

- I didn't work out at a gym in my younger parenting days; I counted housework, yard work, and running after a toddler as enough exercise.

- I don't shop for entertainment; I have neither the time nor interest.

- I didn't have a smartphone until dumbphones became extinct.

- I wasn't nitpicky about my daughter's choice of clothing or hair; I had a simple goal of clean clothing in good repair and appropriate for an occasion (I lost control of that in high school, though).

- I didn't attend after-work social events when my daughter lived at home; social interaction with colleagues is important at work, so I would eat lunch with them and avoid the "desk sandwich."

- I don't game (on my phone or elsewhere).

- I don't watch much TV; I might watch one hour in the evening.

- I didn't have competing demands on my time without family nearby (the upside of no family support).

- I chose not to engage with my ex—that was a waste of time.

- I didn't (and still don't) take on volunteer leadership. Volunteering is an important part of community-building, and I *did* choose evening and weekend gigs, where my daughter and I could work together.

ESTABLISH YOUR PRIORITIES AND SCHEDULE FAMILY NEEDS AROUND THOSE

Everyone sets their own time boundaries, and my time boundaries were designed for chaos-free home life, given my job. Yours may be different.

One friend chose as her parenting goal to set her children up for success. Every decision she made centered on that goal. She accomplished it. Her trade-offs were self-care, in which she had little interest, and socializing.

A much younger single parent near me lived with her mother. With childcare built in, she chose to have an active social life. She reconnected with an old high school friend. They married and expanded their family, happily ever after.

A school parent friend divorced her well-off husband. He coparented, sent a check every month, and paid education costs. With financial security set for her kids, she could turn her attention to activities that would rebuild her professional life, including networking, personal appearance, and returning to school.

I omitted activities in order to focus on quality family time at a low cost. We camped, hiked Sunday afternoons, and visited museums. In high school that was supplanted by a heavy sports schedule.

These are some examples of goals other single parents had, such as a contained job, more learning support, and career building. Other priorities might be school/certificate achievement, special needs attention, outside interests, income improvement, savings, professional development, and launching a child to independence.

The point is that you have a goal or two even when time is scarce.

CHOOSE ACTIVITIES IN SERVICE OF YOUR GOALS

Everyone is busy. The world is revved up with endless possibilities of stuff to add onto the to-do list. Single parents are worse off than two-parent households, but complaining falls on deaf ears. Reallocate complaining time to something more essential and reap the rewards.

Add only those activities that take you in the direction of your goals. As a single parent, I put the greatest importance on activities that would create a community for the two of us or satisfy one of my interests. I considered those essential uses of my time. I would:

- *Socialize with other families consistently.* This would generally be on Sunday afternoons, holidays, and, later on, Friday night dinners. I gained strength from in-person interaction.

- *Double up on resources.* For example, I hired graduate education school students who doubled as babysitters/tutors. They had much more patience than I had to help with homework.

- *Chauffeur my daughter to friends' homes.* If a sane person offered kid duty, I'd jump. Likewise, I'd happily host playdates where my single child could be occupied.

- *Engage in an hour-long bedtime ritual.* Because I worked out of the home and was busy the rest of the time, this was the time to connect. I'd read any number of picture books, transitioning to chapter books. (This continued to middle school, and I still have by my bed the last chapter book we were reading until she decided to read by herself. I still hope to finish it with her.)

- *Volunteer as a worker, not a leader.* I preferred to contribute on a time-limited basis. This included cleaning up at a PTA potluck, working a tag sale, selling bake sale cookies, or being the chaperone assistant for Scout camping.

- *Read.* A lot. Novels, newspapers, magazines, reports, and so forth. Since my commute was ninety minutes each way on a streetcar, I had a lot of dead time I could fill. Standing for hours each day, I mastered the art of reading while strap hanging.

- *Make a sit-down dinner.* But breakfast was grab-and-go, protein-based fare that could be eaten on the car ride to school.

The choices you make won't necessarily be the ones I've made. What's important is that whatever time management strategy you do choose is made consciously, with a focus on reducing nonessential activities. I find most people who say they are overwhelmed need to consider the importance of where they do spend their time and eliminate what won't serve them.

Sticking to your time-management strategy is crucial, but also, as single parents, flexibility has to be built in. Predictability in our lives is a pipe dream, so the key is to consciously reduce less important tasks and be able to bend. Also, those dos and don'ts will change as kids change, so be willing to reconsider and adjust as needed.

CHAPTER 9

Creating Time

Constructively Procrastinate

Get Help with Chores

Create More Time Through Karma

Make Life Easier

Lose the Time Wasters

Put It on Autopilot

Establish Routines

Invest in Time-Saving Equipment

Do It Once, Use It Twice

Cook: It Saves Time

"How do you do it all?" —Reddit single-parent community user

FOR MOST OF MY DAUGHTER'S UPBRINGING, I worked in a fast-paced start-up and had no family help. My daughter had learning needs, and then in middle school, she decided to play ice hockey (an all-in sport requiring vast amounts of time and money). No one ever asked me "How do you do it all?" like this person on Reddit, but in case you are wondering, the following ideas worked for me and offered both dignity and time savings.

CONSTRUCTIVELY PROCRASTINATE

The point is not to finish a to-do list. It's never finished. The point is to *have* a list. Limit your tasks to five per day.

Make the first task something *important to you*! If you don't do it, it will never get done, so make it the first item. I write first thing in the morning, after coffee. Those are the first two things in the day for me. That order has shifted over the years. You may have to focus on getting out the door for school and work first, but the dishes can wait.

GET HELP WITH CHORES

In addition to to-do lists never ending, neither do chores. Don't let yourself drown in this endless cycle. There are many ways to make chores more manageable.

Recruit the Troops

I gave my daughter age-appropriate chores. It developed lifelong habits. Did her college roommates have these? Not so much.

Children and Chores

These charts list what kids are capable of. What you ask them to do may be limited by how many stickers you have to put on a chore chart. Even the youngest child can get into the chore habit.

It can be a struggle sometimes, but it gets easier and is worth your time. Besides, young children love working alongside their parent. Here's a list of what they should be able to do by age. You can choose some or all of these chores to work into their schedule.

Under Age 2

Get diaper (preschool will make them do this so may as well start now)	Put toys and books in bins
Put dirty clothes in hamper (use low baskets)	Turn off the TV
Wipe feet before coming inside	Close low cabinet doors and drawers
Hang up towel on hook	Pick up and dispose of trash

Ages 3–5

Previous chores (except diaper) plus:	
Make bed by pulling over comforter	Put games and pieces in boxes
Put books on bookshelves	Take dirty dishes to kitchen counter
Help unload dishwasher	Wipe down play table
Mop up spills	Take backpacks to and from car
Fill pet water and dry food	Rinse out sinks and tubs
Remove clothes from dryer	Take clean clothes to room
Dust low furniture	Help fold laundry (if you do that)

Ages 6–9

Previous chores plus:	
Make their bed	Help make breakfast
Set and clear the table	Simple cooking tasks (e.g., rinsing vegetables)
Put dishes in the dishwasher	Wipe kitchen table and counter
Wipe inside microwave	Pick up trash in car

Ages 6–9 (cont.)

Take out trash	Sweep or vacuum kitchen and bath
Clean smudges from walls and doors	Put away groceries
Bring in groceries from car	Sweep or vacuum floors/shake rugs
Straighten their bedroom	Prepare recyclables for pickup
Empty wastebaskets	Match socks from dryer (unless of course all the socks are the same color for simplicity)
Put dirty clothes hampers with household laundry	Vacuum car

Ages 10–13

Previous chores plus:	
Pour meal beverages (yes, I left this for older kids to avoid mad-rush morning disasters)	Help hand-wash dishes
Make lunch for school	Unload dishwasher
Wipe down kitchen counters	Clean pet spaces
Sort, wash, and fold laundry	Clean bathroom and shower
Vacuum	Take out trash and recycling
Clean bedroom closet	Vacuum furniture

Ages 14+

Previous chores plus:	
Clean bathrooms	Prepare meals
Sew on buttons and mend clothes	Organize closet

Seasonal/Yearly Chores

Following is a list of chores that need to be done only in certain seasons. As soon as she could walk, my daughter loved to work outside with me.

With a tiny urban garden, we could have plants and flowers. Younger than age two, my daughter loved any bug. We had snails, common to poor urban soil. Gardening wisdom is to countersink a small container, fill it with beer, and let the snail drown happy. I thought drunk snails were a bad example. Instead, her job was to collect them in a pail, which we would then relocate during a walk in the woods later.

She could also pick up outside toys. I must not have been that firm because one early morning, I heard a radio blaring. I tracked the sound to a plastic Fisher Price radio that had been left out in the rain and short-circuited. All night long, apparently. The radio was toast, but the upside was that the raccoon family under the porch moved out.

Older-age seasonal chores can include the following:

Help with planting (3+)	Clean garage (14+)
Putting away toys (3+)	Mow lawn (14+)
Shovel snow (9+)	Wash the car (14+)
Maintain the compost pile (9+)	Turn mattress (14+)

My daughter loved chore charts. Even during high school, she enjoyed banging through them and the satisfaction of checking them off.

Reading this list can also make you feel better for all that they are contributing already.

Hire Out the Worst Chore

Even if it is just one task. I hire someone to vacuum once a month. I despise this chore. Lugging a 40-pound gangly machine creates vast amounts of resentment. The canister bangs against my legs, leaving permanent bruises. (On a note of irony, I recently bought a 7-pound stick vacuum in installments and now gleefully attack tumbleweeds of cat fur multiple times a week.)

I understand it is cost-effective in New York City to send out the laundry. Washing machines in dank basements require multiple trips. Do your own time/cost analysis to see if this works for you, but it serves here as a good example.

Be Flexible

During busy times like back-to-school or tax season, housework takes a back seat. I prioritize the have-tos (dishes and pet care as daily chores) over the nice-tos (cleaning the refrigerator). Laundry, for me, is an easy chore and represents a task I can complete in fifteen-minute increments when I need a short break from more mentally challenging work.

CREATE MORE TIME THROUGH KARMA

Being an appreciative customer repays you with time. Really. Show gratitude to those who provide good service at a fair price, and you could be rewarded with *time.* Cherish those relationships. It doesn't have to mean giant Christmas tips (although there is nothing wrong with cold hard cash if you have it). Examples of low-effort, highly appreciated ways to show appreciation include the following.

Scribble Thank-You Notes to Include with Your Invoice Payment

I have included notes to service workers like the plumber, heating and air conditioning technician, and so forth, thanking them for making me feel safe and secure. As a result, I get prioritized for emergencies.

Nominate for Awards

My daughter used special reading services through elementary and middle school. Every year, I filled out the special education department parent nomination forms. My nominees were flabbergasted that someone would take five minutes to acknowledge their work.

Post Online Reviews

I will give a shout-out if I feel someone helped me with timely and fair-priced service. Financial and legal service providers are especially grateful when you take the time. Reviews are their currency for new clients. (Be careful with nonanonymous negative reviews, though.)

Mention by Name in Customer Surveys

Try to call out by name, if possible, a helpful person in surveys.

Give Referrals

My daughter sent so many friends to her hairdresser that he cut her hair for free.

Gift Cookies

I make Christmas cookies as a holiday activity at home and pass them out. I bought Girl Scout cookies for tradespeople. This helped both the troop sales and my standing with vendors.

Leave a Cooler Filled with Cold Water

On hot days, I leave one on the porch. I'll scrawl a note on top to delivery drivers to help themselves. I always get my packages delivered with care.

People to Consider

A sample list of service vendors and professionals to whom I have demonstrated my sincere appreciation include:

Hairdresser	Dentist
Auto mechanic	Delivery driver
Plumber	Parking lot attendant
Heating and A/C technician	Postal carrier
Pharmacist	Lawyer
Locksmith	Doctor

In return, they reciprocated with:

Free haircuts	Free consultation to open an accidentally locked door
My car parked front and center in a parking lot	Priority for plumbing emergencies, heating and cooling systems
Fair repair estimates	Honest repair advice on my old car
Free furnace repairs	Low-cost or free legal advice
Free dental care	

Spread around the karma. It will come back to you. It costs very little time to show appreciation.

MAKE LIFE EASIER

Lessen the Commute

While I was never thrilled with living in an urban area, it had good schools and was located on the transit line to where I worked. Taking the streetcar was lengthy (ninety minutes on the rickety Boston MBTA) even though it was only seven miles from door to door. However, if I ever did need to get home quickly (such as that inevitable call from the school), I had options. I could hop in a taxi/rideshare and be home in thirty minutes. Likewise, if something complicated an on-time home departure, I could make it to work on time using a taxi or rideshare.

I drove to work once in a while, but parking in Boston was $40-plus per day, so it needed to be reserved for special occasions. Again, I had that parking lot attendant who wouldn't bury my car, and I could make fast getaways because I tipped (see section "Create More Time Through Karma").

Use the Pharmacist as the First Medical Stop Versus the Last

Over-the-counter (OTC) medicines are surprisingly effective. Before child (BC), I traveled quite a bit for work. In countries where medical care was not as readily available, the local pharmacist held cult status as a healer. In the United States, we tend to call the doctor's office and be squeezed into a five-minute appointment that takes half the afternoon and could *still* end up having to get something OTC, anyway.

Consider reversing the provider chain.

Use Your Hotlines

Call the doctor's office, speak to the on-call nurse, or call the twenty-four-hour hotline with your health insurance. All can give you immediate feedback because, of course, no one gets sick nine to five. If any of those providers think it necessary, they'll advise a doctor's visit.

Of course, if you have a wise woman in your circle, call her for advice.

Be Realistic About How Much Is Doable in a Day

After years of gathering the data, it's clear that I generally can finish *five care tasks* per day, assuming no crises. I keep a running list in an organizer. I'll carry over tasks not completed to the next day, so they don't get dropped.

It bears repeating. The point isn't to *finish* everything on your list. The point is to *have* a list.

Find Your Organizer

This is the tool you use to remember tasks. If you don't feel that your current organizing method is your friend, dump it and find one that is.

Late in life, I came to discover *Bullet Journal*. It works for me. I love the physical design of the notebooks. They feel good in my hands and have dotted grids on the pages. It's just a blank notebook, but the concept changed my life. (That and realizing that five daily tasks should be my maximum number of daily goals.)

BULLET JOURNALING

The description of bullet journaling can be found by the developer (Ryder Carrol, self-described as ADHD) in his book, *Bullet Journal Method*, available in your public library. I recommend experimenting first before investing in journals. Try out the process using scrap paper stapled into a book format.

When I was gifted a blank *Bullet Journal*, it looked complicated. I needed time dedicated to reviewing the instructions. Fast-forward to the pandemic lockdown. With forced inactivity, I pulled out the blank journal, took a deep breath, and read what, in reality, were very brief instructions. It turns out it is a very simple and easy tool. I had needed only focused time to read the instructions to grasp how to do it.

I've seen entire websites devoted to the artistic use of journals. If it gives you pleasure to decorate your books, a nice set of colored markers is in your future.

I keep a running list of tasks needing completion, goals for the month, and visions for the future. It also represents documentation that I can refer back to should I ever need to remember a client or service.

Any organizer should be a friend. Your best friend. It's the last thing I interact with at night and the first thing in the morning. It can be whatever works for you.

LOSE THE TIME WASTERS

Smartphone

Partly financial, partly ideological, I resisted a smartphone for ten years. As a Luddite who resents technology, it was easy for me to stay off the smartphone bandwagon. I know full well that my colleagues laughed at me behind my back. Actually, they laughed in my face at the free candy cane phone I sported.

MY SMARTPHONE-BUYING EXPERIENCE

When the candy cane phone finally died, I went to the Verizon store to scope out its replacement. No dumbphones were on display. While I can be oblivious to fashion trends, I didn't want to look like a dork with an AARP Jitterbug phone. I had to ask to see the flip phones, which a guy hoards behind the counter. He cautiously rolled out the few clamshell-style flip phones. "Who asks for these?" I asked, hoping to find my tribe of phone haters. "Construction workers," he quipped.

I witnessed firsthand the addictive qualities of a smartphone's "always-on" draw as I managed a digitally native staff at work. I waited until my daughter went away to school and then bought myself a smartphone. It was getting increasingly difficult to get by without one. Sure enough, I catch myself mindlessly scrolling. My addiction is the news cycle. I turned on the screen time count and was horrified. I actively work to reduce my online time.

TV

No surprise, given my antitech declaration, that I wasn't plugged in while raising my daughter. Lousy programming made that easy. Movies came from the library, then DVDs in the mail from Netflix. Now with streaming, I have two services and still nothing to watch. I have explored cutting cable, but I am unsure how this saves money or makes my life easier.

PUT IT ON AUTOPILOT

Auto Pay (vs. Auto Debit)

I prefer auto payments from my checking account where *I* initiate the action versus giving a company permission to grab a payment amount from my checking account every month. This gives me control and an easy way not to pay a bill if I want to challenge a charge. Schedule push-pay bills that generally have monthly payments, such as the mortgage, health insurance premium, and so forth.

But Do . . .

Sign up for auto debits from your bank account if the risk of forgetting is high. You are better off having bills auto debited from your account. A good way to avoid overdrafts is to keep one month's worth of expenses in that account and have your paycheck or other income direct deposited there.

ESTABLISH ROUTINES

"Some folks view a predetermined plan of action as a limit to personal freedom. In reality, the opposite is true. We free ourselves by planning our activities and following through on that plan."
— Tracey McBride, *Frugal Luxuries*

In the BC era (before child), I didn't have great organizational skills. I worked demanding jobs in a competitive profession and worked harder because I didn't work smarter. Necessity as the mother(hood) of invention pushed me into developing repetitive activities as a single parent.

"In the beginning, it takes a good deal of effort to perform a routine. With enough practice, it gets easier."
— James Clear, *Atomic Habits*

ROUTINES FOR NOW, ROUTINES FOR LATER

1. My morning routine was (and still is) ninety minutes. Never less. Up, shower, change, feed the cat, clean cat box, empty dishwasher, make breakfast, make lunch boxes, roust kid, eat breakfast on the drive to school.

2. Nightly pickup. I used a laundry basket and threw everything in it that was taken out during the day and not returned to its assigned location.

3. Weekend catchup. While weekends were full of sports, fun activities, and meeting up with a friend or family, we still depended on a house schedule to keep up with housework. We'd clean the high-traffic areas like the kitchen and baths and throw the laundry into the machine before heading out.

Saturday meals were generally "everyone for themselves" to use up leftovers and give me a day off cooking.

Sunday's schedule was weather dependent. If it was too cold, rainy, or snowy, we opted for a museum visit with free passes from the library. In nice, or even just tolerable, weather, outside activities were the priority. We had friends happy to go hiking in nearby hills or head to a beach.

Grocery shopping for the week piggybacked with our outings, often happening after sports events or time with playmates.

Note: If you suffer from depression, have executive functioning issues, have ADHD or another condition, you may benefit from a little book titled *How to Keep House While Drowning*. As a recovery therapist and former addict, the author describes a self-compassionate approach to managing your home life.

INVEST IN TIME-SAVING EQUIPMENT

Cordless Vacuums

I have related elsewhere my battle with the vacuum cleaner. It is my most loathsome chore. I found, though, that a lightweight stick vacuum added to my arsenal partially solved the problem. With a lighter-weight Dyson, I vacuum more and am happier with the cat.

Kitchen Electrics

Investing in these machines is an excellent time-saving strategy, but *only* if you cook at home. I see many like-new small kitchen appliances at thrift stores. Buy one there if you want a low-cost experiment and see if that intimidating KitchenAid mixer or bread machine will save you time in the long run. Slow cookers require you to decide on a meal the night before, but they will save a ton of time if you can organize the ingredients.

Dishwashers

These appliances use less water than washing by hand and save time. Remember to clean the filter regularly.

DO IT ONCE, USE IT TWICE

Production Lines

Many of us are familiar with the mass-production concept of holiday baking. It's easy enough to make six loaves of cranberry bread at once or two dozen sugar cookies versus one dozen. It is more efficient to perform the same task repeatedly rather than take a project from start to finish and then repeat it with another similar one. When I make dinner, I make extras to freeze.

Extras on Hand

This applies to purchasing household items, either consumable or not. I don't advocate warehouse clubs (except for disposable diapers). My family isn't large enough for this to be a significant time-saver. Also, I have found that warehouse clubs aren't cheaper than buying on sale at my local supermarket (on a per-unit basis).

Once I found a great deal on Campbell's Chicken and Rice Soup in the quick sale rack at my supermarket for twenty-five cents each. My daughter loved that soup. I grabbed all twenty-five of them. (Of course, Murphy's law dictates that your five-year-old then decides she is sick of that soup.)

Reap the advantages of having extras on hand. The pandemic lockdown of March 2020 showed the wisdom of having extras on hand. Shortages occurred from panic buying. Toilet paper, especially, was in short supply. At that time, I had enough nonperishable supplies on hand for myself and to ship to my daughter, who couldn't source food, much less toilet paper, where she was living.

I can't tell you when a disaster will hit or what it will be. I can assure you, though, that one will occur. Knowing that I don't have to panic buy when an event looms reduces my stress and increases my confidence.

COOK: IT SAVES TIME

It takes the same amount of time to order food, wait for delivery or pickup, return home, and then eat as it does to cook. I am a basic cook. I never developed past the fundamentals, but I am not afraid of trying something from a magazine or cookbook.

I've timed the prep of crockpot beef stew—forty-six minutes, including recipe review, chopping, prep, and cleanup. When browning the meat, I make extra and throw it in a zipper freezer bag for another beef dinner, such as stroganoff, later. That's two meals for forty-six minutes of work. It would take at least that long to choose, order, and pick up from a restaurant. Plus, I won't have the fat and salt from restaurant food.

MEAL PLAN BASICS

At the grocery store or local market, zero in on two basic proteins—a rotisserie chicken and 90 percent lean, organic ground beef. That will take two people through the week and provide the main course around which you can meal plan for the next seven days. Adjust the quantities for larger families.

Rotisserie chicken. Get it precooked, and it takes less time.

Here are some fifteen-minute meals for the rotisserie chicken:

- Chicken breasts with potatoes
- Chicken salad for lunches
- Drumsticks for snacks
- Dark meat diced and mixed with cooked rice; stretch with canned beans or lentils to make chicken seasoned with Mexican flavors and rolled into burritos or tacos
- Chicken stir-fried with rice, scrambled eggs, and frozen peas

Ground beef or turkey. Make one of the following and rotate with chicken dishes during the week.

- Meatloaf stretched with any leftover starch on hand (oatmeal, crackers, breadcrumbs, etc.)
- Swedish (or Italian, depending on your flavor preference) meatballs
- Browned meat for tacos/burritos; stretch with rice

This is good for six dinners and leftovers for lunches. Add seasonal or inexpensive fruit such as bananas, apples, and oranges. Canned fruit can be substituted.

The seventh day you can rest and get takeout.

CHAPTER 10

What Is the Value of Your Time?

TIME VERSUS MONEY

We have a finite amount of time in the day and always more tasks to complete than hours available. Therefore, it's worth calculating whether an activity is worth doing yourself or hiring out in order to know where to focus your energy. This is true even in the most limited-income situations.

A basic calculation of our time's value can also help us choose between many competing demands. It shows how time may be better used invested elsewhere for a higher expected payback in the future (e.g., training for the next job).

This also reduces "decision fatigue." Understanding the value of your time makes it easy to decide between cooking versus takeout, cleaning versus hiring a service, grocery shopping versus online delivery, and so forth. Once you understand the value of an hour, decisions become less numerous and more guilt free.

While raising my daughter as a single parent, I freed up my wallet by understanding my time's value. Hiring out my worst chore or picking up the occasional take-out meal would allow me to focus on generating more income. But by understanding the actual value of my time, I felt less extravagant with regard to getting help.

The most straightforward approach is to look at your last pay stub or other earnings statement and find the amount paid to you after taxes. Then find the total number of hours you worked (also located on the pay statement). If you don't get a pay statement, check your schedule and tally your working hours. Divide those hours into your net (after tax) pay.

Net pay divided by hours worked equals your wage per hour.

For example, the median US pay in 2023 was **$51,000/year**. Assuming a 10 percent tax rate,[1] that net pay after taxes is **$45,900**. If you work 2,000 hours per year, your hourly wage translates to **$23/hour** ($45,000 / 2,000 = $22.95/hour, rounded to $23/hour).

Theoretically, tasks that can be hired out for less than that $23/hour represent a positive return if you are short on time.

HOW TO DECIDE WHAT IS WORTH YOUR TIME

Here's a real-life example to help you figure out what is worth your time. My daughter came home from college with an armful of clothes needing alterations. With my sewing skills, I can hem, take in seams, repair some zippers, and replace buttons. (She thinks I am fantastic. I feel that I have neglected a parental duty to teach her a basic life skill.)

---

1 I use 10 percent given this wage's tax bracket. Even if you earn minimum wage for federal income taxes, you may still have other taxes such as social security and state or local taxes. Using 10 percent seemed the easiest way to estimate the net pay per hour.

It takes me two hours to measure, cut, and hem a pair of pants. Three pairs of pants needed to be shortened, including a hefty denim pair. I saved that for last. We were running out of time before she had to leave. Denim is hard to sew without the right needles, and I am not versed in how to retain the original stitching. I called a local dry cleaner and asked how much they would charge for hemming the denim pants. They quoted me at $18.

Since it takes me two hours to hem pants, it is more cost-effective for me to send out this chore if I make more than $9/hour after taxes. The Massachusetts minimum wage is $15/hour ($12/hour after tax). The dry cleaner charge would cost me $9/hour. I would *gain* $3/hour if I spent the time working a minimum wage job instead of hemming. I would also gain the time to spend on other things.

The higher the value of my time, the more it makes sense to hire out the hemming. Even if I make the *median* after-tax hourly rate of $23/hour, then having the jeans sent out for hemming for $18, which would take me two hours of work, makes complete sense. I would be paying $9/hour for the job, and I could work two more hours and earn $46.

WHAT IF YOU CAN'T WORK MORE HOURS?

"The hours' thing doesn't work for me because, in reality, it doesn't take into account the reality that I can't work any more."
—Reddit r/frugal post

I realize that it's not always viable to work another hour. Maybe we're not paid on an hourly basis. Maybe we run out of time to work more because before us lies cooking, homework, and bedtime duties as a parent. Single parents always have to weigh the trade-offs between time and money. We don't have reinforcements or substitutes to step in if necessary.

If I can't work additional hours, I have other tasks that would cost more than the $9/hour. For example, I am comfortable filling out my own tax return, and it would cost more than \$9/hour to hire a tax preparer. If I spent the time hemming the jeans, I could possibly run out of time to do my taxes. Tax preparation services start at \$80/hour.

If this is your situation, ask yourself whether it makes more sense to:

DIY a task or chore, no matter how small the job (e.g., hemming pants or cooking dinner)

OR

Hire help and devote your time to a task that would cost more to hire out.

Examples of time trade-offs that come to mind:

DIY mending *versus* seamstress

House cleaning *versus* house cleaner

Snow shoveling *versus* plow service

Tax filing *versus* tax preparer

Laundry at home *versus* wash-and-fold service

Manicure at home *versus* nail salon

Meal prep *versus* takeout

Picking up someone at the airport *versus* paying for them to use a rideshare

CALCULATING THE *REAL* VALUE OF YOUR TIME— *ADVANCED METHOD*

If you have mastered the basic method to value your time, move on to the advanced calculation method.

Many people think of their hourly value in terms of their gross pay but need to consider all of the costs they incur to earn that wage, such as taxes in the previous basic method. We also incur other costs to earn our wages.

Total Costs to Earn an Income

As a single parent, you probably incur childcare costs paid to a provider. Add up those childcare costs, making sure you include occasional late penalties, early drop-off options, and so forth.

Add to the childcare costs the other costs to work, including transportation, meals out of the home, and a wardrobe.

Subtract these cost-to-work expenses to calculate the *real wage* earned.

Calculate the Real Total of Hours Working

In addition to the nominal hours worked, add additional hours, such as commuting time or work brought home. Time for pickup and drop-off at childcare should also be added.

In the hypothetical example below, my commuting time door to door would be 3 hours a day or 600 hours per year. Now my wage-earning time is 2,600 hours.

Working hours for a full-time year	2,000
Commuting hours for a full-time year	600
Total hours incurred working	**2,600**

Example to Calculate Real Take Home Wage

In the hypothetical example that follows, I earn the median wage for a worker in the United States, $51,000. I pay for after-school childcare and commute ninety minutes each way to work. I assume my effective tax rate is 10 percent.

Gross annual wage	$51,000
Less expenses (annualized)	
10% taxes	$5,100
Commuting cost (12 monthly passes @ $100 each)	$1,200
After-school childcare	$6,000
Office gifts/clothing	$ 100
Meals eaten away from home	$2,400
Total expenses	$14,800
Net annual income after taxes and expenses	**$36,200**

In addition to commuting and clothing, running on fumes at the end of the workday may see me succumbing to convenience food or purchased lunches. I use $200/month here, which is the average American expenditure for "meals purchased outside the home."

For the numbers in the chart, I used the monthly estimates provided by the USDA publication, "Costs of an Average Family."[2] Your actual costs will vary by region, age, and multiples, if any. The average cost of full-time daycare annually in Massachusetts is $20,415. (My example uses the cost of after-school care vs. all-day care.)

In this advanced method, you will divide the $36,200 net earnings by the total hours incurred of 2,600 to calculate your real hourly wage. With these adjustments, I earn a real wage $14/hour ($36,200/2,600 hours = **$14 real hourly wage**).

---

2 https://www.usda.gov/media/blog/2017/01/13/cost-raising-child.

Any task I can hire out for less than $14/hour makes sense because I could hypothetically earn more by working more hours instead of hemming pants. Even in this circumstance, sending out a two-hour job that costs $18 ($9/hour) is still a better use of my time.

I can theoretically redirect two hours of my time to working more hours or concentrating on a task that would cost more to send out.

SHOULD YOU WORK ANOTHER HOUR?

We may have already put in all our mental time at work. There is a reason airline pilots are subject to "flight time limits" and rest requirements. Boston limits all its snowplow drivers to sixteen-hour shifts with two thirty-minute breaks. Our cognitive functions slow down after a certain time point, making mistakes more common.

Wondering if you should work another hour? Here's a good rule of thumb:

> "You should stop working if it's a net negative hour on average. Working hard on a project is good until the next hour of work burns you out more than it produces something valuable."
> — James Clear, Lifehacker.com

WHAT IS YOUR TIME VALUE IF YOU DON'T WORK?

The Bureau of Labor Statistics reports that 28 percent of female and 17 percent of male single parents may *not* be employed in a wage-earning situation. If you are in that situation, then you can use an approach known as the "expected value" to estimate a wage equivalent. Here are two ways to calculate the expected value.

- Determine your salary if you *did* go back to work. In my case of the hypothetical median wage earner, that would be $15–$23/hour.

  OR

- Calculate a potential new hourly wage as a result of gaining skills during nonemployment. This is known as "the expected value method." Skilling-up activities might include learning:

  Basic coding skills

  Microsoft Office skills such as Excel, PowerPoint, or Word

  Language skills, either as a native or nonnative speaker

  Validation of skills either with a degree or certificate

  Public speaking

  Social media

  Writing

  Website building

You can quickly search potential earnings with these skills by looking at Salary.com and then calculating the real wage value, as we did previously.

DIY VERSUS HIRING SOMEONE

Compare your net hourly wage against the net hourly cost to hire someone. The goal is to identify the best use of your time and money. Some activities are faux frugal and should only be done for other reasons, such as enjoyment or values.

Activity	DIY Cost of My Time ($14/hour)	DIY Out-of-Pocket Cost	Cost to Hire Help	Cost Comparison
Grocery shopping	2 hours = $28	$2 (gas)	$50 for delivery costs and upcharges	DIY = $30 vs. delivery = $50 DIY savings = $20 or $10/hour
Vacuuming	1 hour = $14	None: own vacuum	$30/hour	DIY = $14 vs. hire = $30 DIY savings = $16/hour
Laundry at home vs. service (3 loads)	.75 hours = $10.50	$3/load x 3 loads = $9	$11/load x 3 loads = $33 for a drop-off service	DIY = $19.50 vs. service = $33 DIY savings = $13.50/hour (less than a $14 hourly wage)
Laundromat vs. service	4 hours = $56	$11/load x 3 loads = $33	$11/load x 3 loads = $33 for a drop-off service	Laundromat = $89 ($56 +$33) vs. service = $33 No DIY savings
Exercise (3x per week or 12 hours/month)	12 hours per month = $168	$0; you walk to work or use YouTube videos	Gym + travel time = 20 hours/month @$14/hour = $280 +$100/month membership +12 hours childcare = $180 Monthly cost = $560	DIY = $168/month vs. gym = $560/month *Using a gym is cost-effective only if no travel time is incurred and you get reduced fees and free childcare*
Shorten one pair of pants	2 hours = $28	$0; I own the materials	$18	DIY = $28 vs. send out = $18 No DIY savings; send out
Comparison price shop dental braces	4 hours = $56	$1,000 savings	$7,000 high-priced orthodontist	Return is $944 net savings for 4 hours of work or $236/hour
Clipping coupons	1 hour = $14	$5 savings	0	No DIY savings; you spend $14 of time to save $5
Pizza	.25 hours = $3.50	$8 ingredients	$25 delivered	DIY = $11.50 vs. ordered = $25 Make homemade; saves $13.50/pizza

The previous chart shows the high value of comparison shopping big-ticket items such as orthodontic braces. Low-priced things like food, cleaning, and coupon clipping don't provide high returns, if any, to do yourself. Doing this exercise for some of your more common tasks could be eye-opening.

"BUT I DON'T HAVE THE CASH TO PAY OTHERS"

You simply may not make enough and can't cover the basic cost of living without subsidies. In that case, your "free" time is still better spent to increase your earning potential rather than trying to save every dollar. (That is if you use time versus killing time.)

You can advance your earning potential through getting more education, gaining skills, interviewing for new jobs, or accessing subsidies for low-wage earners. Here are a few ways to potentially yield higher future household income:

- Researching skills that would earn a higher wage

- Talking with supervisors about what it takes to get promoted

- Earning degrees or certificates

- Applying for income-based subsidies (utilities, phone, healthcare)

- Managing mental health challenges

- Improving physical health for yourself and your family

- Networking for new jobs

- Creating household routines to save time, thereby saving money

To explore this more in-depth, refer to chapter 13.

Essentially, your actions from these activities will drive growth over the next twelve months, so the value of your time is higher than your realized income indicates today.

FACTORS MORE IMPORTANT THAN MONEY

"Many people cheat the opportunity cost arithmetic when they don't want to do something." —Reddit r/Frugal community user

I consider other intrinsic but not quantifiable factors, such as "enjoyment" or "sustainability," to decide whether an activity is worth doing. My example of paying $18 for jeans hemming versus my labor worth $28 makes it obvious that I should have sent out all three pairs of pants for alterations. However, I wouldn't have had the opportunity to teach my daughter a life skill with the two pants we did hem together.

The return on time chart on page 94 tells me that I should do my own vacuuming since I would save about $14 each hour. However, I loathe vacuuming and would rather do my own taxes. (That tells you something.)

In the food-shopping example, it takes me two hours to drive to the store, shop, bag my purchases, load them into a car, and then bring them into the house. This saves me $20, or only $10/hour versus ordering online and having the food delivered. For anyone making minimum wage or more, it makes more sense to have the groceries delivered.

For me, personally, the intrinsic enjoyment value is high. I enjoy cooking and picking out ingredients, so I assign it an intrinsic enjoyment value of 4 out of 5. (Vacuuming gets a 1.) For that reason, I do my own shopping. But others can feel vindicated for ordering delivery.

TALE OF TWO LAUNDRY DECISIONS

The return I get from doing my laundry at home versus sending it out is $13.50 per hour for three loads of laundry. I have laundry machines in my home and can fit in a load between most tasks. I even have a permanent setup for line drying.

My daughter, on the other hand, has a different calculation. She doesn't have a washer/dryer in her college apartment. Without a car, she trudges the items for five blocks to a laundromat and sits there for three hours. She needs to be there to switch machines and make sure no one steals the clothes. The machines will cost $33.

The alternative is to send out the laundry with a wash-and-fold service. The service picks up and delivers the clothes for $33, the exact out-of-pocket cost of using the laundromat, *and* it gains her four hours. Even before calculating her return on time, it makes sense for her to use a pickup service. She would spend $33 at the laundromat or $33 for wash-and-fold services. Some services are like that.

But in case you are wondering about her return on time, she saves four hours using a service over going to the laundromat. Since she has an hourly $10/hour net minimum-wage job at school, she could work an additional four hours, earn $40, and send her laundry out. Given that the costs out of pocket are the same for either the laundromat or service, the value of her time is $40.

> *"I wish I hadn't been so tight with my money. It would have been better if I had bought services instead of doing it myself. I didn't understand the value of my time."*
> —India, **successful 55-year-old, small business owner**

THE TAKEAWAY

Knowing the value of your time helps you decide what activity is worth doing yourself versus paying someone to do it. Everyone has to decide for themselves what is worth their time.

Don't DIY tasks with negative savings. Instead, use the time to increase your earning potential or do a higher-cost activity. Conversely, some DIY activities' small savings provide enjoyment or health benefits. Homemade versus delivery pizza comes to mind. Also, if those small savings are repeated continuously, they can add up to a sizeable budget contribution.

If something takes an hour to save a few dollars, that is a poor return on time if you don't have extra time to spare. If you feel you have spare time but no money, you can calculate what will be a good use of that time to *get* more money.

The time versus money analysis defies the conventional wisdom that DIY is always cheaper. Knowing the value of your time demonstrates how that thinking can lead to a false economy. With more tasks than time to accomplish them on our own, the calculation could show what is a better use of your time. Now you have the financial method to prove that.

CHAPTER 11

Home Management: Finding Efficiencies on Every Front

The Vision

Embracing Predictability

Food: Consuming, Cooking, and Storing It

Taming the Paper Tigers

Administering the Family's Health

THE VISION

A first step on the road to a calm household is adjusting the concept of time. Instead of thinking in hours, think in terms of **fifteen minutes**. That's how we live our parenting lives and it's how we create a well-ordered life.

Here's what can be accomplished in fifteen-minute increments:

You can put down whatever you are doing and actively listen to your child about their day.

You can arrive at pickup fifteen minutes early, which is enough time to go through your email inbox.

You can sort the clothes into wash types.

You can get dinner on the table upon arriving home from work.

You can find the doctor's number, place a call to the office, explain your need, and expect a call back.

You can prep breakfast to go or have a sit-down meal.

You can take a breather to listen to a friend on the phone because they would do the same for you.

You can minimally walk the dog or put away clean dishes.

IT STARTED WITH THE PILGRIMS

In 1620, the Pilgrims landed on First Encounter Beach, Cape Cod, in Massachusetts. After dropping to their knees and kissing terra firma, they did laundry. It was a Monday. This is where New Englanders started their tradition of doing the washing on Monday.

Getting our home life under control sets a stage for everything else in our life. It can give us a sense of control or chaos. And routine—when scheduled tasks are done on a recurring basis—can be an essential ingredient.

EMBRACING PREDICTABILITY

Rinse, repeat. Routine makes it mindless. And easy.

Household management is "Groundhog Day" for all its repetition. You make the beds and then have to do it all over again the next day. However, once done, you can take pride in a task accomplished, no matter how small. It lets you move on to bigger things.

If starting any task here feels overwhelming, remember fifteen minutes. If fifteen minutes is too much, then do five minutes.

"You can accomplish a lot by doing small things every day."
— Gretchen Rubin, The Happiness Project

If you take care of a small thing, then you start on the road to momentum for big things.

Put your tasks on autopilot. I like a clean home. I breathe better and have less stress.

It's the same every week. The same tasks at the same time, and it doesn't vary. The schedule is the only decision, and I make it once. The rest is rote. The tasks' repetitive nature lets me enjoy music or a podcast.

While predictability may not be ideal in food, romance, or even work, it doesn't always equate to "boredom." Embracing the recurring tasks necessary to maintain a healthy, functioning household can reframe your outlook.

"It's the job." That phrase inspires me. It assumes autonomy. Did I think parenting and household management would be this hard?

Probably not, but now that I do know, my energy should be directed at figuring out how to simplify it, not eliminate it. It's unlikely someone will show up to do it for me. I may get help but not a replacement.

It's not forever. This path that requires me to take care of others is time limited. Things change. Children acquire skills and can take over tasks. Your role will switch to "player/coach."

Meanwhile, though . . .

Get Help

Outsource your worst task until you feel ready to create a system for it. If laundry piles up ahead of you, use a drop-off wash-and-fold service or one that picks up and delivers. If grocery shopping is too much to manage with kids in tow, order online and either pickup curbside or get it delivered. I have animals and need frequent vacuuming. I hire in help for that.

Enlist Your Kids

Infants like to watch you. Younger children, from toddlers on up, like to participate in household tasks. They'll follow you around, imitate your activity, and learn the basics of household management (see chapter 10). Finding ways for them to contribute answers the question about what to do all day with preschoolers and sure beats putting them in front of a screen for hours on end.

Reduce conflict with your teen on the topic of chores with autonomy. In chapter 10, I include age-appropriate tasks that teens can accomplish. If you have successfully created that expectation of participation by your children, the terrible teens shouldn't see much resistance. But then there are teens and there are teens. Some look for conflict. Some can't manage multiple tasks.

By adolescence, I recommend a collaborative approach to task sharing. Home care tasks have to be done, and they can't fall on just one person, you. It simply isn't fair.

Make a list of all the tasks that need to be done in your household. You can use the aforementioned list in chapter 10 as a starting point. Print or type the list, double-spaced, and sit down with your teen. Tell them you need to split up the list evenly and that they can select the tasks they prefer.

Be realistic about chores when you are trying to get out of the house before school. My daughter had one morning job, emptying the dishwasher. Even though the pets were hers, I didn't think it was fair for them to be in the middle of any contention. Most of her chores were after school and on weekends.

FOOD: CONSUMING, COOKING, AND STORING IT

Refrigerator Management

Currently, I have a European fridge in my rented home. It looks chic but was clearly meant for people who go to market every day. (I live miles from any market, large or small.) This fridge holds exactly one week's worth of perishable food for one or two people. It's a challenge to fit American-size containers into it. A Brita water container doesn't fit, and neither does a half-gallon-size milk jug.

Before I moved to the tiny-fridge house, I had a hulking, twenty-year-old, side-by-side fridge in old-school white. It was a workhorse, never broke, and only required that I clean it now and then to keep its seals functioning.

It's to that fridge that I dedicate this section.

REFRIGERATOR MANAGEMENT

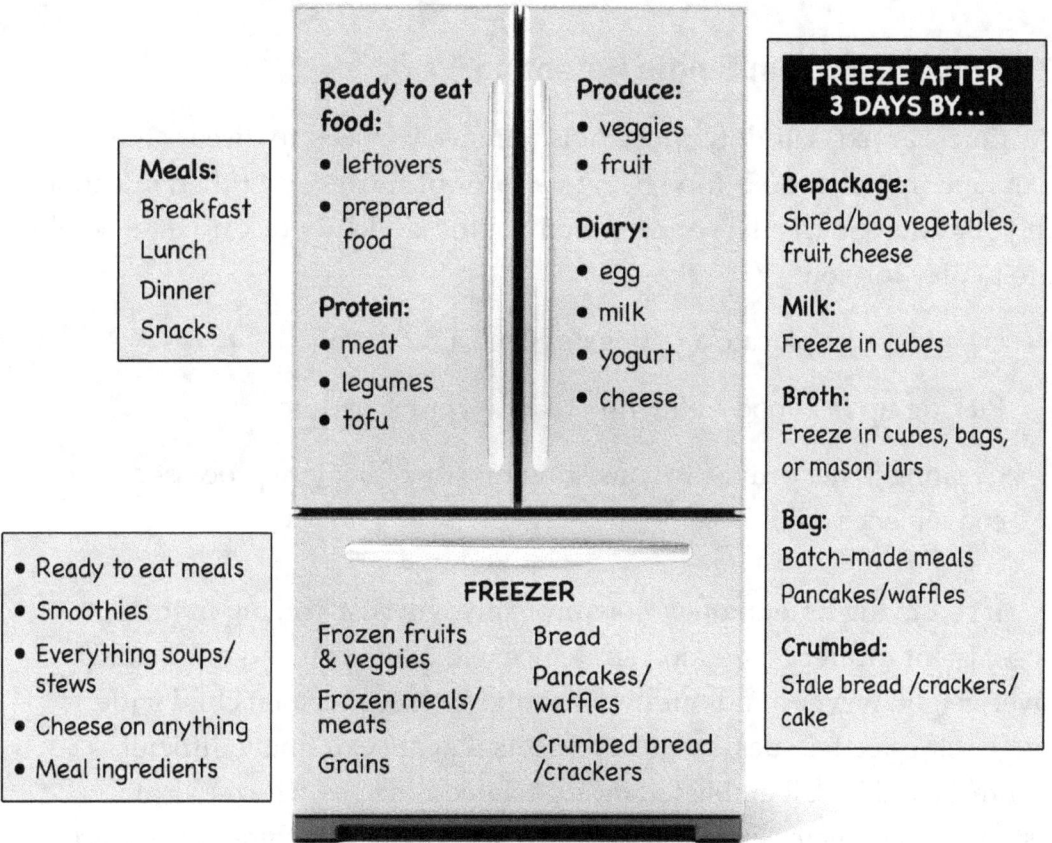

Meals:
Breakfast
Lunch
Dinner
Snacks

Ready to eat food:
- leftovers
- prepared food

Protein:
- meat
- legumes
- tofu

Produce:
- veggies
- fruit

Diary:
- egg
- milk
- yogurt
- cheese

FREEZE AFTER 3 DAYS BY...

Repackage:
Shred/bag vegetables, fruit, cheese

Milk:
Freeze in cubes

Broth:
Freeze in cubes, bags, or mason jars

Bag:
Batch-made meals
Pancakes/waffles

Crumbed:
Stale bread /crackers/ cake

- Ready to eat meals
- Smoothies
- Everything soups/ stews
- Cheese on anything
- Meal ingredients

FREEZER
Frozen fruits & veggies
Frozen meals/ meats
Grains

Bread
Pancakes/ waffles
Crumbed bread /crackers

Refrigerator management is a flow system. All food in the fridge should be moved along.

If you find it piling up, do a "no-shop week" where you eat only what you have on hand. If you need inspiration, there is a terrific website, SuperCook.com, where you list all the ingredients you have on hand, and it gives you hundreds of recipes.

Once a month, clean out the fridge.

This will take twenty to thirty minutes. It's a good kid job.

As far as I know, I coined the term "refrigerator management." It means having a consumption plan for perishable food on hand. It's about being efficient and saving time.

The Role of Food in Single Parenting

As time-starved, self-doubting single parents, we need to discuss the elephant in the room. Is food being used for purposes other than nutrition in your household? Ask yourself if any of these silently ticking time bombs are in play for you:

Using food to placate a youngster from a tantrum

Picking up fast food frequently to ease your schedule

Creating a diet primarily consisting mostly of heavily processed convenience food

If so, saving time/money now probably will cost you big in the not-too-distant future. Those food strategies will make you and your child overweight. Never mind our own health for a second, a fat child suffers huge self-esteem issues, starts bad habits that are extremely difficult to break, and is vulnerable to obesity-related illnesses. The medical establishment increasingly blames our weight on everything from cancer to skin conditions. If you notice, most doctors maintain a healthy weight.

So let's stop disadvantaging our kids even more. The basic "fast fuel" meal suggestions here can get you started on a game plan while you start reading up on ways to stop using bad food in your parenting strategy.

Reducing Food Waste to Save Time and Money

For a decade, I subscribed to the "pantry principle," where I would estimate my family's consumption rate of an item and stock up about a month's worth of the product when on sale. That worked well for nonperishables and long-life products like butter that could be frozen. And making smart use of your freezer is key to both refrigerator management and reducing food waste.

Just about anything can be frozen. This includes:

- Shredded cheeses

- Butter and margarine

- Milk

- Pizza dough

- Eggs (stir in some salt and freeze uncooked in an ice cube tray)

- Chicken broth (homemade or store bought) poured in ice cube trays, too

- Leftover tomato products like sauce, paste, diced, or whole

- Fresh vegetables you haven't cooked yet, packaged in ziplock freezer bags after partially cooking

The following chart lists nonperishable foods that create an ideal pantry—food commonly needed and/or that can be used in a pinch to create meals at home.

THE IDEAL PANTRY

Cereals and Starch	
Oatmeal (old-fashioned)	Box cereals
Rice (brown and white)	Pasta (linguine, macaroni, etc.)
Taco shells	
Dairy	
Dried or powdered milk (for baking, waffles, pancakes, sauces, etc.)	Evaporated milk in can
Nut milk (coconut, almond, cashew)	Dried butter
Canned Protein	
Chicken	Tuna
Soup	Beans (black, kidney, pinto, navy, etc.)
Canned Fruit	
Pineapple	Peaches
Blueberries	Oranges
Dried Fruit	
Raisins	Currants
Oils and Vinegars	
Vegetable oil	White vinegar
Flavoring—Sweet	
Sugar (brown, white)	Syrup
Jam/jelly	Molasses

Flavoring—Salty	
Soy sauce	Salt
Seasonings (Mexican, Italian, Chinese)	Teriyaki sauce
Canned Vegetables	
Tomatoes (sauce, diced, whole, etc.)	Corn (whole and creamed)
Pumpkin	Olives
Baking	
Flour	Spices
Baking soda	Baking powder
Drinks	
Coffee	Powdered flavor drinks
Cocoa	Tea
Never Perishable	
Tissues	Paper towels
Dishwasher soap	Dishwashing liquid
Trash bags	Toilet paper
Plastic wrap	Tinfoil
Bottled water (for emergency use)	Ziplock freezer bags
Disposable litter boxes	Pet food
Floss	Soap
Feminine products	Toothpaste

Leftovers! It's What's for Lunch

If your dinner fare would make good leftovers for lunch, make extra. Mostly, these go to the adult's lunch since you probably have access to a microwave to reheat it.

SCHOOL LUNCHES AND THE STIGMA OF FREE

I was a school-lunch kid. My mother steadfastly refused to make four lunches on top of all the other meals she made. In those days, the school food was prepared by lunch ladies in full kitchens in the back of the cafeteria. The lunch subsidies to all schools back then validated my mother's return on time equation. Healthy and cheap described those lunches.

At some point around my middle school years, family finances got bad enough to qualify us for free lunches. I was one of a few kids that had to inform the lunch line cashier that I got free lunch. Every Day. My defiant teen self-proclaimed "free" out loud, followed by a hard stare daring anyone to make a comment. I had a personal brand that I wouldn't put up with bad behavior from anyone, adult or peer. My younger sister, though, was more socially minded. Her tact was to start making her own lunches the night before. A homemade PB&J was more socially acceptable than free-lunch Salisbury steak.

That fear of being labeled poor deters many students from the subsidized lunch line with its cheaper and healthier offerings. For all your good intentions to provide healthy food for your family, the option to buy food from an a la carte junk food line can undermine that.

Kids are also influenced by what is familiar. To avoid having them reach for fatty chicken nuggets and cheeseburgers, avoid bringing them home on a regular basis yourself.

Most schools provide lunches, and if you receive the subsidized lunch, it can be a terrific time and money saver. Sometimes though, your child won't like the selection (or you forget to put in the monthly order). My daughter didn't like Pizza Friday, so I knew to pack her lunch on Fridays. In high school, she went into a full-scale revolt against the school food, and since I'd pack my lunch for work every day, it was easy enough to make another for her.

Getting Food into Bodies, Quickly

Nourishment affects everything. Good food provides:

- Focus during the day; can't pay attention on an empty stomach

- Steady blood sugar to level moods and focus

- Healthy weight maintenance

- Essential nutrients for growth and health

It behooves us as parents to figure out the "good food conundrum." Sourcing, preparing, and cleaning up meals needs to be as healthy and painless as possible. With all that at stake, I devoted time to figure the most efficient meal process. I developed these guiding principles:

Sourcing Food

As discussed previously, ordering grocery delivery versus shopping yourself provides significant time savings *if you can plan.* The time value of money equation in chapter 10 also demonstrates that if you take home more than $10/hour it can make financial sense to get your groceries delivered.

Preparing Meals

Years of trial and error revealed the following minimum needs for single parents:

- Breakfast needs to be high protein/low carb that is also grab and go.

- Lunches, if not bought at school, should be the same—high protein with veggies; leftovers repurpose well to adult bag lunches.

- Snacks, low in sugar and readily available, or the default is cookies.

- Dinner can be made ahead on Sundays for three nights, and on other nights, use leftover or second-night recipes.

- One night at a restaurant, added on a Friday, transitions from the scheduled week to the weekend.

- Meal kit deliveries are a viable option and can be cost competitive with the other options, especially in high-cost-of-living locales.

- Simple meals can be learned easily; rotisserie chicken and ground beef are in heavy rotation in our house, and after mastering meals based on these two proteins, I could handle six dinners and lunches a week.

A WEEK OF EATING AT CASA PATRICIA

I aim to cook only three days a week for six days and get one night of takeout.

My food week starts on Saturday. I'll plan a weekly menu while sitting at a school sports event. On the way home, we'll stop at the grocery store and pick up the ingredients. The shopping may include dinner from the hot bar for that night, depending on my energy level.
I will spend fifteen minutes before going to bed putting out the ingredients for the next day's cooking. The French have a phrase for this, *mise en place.*

Sunday, I'll cook for the next few days. In an hour, I can prepare meal ingredients for use during the week, using an unpaid sous chef (aka teenage assistant) that day.

Sunday Prep

Hard boil a dozen eggs, chop and freeze onions, prepare a cup of rehydrated milk (cooking only; straight up the stuff that tastes awful), and cook rice and/or potatoes. Make a batch of waffles or pancakes, some to eat now and most to freeze for grab and go for the week.

Breakfast

Protein pancakes and waffles, premade and frozen

Muffins, heavy on protein mix-ins, premade and frozen

Eggs, sausage/bacon on an English muffin, wrapped to go

Overnight oatmeal in a jar

Hard-boiled eggs and toast

Lunches (Work or School)

Peanut butter sandwiches with orange or apple

Rotisserie chicken sandwiches with canned pineapple chunks

Leftover stir-fry noodles with apple or orange

Cheese sandwiches and canned fruit

Tuna pasta salad made the night before with orange or canned fruit

Dinner

Rotisserie chicken breast

Spicy beef pasta (AKA spaghetti and meat sauce)

Meatloaf cooked with mixed vegetables and potato side

Stir-fry noodles with frozen shrimp or leftover rotisserie chicken

Burritos from leftover rotisserie chicken or ground beef

For inspiration, check out the website on the USDA Food at Home webpage for the "Thrifty Food Plan." All menus meet the USDA nutrition guidelines and include easy-to-access ingredients.

Retire These Time-Held Food Myths

Myth 1: You Can Cook Once a Month and Eat Meals in Rotation from Your Freezer

Replace this concept with "batch cooking." Batch cooking means you make extra of a meal, such as meatballs, and freeze it. "Once a month cooking" means that you make large amounts of a dish and assemble it like a production line. The idea of "once and done" appeals to me, but the cook-ahead recipes usually are full of fat and carbs in the form of cheese and pasta. While having a few extra chicken enchiladas or mac and cheese on hand helps in a pinch, a steady diet of those foods isn't healthy.

Myth 2: Fresh Vegetables Are Healthier Than Canned or Frozen

Produce starts to lose nutrients as soon as it is picked. The fruits and vegetables in my supermarket undoubtedly were picked last week or earlier. Some of the fruit is picked green and ripened using ethylene gas, making them taste like cardboard. Eat frozen food guilt free or shop at a local farm.

GUILTLESS GUIDE TO PRODUCE

"Eat more fresh produce!" a health mantra extolls. But does this consider that by the time a produce truck makes it from the California Inland Empire of food factory farms to my supermarket in New England, the food is well past its nutritional prime? I am better off, nutritionally, with frozen produce. Mass farm production also ruined the taste of fresh food for me. It is also a planning, money, and time-saver to switch to frozen produce.

Myth 3: Throw Out All Expired Food

This depends. Milk and other liquid dairy products hold pretty true to their expiration dates. However, I've eaten my fair share of canned foods a year-plus past their "best by" dates. Remember that most dairy foods can be frozen. Cheese crumbles, but if it was going to be melted anyway, then it doesn't matter.

Emergency Supplies

As a Red Cross volunteer, I taught preparedness to vulnerable populations. They bear the brunt of the fallout from accelerating natural disasters. I stopped teaching because I didn't feel I was making an impact. The program I presented didn't really reflect the needs of this population. I should have been presenting specifically to single-parent households.

The disaster fallout hits single-parent households exponentially. Disasters disrupt anyone's best-laid plans. I can't tell you when or what disaster will come next. I can only tell you there will be one. I am in New England. We don't have hurricanes or large earthquakes (well, mostly don't have), but we do have our fair share of disruptions. Here is an abbreviated list of what we've dealt with in the recent past:

2010: a weeklong boil-water order for the Boston area because of a collapsed water main

2010: flooding knocked out home heating and water mechanicals in the Boston area during the winter

2011: Hurricane Irene ripped through Massachusetts, knocking out power for weeks to cities and devastating inland Vermont

2013: the Boston Marathon bombing shelter-in-place order where no cars were allowed on the road and people had to stay inside for eighteen hours

2015: ten feet of snow collapsed the transportation system

2018: a gas leak exploded homes and caused fires in five cities and towns in the Merrimack Valley north of Boston, leaving thirty thousand residents to evacuate their homes immediately and, upon their return, be without gas heat into the winter

2019: a polar vortex where the region issued a stay-at-home advisory in the face of subarctic temperatures

2020: the pandemic lockdown that prompted panic buying of household goods and food where essential food and hygiene products disappeared from shelves

2020 thru 2021: consumer goods shortages from supply-chain lockups caused by the pandemic-induced labor shortage, microchip shortage, and shipping container shortage

Convinced? New England isn't even in a high risk area, so it makes sense to keep extras on hand. It is especially important for single parents as part of the vulnerable population. Remember:

- We can't stand in line at the Home Depot or supermarket unless it is after work hours and we can take our children

- Our support networks have their own family to care for during emergencies.

- Already stretched to the limit, we don't have a margin for error.

The following actions can create a "margin of safety":

- Posting an emergency numbers list on the fridge with your phone and children's phones

- Having three days of emergency supplies of food, water, and hygiene products, including diapers

- Packing a "go bag" with an extra set of clothes, snacks on the run, cash in small bills, plus those emergency numbers; I use an old gym bag stashed in the front hall closet

- Creating a family emergency plan for evacuating the house and identifying an escape route

- Practicing an evacuation drill as a family activity—it's a great activity with younger children when you need something to do; kids love drills, and it can ease anxiety around the "what-ifs"

With the minimal preparation suggested previously, I was able to handle the fallout from the aforementioned list of disasters. I even was able to ship supplies to my daughter whose city's infrastructure collapsed during the pandemic lockdown.

We can't know when an emergency will erupt to disrupt our lives, but we know it will and we will be prepared.

TAMING THE PAPER TIGERS

Rules of Thumb to Manage Paper

Where does all the paper come from? That's a rhetorical question. Healthcare is by far and away the worst offender. The folders marked "health insurance" and "health expenses" take up a disproportional space in my file cabinet. (When I had administrative care of my now late mother, the healthcare paperwork took ten hours a week to manage. Thankfully, we now have fewer physical documents, but the onslaught, whether paper or electronic, still needs organization.)

I use folders both literally and figuratively. I admit to using both old-school paper manila as well as electronic folders.

Why do I keep all this documentation? Probably 20 percent of the bills I get are incorrect. That includes healthcare providers, insurance policies, and rental agreements. Most egregious are monthly charges that hit my credit card. I am beginning to believe this is intentional. They think they have your money and aren't up for a fight. Not true. Get vendors to the bargaining table. In the past, I've had success leapfrogging merchants by hitting "dispute" on a credit card transaction. That has been less successful of late so try to resolve the charge by calling them.

Systems

Here is my file system. It's been the same way for thirty years.

I have three boxes (or piles): incoming, action, and to file.

If you are all digital, this same flow can apply to online documents. After you take action on an incoming document, you create the file folders every year and drag and drop documents in them for recordkeeping.

To File

Every year I set up these folders:

Housing (rental agreement, expenses, mortgage, insurance)

Utilities (heat, electricity, water, cable, Internet, phone)

Taxes (property taxes, excise taxes, estimated income tax payments, donations)

Banking and retirement

Car (payments, leases, maintenance costs)

Sales receipts

Medical insurance

Medical costs (out of pocket)

School papers

Because of the transition from paper to digital documents, I've maintained two systems. I go paperless as much as possible, but when it comes to healthcare, it is still heavily paper based. I am not going to take the time to scan old documents to my computer, but if you are in start-up mode for an organization system, feel free to use any tech available.

The Seven-Year Rule

At the beginning of each new year, I set up a new set of files with the same labels. In April (after I have filed the previous year's taxes), the previous year's files will go into a box, marked with the year. It stays in my office, and the years before that go to the basement, closet, or garage. I keep seven years of files, or seven boxes. When I put the previous years into storage, I pull out the oldest or eight-year-old file box and toss it.

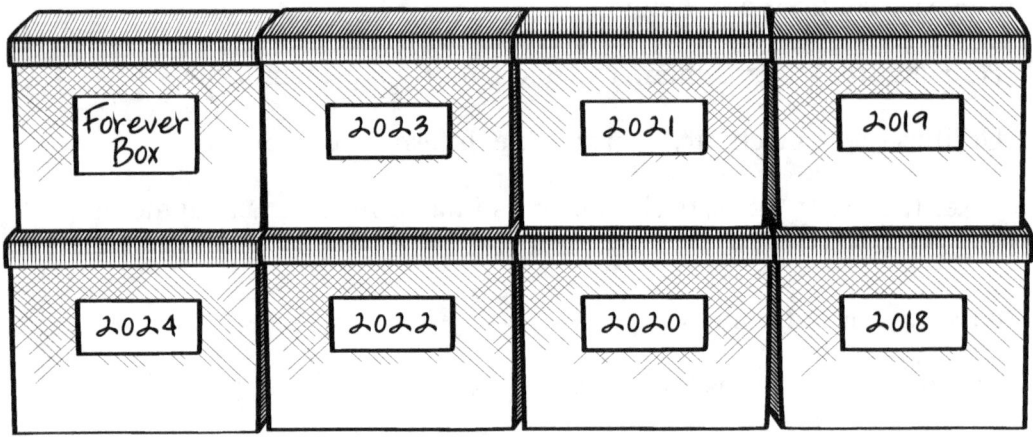

There is one important exception to the seven-year maintenance rule: receipts relating to the purchase, maintenance, and sale of a house should be kept for ten years past the sale. You need documentation to prove the costs of improvements to your home so they can be deducted from any profits from the sale.

Prevent Identity Theft

Most financial and medical companies no longer print sensitive information such as social security numbers or account numbers on their statements to you. However, you should check before tossing. I recently discovered that while my bank doesn't report my account numbers in full on my statements, the brokerage where I keep my retirement account (IRA) does print full numbers, so please check. Also, for a long time, my dentist was using my social security number as the patient identifier. I check those bills as well. Shred these in a machine or tear them into tiny strips.

Fun fact: Shredded paper cannot be recycled. It's too small.

Touch Only Once

Minimize paper shuffling with this simple sequence: inbox > action > file.

Something might sit in the action file until you have time to absorb it and figure out what to do. That's why you need a paper route. Yes, I actually mean a time that you do paperwork. It's mind-numbing work, so I do it in the evening after dinner. As my work schedule lightened up, I moved it to the afternoon. That way if I need to call someone about the paper in front of me, they would be around.

Schedule Time to Go Through Your Inbox

But don't do paperwork during your prime mental acuity time. Prime time is for thinking work, not stupid busy work. When my daughter was very young, I had a mother's helper come in a few hours every week so I could do things that required my full attention like the inbox, both paper and email. For me, that was Saturday afternoon. If you can't afford a mother's helper, then do paperwork while your child is on a playdate, with a relative, or yes, glued to something you actually don't mind them watching on a screen.

Don't Be Afraid to Talk to a Live Customer Service Person

If someone sends me a bill/invoice that I don't understand, I call them and say "I am confused." I don't argue; I have them take the time to explain. Shortcut the interminable customer service IVR computerized system by repeating "associate" or "operator." Talkin' to you, Bank of America.

Put It on Autopilot

Paperwork is "stupid work," so automate as much as you can.

Put bills on autopay *unless* the vendor is mistake prone.

While I pay the total balance each month on credit cards, if you run on really tight cash flow during the month, you could consider a hybrid approach. Set up the card for autopay of the minimum each month. During your weekly paperwork session, you can adjust your coming monthly payment to pay the entire balance when your statement arrives by email.

Get Rid of Junk Email to Reduce Impulse Purchasing and Save Time

Ninety percent of my emails are promos and solicitations. I worked for a decade in consumer research, and I have bad news. We mortals don't stand a chance against the myriad of behavior-based customer research done before those emails ever reach us.

That's why even if I like the store or product, I immediately scroll down to unsubscribe.

Better to resist temptation by removing promos from sight. Luckily, we live in a world where commercial email gets swept aside with the click of a key. If this feels annoying, consider the olden days when we wrote letters to the mass mailing association in order to get off a mailing list. My brother kept a recycling bin right inside his door to toss junk mail before it could enter the house.

The following steps should get you started on the road to sanity:

- *Unsubscribe from nonprofits, even if you love them.* This doesn't make you a bad person. It makes you a good parent. If you want to donate to an organization, you will know where to find them.

- *For memberships such as the zoo or Audubon, set preferences.* This is a tragedy of gigantic proportions that worthwhile nonprofits have gotten into the email business. Most of mine comes from four nonprofits. You can click on email preferences and set what you want. I am so fed up with some of them that I have not renewed.

- *Unsubscribe from blogs and newsletters.* Blogs have become a side hustle for many and are annoyingly full of affiliate links. You click on a product the blog or newsletter recommends, and the blogger gets a commission if you buy.

- *Newsletters, likewise, have become another form of advertising.* However, I will caveat that some provide value. One that comes immediately to mind is ADDitude.com. This is a for-profit organization that curates some of the country's leading experts in learning styles and neurodiversity. It is a mega resource. Mayo Clinic's newsletter similarly provides worthwhile health information. If you derive value from the time you spend reading newsletters, then keep them coming. However, if you find yourself ignoring them for lack of time, you can either unsubscribe or direct them to a specific box.

- *Use "mail preferences" to direct specific mail to a specific folder.* I don't use this function. I'd rather intercept nonvalue emails from entering my vision in the first place. But if you can't bear to leave unsolicited emails unexamined, you may find redirecting emails to be a valuable use of time and good time management.

What's left should be necessary email. I know some people have two email accounts. One for shopping and the other for bills and personal mail. If that helps you tame this beast, that's a valid strategy. Just don't merge your mailboxes because you will be right back to where you started.

ADMINISTERING THE FAMILY'S HEALTH

As the family chief medical officer, the responsibility to manage, schedule, track, maintain, and pay for healthcare consumes significant time for me. If you have a true coparent, this role should be the sole responsibility of one party, preferably the custodial parent.

Respect that person's skill set to manage this, and peace will reign. It is a thankless job. Besides my child, I had financial responsibility for an infirmed parent. This included managing medical billing and payments for her retirement, assisted living, and, ultimately, nursing homes. Until she went on Medicaid, my life was a torrent of paper-generated bills.

Paperless settings, auto-calendar inputs, and text reminders have made the chief medical officer role easier and less paper intensive. I can review accounts, payments, past appointments, and medications online now. I only have two folders at this point: medical insurance documents and out-of-pocket medical expenses. The latter includes receipts for medications (both prescription and over the counter). That documentation is necessary for reimbursement from a Flexible Spending Account (FSA) or itemizing medical deductions on your taxes.

PART 3

Money

CHAPTER 12

Increasing Your Income from Wages

The Good News for Single, Working Parents

How Soft Skills from Parenting Translate to the Workplace

Job Strategies for Single Parents

Improving Your Earning Potential Versus Working More Hours

How to Increase Your Job Income

Handling Work Conflicts

Skill-Up for Success

How to Start Searching for the Right Job

WHILE INCOME DEFICITS ARE NOT UNIQUE to single parents, we pay a disproportionately higher share of income for childcare. Single parents need more childcare hours and may need to take lower-paying, more contained jobs. Often, we can't travel or work overtime since it is rarely financially viable after subtracting the costs incurred to work.

More than half the country has this problem. In the single-parent household, it's aggravated by our poor childcare system and the rigid nature of many jobs.

After a forty-plus-year career, I have a few things to say about working for wages. Work rules have changed dramatically between when I started to work and now. I like to think they've changed for the better. What follows are my most useful tips, acquired not only as an employee and employer but also as a job mentor.

THE GOOD NEWS FOR SINGLE, WORKING PARENTS

Trends in the job market are moving favorably for single parents:

- Low unemployment rates, rising turnover, and record job vacancies create high demand for workers.

- Shifting demographics have resulted in fewer workers, which in turn makes workers better positioned to negotiate with would-be employers.

- The advent of remote and hybrid work helps to address the all-too-familiar logistical and commuting challenges faced by single parents.

- Online training opportunities make it easier for workers to acquire new, marketable skills.

- Though the pace is still glacial, the government and employers are starting to address the shortage and cost of childcare.

HOW SOFT SKILLS FROM PARENTING TRANSLATE TO THE WORKPLACE

Keep in mind, employers desperately seek soft skills, which we have in abundance. As a single parent, you have had to develop a range of these skills, and they are transferrable to the workplace. Do a search for soft skills plus the word "resume," and you should get examples of how to put your abilities in a resume.

My goal for this section is not to write your interview script. In fact, it's never a good idea to lead with parenting stories in a resume or interview, single parent or not. You don't know your interviewer's biases, good or bad.

Instead, I am pointing out all the strengths you bring to an employer. Have confidence that you have a lot of skills they need. (Come to think of it, confidence is a soft skill.)

For example, as a single parent, you've had to master:

- Listening skills. You are attentive to your family's needs. Demonstrate on a resume that you are understanding because you can listen to another point of view before acting.

- Punctuality. You meet multiple needs simultaneously and still get to places on time. Demonstrate your own on-time percentage. Do you clock into a job a few minutes early every day?

- Organization. As a parent, you've tapped into the executive function part of your brain, providing for daily care tasks. On your resume, demonstrate how you have managed multiple projects, made a habit of being punctual, or delivered a project on time.

- Collaborating with others. This is a biggie for an employer. These days, few people work as an island onto themselves. You've learned this skill as a parent, who needs everyone pulling in the same direction to move ahead. On your resume, mention joint projects, committees, and volunteer groups where together you accomplished a goal.

- Motivating others. Well, if you haven't yet learned this, your toddler will teach you soon enough. Young children express their primal needs, and you need to be a genius to keep up with them. In the workplace, this means moving peers, subordinates, and, yes, superiors to work with you on an idea. Give examples when you took an idea to fruition by helping teammates find their inner "why."

- Trustworthiness. This means that others can depend that you will do what you say you will. Clearly, you are trustworthy enough to get a young child to school or yourself to work on time. Highlight when you have represented an organization's brand and upheld its reputation. Mention roles where you have handled money, volunteer or paid.

- Creativity. Every day single parents have to write a playbook on solving problems. Think back to any challenge where you've gotten around a bureaucracy, adapted a nontraditional role, or MacGyvered a solution. Do it enough, and problems won't phase you.

- Patience. Do I need to spell this one out? It's an important managerial skill that I got much better at as a parent. Junior people make mistakes that freak out managers and clients. With parenting experience, I could listen to the complaints, debrief with the offending party, then tell them about my biggest goofs. It went a long way to defusing the situation.

"As single parents you are advantages to companies, not hindrances. The skills single parents use to manage life—arranging care, handling bureaucracies, constantly adapting—are perfectly aligned with what businesses need. From the moment you awake, you have to organize yourself and the families for the day, figure out how to communicate, and how to live in a world that is not built to fit your needs. The mindset is innately collaborative and communicative, oriented toward problem solving, good at working with limited resources, and used to overcome daily challenges." —**Harvard Business Review**

- Dedication. You could have resigned at this parenting gig at any time, but you didn't. In the face of adversity, you drew on role models, got information (buying this book), and soldiered on. Companies don't like turnover. Mention your longevity in previous jobs, spending overtime to fix a problem, and working with previous colleagues.

JOB STRATEGIES FOR SINGLE PARENTS

While all of the factors discussed previously may help you get a job, as single parents we also need solid strategies for thriving, or at least surviving, at whatever job we get. I detail a few strategies here.

Choose a Job That You're Already Good At

This strategy is to work fewer hours than required by working at a job you could do blindfolded. During my daughter's childhood, I was, at times, unemployed, overworked, or underworked. "Underworked" meant I could perform my work in half the allotted time and use the remaining half to run my life. In other words, I was paid full-time but did the work in half the time as others. I was very overqualified for a position, but the happiness from less stress and the feeling of mastery assuaged my ego.

Hold Your Work Boundaries (Overtime, Outside Meetings, Etc.)

Again, referring back to my "underemployed era," my colleagues were all generally younger and, if married, in a two-parent family. I didn't expect much sympathy. I held to those boundaries that were right for my situation and didn't make a big deal of it. These included:

- No work trips. It cost too much for overnight care.

- No supervisory roles. The extra work wasn't compensated. While I would willingly mentor junior folks on the job, I no longer wanted to write performance reviews or be responsible to pick up any slack from underperforming team members.

- No special projects. I learned that the hard way.

- No before/after work engagements with the office.

- No monetary contributions.

I didn't win any popularity contests, but the low salary did not allow for extraneous childcare costs or donations to causes like birthdays and charitable donations.

Live Close to Work or Work Remotely

Live as close as you safely can to your workplace. It may be that you have to downsize your living space, but it will be worth it. Once the kids are in school, the quality of the school district will matter the most. In some cases, you may get both. In Boston, the inner city has expensive housing and lousy public schools. However, you can apply to "bus" to schools in the leafy suburbs. The Boston Metro Area is small, so it is also possible to live within ten miles of the office by public transportation and still enjoy a town or city with good schools.

Being close to my office made for quick and inexpensive getaways following those dreaded calls from the school nurse that my child was sick. I could take a ride share back home and be there in thirty minutes.

Be Selective About Your Employer

Hold out for positions that will work for you as a single parent. Talk to former and current employees about flex work, attitudes toward families, and so forth. In the end, it works best for you and the employer if the culture is one in which you can succeed.

Work for a Reasonable Person

The definition of "reasonable person" is one who can understand work/life complications and accommodate flexibility. This isn't to say that they grant every wish, but rather, they can listen to your proposals and work toward a mutually acceptable solution. In the sidebar, I share an exchange I had with a supervisor when summer childcare plans fell through last minute. Notice that no one plays the victim here; rather, we talked about what was important and what could be modified. We reached a joint solution.

WE ALL NEED A "MIKE"

When childcare problems arise (which they will), it helps to be proactive as well as have a reasonable supervisor who can objectively weigh options.

While in middle school, my daughter attended a summer environmental science camp. It was a terrific program that was all day long and very physically demanding. If I could give an award for the best camp ever, it would be this one. It was within walking distance from the house, which meant I could leave for work at 7:30 a.m. For two years, we managed this. Then, in the third year, a week before camp was due to start, the school department shifted the program to another location, clear across the city.

I had to request flextime on short notice. I negotiated with my supervisor, Mike, explaining the situation. Even with a "Mike," I took responsibility to consider the options and related impacts. I thought out options, pros and cons, and stated my preference. I acknowledged that the decision was ultimately his. Mike came back with a few requests like coming in especially for company meetings, and we cobbled together a plan that worked. Look for supervisors with whom you can have constructive dialogue.

Understand Your Value and Hold Out for It—
Conditions Are on Your Side

The pandemic wrought "The Great Resignation." After remote work or government-sponsored unemployment pay, workers (not just single parents) realized that "The Great Exploitation" had been going on. For the previous forty years, working hours increased, and salaries stayed the same. This massive rip-off relied on automation, an abundance of workers (Baby Boomers), and Asian offshoring (Daniel Pink, *A Whole New Mind*).

The pandemic lockdown happened just as the working-age population started declining with Gen Z. Then the middle cohort of Boomers retired early and 2 percent of the population died of COVID, half of whom were working age.

This decline in the working-age population shifted the status quo in favor of workers. I feel this advantage to workers will hold out. While I always had the mindset to "keep my job at all cost," I counsel my own daughter differently. She and her twentysomething cohort are entitled to reasonable work expectations and employment with dignity.

Be Confident About Your Skills

As a single parent, you become endowed with some level of time-management skills. You also have social skills. Cut yourself a break. You'll get better as you go along. No one is born knowing how to juggle, and few of us had parental role models for single parenting. We may have had single parents, but their times and situations were all different.

You be you. You do you. Only you know what is required in your situation. Don't judge yourself by others. They may not be in your situation.

IMPROVING YOUR EARNING POTENTIAL VERSUS WORKING MORE HOURS

Overtime and extra shifts may be the easiest source for extra income. You know the company, and they know you. For you, this may be a no-brainer. But do you really have the bandwidth to work more hours? Again, the most important question to answer is "What's the best use of your time?"

Is Your Time Better Spent Training for a Better-Paying Career?

An assessment of the cost associated with a second job commitment and your return on time probably is a net negative calculation for you. It costs money to work. Besides commuting costs, there is childcare. Go back to chapter 10 and calculate your return on time. That is the bare minimum you will have to earn for it to make any sense at all to take a job.

But the other important consideration is: Is your time better spent training for a more lucrative and stable career? Or maybe a second job introduce you to a new career?

Enter the Growth Multiplier

Some people just don't make enough money. They can't cover the basics without subsidies. In that case, their "free" time is better spent in the pursuit of bettering their earning potential rather than trying to save every dollar. (That is *if* you use that free time productively versus killing time.)

Advancing your earning potential can include getting more education, gaining skills, interviewing for new jobs, or accessing subsidies for low earners. Here are examples of nonwage-paying time that could lead to more future household income:

- Researching new skills

- Talking with supervisors about what it takes to get promoted

- Earning degrees or certificates

- Applying for income-based subsidies (utilities, phone, healthcare, education)

- Managing mental health challenges

- Improving physical health for self and family

- Networking for new jobs

- Creating household routines to save time, thereby saving money

Essentially, as James Clear states in *Atomic Habits*, "Your actions from these activities will drive growth over the next 12 months, so the value of your time is higher than your realized income indicates today."

HOW TO INCREASE YOUR JOB INCOME

Emma Johnson, in her book *Kickass Single Mom*, discusses improving single parents' income in great detail. While her book generally is geared toward professional, single moms, her advice on improving your income holds for any level of employment. Her philosophy is that you are far better off spending your time on a job search than penny-pinching. However, that comes after you take an axe to your spending (see chapter 14, "Expenses").

Upgrade Your Work Situation

Two pathways to making a better wage or having a more contained job include:

1. At a new employer   OR   **2.** At your current employer

At a New Employer

A first job, new job, or new employer—luckily the pathway to get what you want is similar for all three.

Quick, online research can be a low risk to start thinking of your direction. You can look up companies in the fields that interest you and then either look at their job listings or their employees on LinkedIn.com. You will quickly get a feel of the skills and/or experience needed in those jobs that interest you (or your child, for that matter).

WHAT EMPLOYERS GET WRONG WHEN HIRING AND WHAT YOU CAN DO

For all the hand wringing about the current labor shortage, you'd think employers would change up their game to find the best talent. But I see the same mistakes being made now as in the previous decade:

- Creating unrealistic requirement lists for job descriptions

- Wanting a candidate who has the exact same job at a competitor

- Punting job descriptions to human resources vs. hiring managers

- Overreliance on applicant tracking software

- Not considering how to rearrange responsibilities among their workforce so as to meet the needs of the labor market

- Not hiring ahead of the curve but waiting until someone quits

- Having one-size-fits-all job structures (i.e., only full-time employees)

Use the following strategies in your job search to overcome employers' blind spots:

- Ignore the job requirement laundry list. Focus on your key skills' alignment with the job description. Emphasize "transferrable skills."

- Use your network (or LinkedIn.com) to email directly someone in the company who interests you. You could start with the five most powerful words, *Can I get your advice?*

After receiving an offer, discuss your needs in terms of flexibility and offer possible solutions to accommodate them. But only do that with a hiring manager.

Don't get bullied into taking a job. True story. I once turned down a job because one interviewer told me he worked all night to do his project. I am no stranger to hard work, but as a single parent, that didn't feel like a good situation. The human resources representative called me, furious, and demanded I reconsider. I offered to consult until they found someone, but she was too disappointed to see my offer as a solution.

Job Hunting

Thousands of books, videos, and podcasts provide detailed advice on how to find your ideal job. It may not be your parents' job market, but some old things are new again. Here, in summary, are the six basic, time-honored steps for job hunting:

1. Know what you want.

2. Do some amount of research to discover who offers what you want.

3. Talk to everybody in your social circle about what you are looking for, and ask to meet anyone they know who may have the type of job that you want.

4. If you don't have a skill an employer wants, skill up with credentialing.

5. Avoid applying online through the company's online applicant tracking system. Only use it if you don't have any other route.

6. Send follow-up thank-you notes to anyone you meet who talks to you about a job.

Five Steps to Starting Your Job Hunt

1. Find Your Local Library

Even if your local library branch is limited, it probably belongs to a larger system, and you can order any book you want online.

To borrow physical books, you'll need proof of address. To access digital assets such as ebooks, music, movies, and so forth, you can apply online.

2. Borrow and Read Warren Berger's The Book of Beautiful Questions

I recommend this book to everyone, from job searchers to company presidents to friends.

3. Figure Out How Much You Need to Earn to Be Self-Supporting (Eventually)

This requires a budget. Find out how in an app such as You Need a Budget *or* use a study to find the cost-of-living calculations from Massachusetts Institute of Technology.

4. Identify a Few Career Path Options and Compare What They Involve and Their Salaries

Download from your state's employment website a list of careers and salary ranges. In Massachusetts, I found the state career information site to have a wealth of information.

State websites have financial aid for job seekers, lists of occupations and salaries, CareerOneStop centers, and unemployment assistance.

5. Talk to Live People

I understand that, for some, talking to a live person feels life-threatening. However, if you find a knowledgeable person, it saves a lot of time. Keep in mind that, in their hearts, people want to be helpful. Suggestions include:

- The reference librarian (phone or in person); the librarian can recommend books, and classes may be held at the library

- Admissions and financial aid offices at the local community college

- Employees at state job and employment offices

- People who have the job you want

Sometimes you get a dud. If so, politely end the conversation. Return (or call back) at another time and keep doing it until you find a helpful person.

Finding Time to Job Search

Job search professionals will tell you that finding a job is a full-time job. I won't go that far. Knowing what you want will narrow the field to employers who match your need. It's a time-saver.

Since most of this can be done online, it's a good after-kids-go-to-bed activity. Replace a few nights of streaming with the tasks here.

THE PITFALLS OF LOOKING FOR NEW WORK AT YOUR CURRENT JOB

Looking for another job while at work is perilous. If your employer finds out, you could find yourself branded as "disloyal," potentially affecting raises, promotions, or bonuses. Also, since employers can track employees' use of company computers, there is a chance your nonwork activity can be reported to your supervisor.

Review part 2 of this book and see if some of those suggestions of how to find time can help with job searching.

If your motivation flags, ask yourself why. Is the thought of change intimidating? Then consider how well you shifted during the pandemic or when your child was born. *You are already a change maven.*

At Your Existing Job: "Love the One You're With"

This represents the path of least resistance. The company knows you and doesn't want to incur the expense to replace you. It goes without saying that the larger the company, the more room to move around or up. However, even the smallest family-owned business needs reliable workers who know their jobs.

Remember the exchange with "Mike" earlier in this chapter? Start with thinking about what your company needs and look for overlaps with your own needs. If you are unsure of those, it helps to talk to people, asking their ideas on how you can improve your situation.

Start with the Five Most Powerful Words: "Can I Get Your Advice?"

It feels pretty good to be asked for your opinion. Open the conversation with your employer with broad questions, always phrased in terms of what is best for the company:

"I am looking at adding to my skills. What do you think the company needs most right now?"

"I see Janelle is retiring soon. What is needed to move into her position?"

"You know my work. Where do you see the best match between my abilities and the company's needs in the coming year?"

Talk to people who have the job you want and learn about their career paths and the skills needed for that job. Talk to human resources if there is one, or talk to a career coach online. States also sponsor the CareerOneStop centers. (I haven't heard if job seekers found the advice valuable. The online tools, though, are a good place to start.)

The goal here is to open up the world of possibilities for you. That begins with some research on your part.

It bears repeating. Any position needs to be within the parameters for you to manage life as a single parent. Make sure you make your own list of "wants." You don't have to share those during the career discussions but keep them in the back of your mind as you listen to the advice given.

Look for Free Training In-House and Outside

Your employer *may* have an established training program for employees. This was a matter of course for the largest US employers for years. Starting in the 1980s and accelerating into the twenty-first century, those programs were cut, and employers relied on poaching talent or crossing their fingers and hoping that educational institutions could give them what they needed in terms of skills. If demographic trends continue, in-house training could make a comeback.

If you find an outside training program, then consult your employee handbook for the policies. If your program falls within the reimbursement guidelines, it's an easy discussion with human resources. However, if you want to "color outside the lines" (such as time off to study), talk to your manager. I was a pushover for any kind of education and approved reimbursement for everything from foreign language to computer language classes. I also approved study time before exams (as long as the workload didn't fall on me).

HANDLING WORK CONFLICTS

It takes effort to look at a conflict from both parties' sides. It's easier to understand your boss's point of view once you've had their job for a while.

Understanding another's needs can help you negotiate conflict resolution. What is it that your boss needs that you can live with giving?

Remember, a goal is to keep your employment reference. If you do decide an agreement can't be reached with your employer, act professionally and give at least two weeks' notice and offer to train your replacement.

At age sixteen, my daughter started working teenage beginner jobs. I was less concerned about the wage and more interested in her learning how to be a worker. This meant coming to work on time, getting along with colleagues, and staying present in her job (i.e., putting down the phone).

I witnessed rotten behavior from her multiple employers. Employers never disclosed they would cut her hours in August because customers went on vacation. The worst happened when her university ghosted her after committing to a summer position. "Bad employer behavior" appears not limited to small companies.

Learning to stand one's ground in the face of potentially exploitative behavior is a valuable life lesson. Part of that is examining your own needs opposite the employer's agenda and deciding on a path.

When to Hold 'Em

For three summers, my daughter coached youth ice hockey for the largest US development program. It was exciting to get all that free ice time, hang out with other college kids, and travel to beautiful locales. Camps have always relied on the cheap labor of students. For the world of hockey, it's valuable for all parties involved, except that the hours are incredibly long, making the net pay about $2/hour—all while using skilled workers who have trained long and hard to reach this competency level. It's also incredibly physically demanding.

I held my tongue over the low pay and its inequity between the girls and boys. My daughter's goal was to learn to be a worker. This meant taking direction and ownership of her charges' experience.

One particular camp vexed her. Held at the Boston Bruins Warrior ice rink, the site practically blazed from the halo of hockey heroes practicing there. Unfortunately, it also meant parents liked to be there, too, basking in the glow of their children on hallowed ground.

The more involved the parent was in their child's hockey development, the worse the kids behaved. One day, my then twenty-year-old called me in tears, telling me she wanted to walk out. Even after years of handling prepubescent boys on the rink, she was at wits' end over this particular group's behavior.

"It's up to you," I replied (always acknowledge autonomy). "Be sure to think about the consequences. Your fellow coaches will be left shorthanded, and you won't get a reference even though you have been there for several years. Another option is to finish the day and resign tomorrow with notice." She finished out the day's session, took a mental health day, and then returned to finish the season.

When to Fold 'Em

A different work conflict elicited different advice from me. My daughter worked in the university student call center soliciting alumni donations. In her second month, she ascended to the top of the leaderboard. Proudly, she pulled out her phone to snap a photo and send me. A colleague reported her for having her phone out. Three supervisors, all upperclassmen, pulled her into an office and screamed at her. She called me, shell-shocked.

Nobody should scream or be screamed at. It's unprofessional. I didn't have to listen to who was right or who was wrong. Screaming from a supervisor is unacceptable. Three-on-one with a junior employee was abusive. My response now was swift: "Aaaand, this is how you quit a job. Go in the next day. Resign. Say you will be professional and give two weeks' notice, but you don't want to work there anymore with such unprofessional behavior."

There are plenty of jobs out there at any level. Go for the flexibility and parameters you need. Everyone can be up-front about needs and work out a common agenda. It won't always work out. Just remember, if someone screams at you, move on. If you feel frustrated, talk to someone, and think it through. There is a situation that works for you.

SKILL-UP FOR SUCCESS

One can now attain skills needed for a job less expensively by pursuing certificates and credentials. "Credentialing" meets employers' needs in the shortest period of time and meets workers' needs to demonstrate success. From Microsoft certificates to med-tech programs in community colleges, you can gain advancement with a range of time commitments.

Certifications

To get those skills in-house, some employers are willing to pay for you to attend classes. Asking your employer to pay for and give you time off to attend school is the obvious preference. Depending on the scarcity of workers for a particular job, an employer may educate even a new hire on the skills they need.

> "First, they get a credential in a skill they need, then another, and another. Each can quickly pay off on its own by helping to get a job, raise, or promotion. Over time, they can add up to a bachelor's degree. . . . A lot of people will need more education to get back into the workforce, and they'll need to get it quickly, at the lowest possible cost, and in subjects directly relevant to available jobs."
> —Wired.com

The trend of "credential stacking" appeals to my sense of efficiency. Employers want specialists now, not generalists. If obtaining a credential proves to an employer you have the skill, you'll make it easy for them to make a hiring decision.

Credentialing isn't just for information technology and healthcare professionals. If you want to moonlight as a youth sports coach, childcare provider, or home health aide, having a credential will give you an in, a resume advantage, and probably higher pay.

One Word for the Community College Option—Childcare!

Completing your general education requirements at community college has several advantages over a four-year university. You will pay much less money to attend smaller, more flexible classes that provide the same quality education. Plus, you can do the program in person or remotely. You can switch careers for minimal cost. And childcare is sometimes provided on campus.

WATCH OUT!

Avoid for-profit, unaccredited training schools. This trillion-dollar industry is now in hot water for taking vast amounts of money from students and delivering on neither a marketable skill nor any skill at all. Talk to your state department of employment for training suggestions in an area that interests you.

I differentiate between accredited online colleges such as Southern New Hampshire University and false for-profits. For any college, private, public, or online, carefully read reviews. Oftentimes, a low-cost community college can be the preferred path to higher skills.

Affording the Cost of Training

Many organizations offer scholarships in the $500–$2,500 range. These are listed in scholarship search websites, which your library can point you to. However, these are small dollar amounts, require considerable effort to apply, and are very competitive. Instead, seek merit aid directly from the school you apply to or financial-based aid from your employer and/or US government programs. These include:

■ Employer-paid/sponsored

■ Graduate school scholarships and loans

■ State employment training programs

■ Community college programs

■ Trade union apprenticeship programs (local unions)

■ Technical high schools (high school and adult learners)

■ Federal government grants (FAFSA.org)

■ Private industry product training (e.g., Microsoft)

■ Trade associations (data analytics, app development, etc.)

■ Affinity group scholarships (Black Engineers, Daughters of the American Revolution (DAR), etc.)

Affording the Time for Training

Chapter 9 gives you ideas about finding time, including for job hunting. For learning time, you have a few extra resources:

■ If your employer is sponsoring your education, they may give you time off for classes and travel. This usually works when they are training you for a skill they need. If they don't offer, ask.

- Colleges and universities very often offer childcare. Even many prestigious universities offer distinct programs for adult learners and may offer childcare.

- Depending on their funding, state employment offices frequently provide childcare vouchers for school returners, so check there.

THE LONG VIEW

"I had my kids very young. I worked 2 jobs and went to school. I struggled for a long time, I did not have support from my kids' dad, just me. I wanted to be the best parent I could be, which to me, meant going back to school to make more money to take care of them . . . I'm 36 now and people think I'm so successful and I am, just very exhausted that I pushed myself for so long."
—Reddit single-parent community member

"How did u do school with 2 kids?"
—Reddit single-parent community member

"I went back to school when my daughter was 13 and she could watch her brother. The university also had a great daycare program and I received a discount. It was tough, but I stuck to a schedule during the week." —Reddit single-parent community member

---

HOW TO START SEARCHING FOR THE RIGHT JOB

First: Focus on Strengths

This book is about helpful, positive changes. By knowing your strengths, you can exploit them.

It is a myth that your greatest potential for growth is your area of weakness. Focusing on deficits will demotivate you while focusing on your strengths will help you feel more positive and give you energy. Inventory your strengths, if only to feel good.

To achieve the goal of increasing income, we need to build from a position of internal strength. A classic strength identification exercise has you writing each strength idea down on a separate sticky note or index card. (You can find comprehensive strength lists on many sites. See CareerOneStop.org for basic strength and skills inventories.)

Next: Inventory Hard or Technical Skills

Technical skills relate to a particular occupation. You may have learned technical skills from past work experience, school, or training, such as writing code or operating equipment.

Finally: Take an Interest Inventory to Match Up with What You Find Stimulating

Your strengths, skills, and enjoyment in these categories comprise the most immediate areas where you stand to do well financially. It's a fun exercise to rate your level of interest to do various tasks. After you take the self-assessment, you will receive results listing all the various careers and jobs that match your interests, the future prospects in those careers, and what they earn.

In our online Reddit community, members frequently asked what career would *make them more money and what training they needed.* An interest assessment answers those questions. The questions are longer than a magazine quiz but can still be enjoyable.

If you search "interest inventory for adults," you'll find that the job site Indeed.com has the inventories, as well as CareerOneStop.org. Take a few if you wish and see what excites you.

CHAPTER 13

Other Income Streams

The Importance of Multiple Income Streams

1. Wages

2. Child Support and Alimony

3. Subsidies

4. Private Grants

5. Income-Related Subsidies for Health Insurance, Medications, and Utilities

6. Sliding Scale Payments

7. Family Support

8. Side Jobs

9. Savings

10. Selling Unwanted Goods

11. Borrowing

12. Teen Labor

THE IMPORTANCE OF MULTIPLE INCOME STREAMS

With all due credit to financial planners, I've adapted their mantra of "five streams of income" for single parents, rounding up an even dozen. The "twelve streams of income" that follow don't mean to suggest you need scads of part-time jobs. It means that you create multiple sources of income to:

- Reduce reliance on one source and the risk should that source dry up

- Recognize how essential subsidies are for stabilizing household finances

- Look at your potential income earnings as a "portfolio" of opportunity

1. WAGES

As in the previous chapter, this refers to working as a W-2 employee for a company. Ideally, this is a position with benefits. I also include self-employed workers who receive 1099 wage statements. These workers, such as myself, generally do not receive health, dental, and so forth. Steady gig workers, such as full-time rideshare drivers, also fall into this category. (Occasional workers fall into "side jobs," described in number eight on page 156.)

2. CHILD SUPPORT AND ALIMONY

Child support counts as a stream of income. Below I have discussed some of the oft-mentioned problems with collecting that income. Before getting into that, I want to caution readers not to waive child support from the other parent. No matter how much you make now or how difficult it is for the ex-partner, realistically, it's not your right to waive this support away—it is your child's. Even if the court only awards $50 a month, take it. Your income could decline or disappear. If you don't need the cash to live on, then bank it for your child later on. Education is expensive.

Ethically, the responsibility of having a child needs to be met by both parties. Both must contribute. Waiving that right absolves the other party from feeling the obligation's full weight. It may not be obvious now, but someday, an errant parent could wake up to their emotional responsibility.

I don't know if they will be better parents for it, but at least you don't make it easy for them to walk away.

AIMING FOR FINANCIAL INDEPENDENCE

While Emma Johnson's book, *Kickass Single Mom*, targets the upper socioeconomic segment of women, she makes some universal points about alimony and child support.

"Kick-Ass Moms do not depend on either [about 60 percent of custodial parents receive the total amount of child support] . . . and alimony is increasingly being limited by court reform. Also, both are contingent on another person's income—a person who very likely does not like you and is motivated to find ways not to pay. In other words, it is irresponsible financial planning to count on money that you may never see. The goal is *financial independence* [my italics]. Solely focusing on [child support and alimony] has impacts:

Ramifications on co-parenting

Disincentives

Focus on a piddling amount of money

It holds you back in every way.

You cannot live your potential as a . . . person if you choose to be financially dependent on anyone else, much less [someone] with whom you are no longer romantically entangled."

— Emma Johnson, *Kickass Single Mom*

Having a support agreement is essential because you cannot get government transition support without one, even if you qualify. But don't get consumed by it, either. While I advocate for taking steps to ensure the support is sought and paid, I don't advocate for making it a focal point of your life. Anger and frustration have both financial and emotional costs.

IF THEY FAIL TO PAY CHILD SUPPORT

"My ex-wife is getting in the way of my visitation rights with my children. What should I do?"

I will tell you what you should not do, and that is withhold money that the court ordered you to send her for child support. That is not only breaking the law, but it could also threaten your children's well-being. If you and your wife aren't speaking to each other and can't work this out in a civil way, then you must bring a contempt of court action against her. Unless your ex can prove that she has very good reasons for keeping you away from your kids, she will be ordered by the court to do what is legal and may have to pay your legal costs and a fine and possibly face going to jail in a short period.

"My husband is continually late with his child support payments. Is there anything I can do?"

Unfortunately, you are not alone. The legal term for past-due child support is arrearage, and it is a national shame. If I were you, I would hire an attorney to go after your husband, assuming he has some money to chase after.

A less expensive method is to contact your state's Child Support Enforcement (CSE) program. The federal website https://www.acf.hhs.gov/css has links to state agencies.

"My spouse is officially in arrears and is threatening to claim bankruptcy so he won't have to pay. Can he do that?"

He can try, but he most certainly won't succeed. Delinquent child support—along with back taxes and outstanding student loans—is a kind of debt that cannot be eliminated in a bankruptcy proceeding. All that filing can do for your spouse is to delay the day of reckoning. While it is true that in the midst of a bankruptcy hearing, all active attempts to collect a petitioner's debt must cease when the proceeding is finished, he will still owe back child support, and he will still have to pay.

— Suze Orman, *The Road to Wealth*

Find a low-stress way to receive the money or share expenses. While I disagree with Johnson's idea of a joint credit card you split up each month, I can get behind any idea that keeps you one step removed from the other party. Have the noncustodial parent pay their sums into a college account or other child-focused goal.

If the money isn't getting to you, you can hand it to the state child support enforcement agency. They have powers (to attach income to tax refunds, withhold passports, etc.) that you don't have. Let them do their job and take on the responsibility to chase the check.

For income advice on spousal and child support, I recommend Suze Orman's comprehensive money guide *The Road to Wealth* and its chapter "Financial Intimacy." It gets into the nitty-gritty, especially divorce, cohabitation, separation, and support payments. Libraries usually stock multiple copies.

3. SUBSIDIES

The Massachusetts Institute of Technology 2022 Cost of Living study showed that a single parent had to earn $120,000/year to support one child in Boston. Mostly, this is attributable to the cost of housing and childcare. If your current household income doesn't total that kind of money, subsidies will need to be considered for your revenue stream. Hopefully, your area has a lower cost of living.

Once you receive one government assistance program, you automatically qualify for many other programs, including transit, housing, school lunch, and utility subsidies.

Some of the better-known subsidies include SNAP, WIC (Women, Infants, and Children Grants), and TANF ("welfare"). WIC helps parents pay for food, healthcare, and education. TANF helps families. The Affordable Care Act ("Obamacare") will provide health insurance with premiums on a sliding scale.

Call 211 in your area and be connected for advice on what programs you qualify for and how to access them. 211 is the most comprehensive source of information about local resources and services in the country. Many different kinds of organizations operate the 211 service, including United Way, Goodwill, Community Action Partnerships, and local crisis centers. The phone banks are staffed with compassionate volunteers who could give you good information.

If you get a dud, politely depart the conversation ("Oh, I'm sorry, the baby is crying. Gotta go.") and call back at another time.

4. PRIVATE GRANTS

Small foundations and religious organizations such as St. Vincent de Paul award grants for emergencies such as past due electric bills, but consider this more of a one-off than a revenue stream. Funding is not ongoing. You need time to apply. There are applications and depending on the request, the grant requirements might include house visits. Consciously decide if this is a good use of your time and your level of need.

5. INCOME-RELATED SUBSIDIES FOR HEALTH INSURANCE, MEDICATIONS, AND UTILITIES

This stream of income comes in the form of reduced costs for essential living needs such as housing and utilities. Technically, subsidies are not a revenue stream, but they are recurring, and any reduction in expenses has the same effect as raising income. You apply once and, if eligible, receive reduced and fixed costs.

Housing

Affordable home ownership and rental subsidies vary town by town. Go to your city or town website and search for "affordable housing" to find the eligible housing for your family size and income. The income limits are also made for working families. In some states, developers are required to designate a portion of their units as affordable housing units in rental and for-sale developments.

Utilities

Electric, heat, and telephone providers offer subsidies through assistance programs. You can inquire through the 211 service or directly on each utility's website or from customer service. The Broadband Accessibility Act recently required Internet providers to make income-based subsidies available in their operating areas. (This federal Internet subsidy program is going away but may be locally available.)

Health Insurance

Go to Healthcare.gov to be connected to health insurance. Premiums are income based, thanks to the Affordable Care Act. Some states, such as Massachusetts, where I live, have their own health insurance gateway. Other states use the federal program. Either way, if you don't know your state's program, start at Healthcare.gov, and it will redirect you.

These assistance programs can be also considered for anyone over the age of eighteen. Children over eighteen can also apply for their own policy through the state health insurance program. And if your employer provides health insurance, children can stay on your employer's plan until they are twenty-six.

APPEAL IF DENIED

If you are denied benefits from any assistance programs, file an appeal. I have successfully filed appeals for multiple programs, including my daughter's and my respective health insurance premium subsidies and even property tax assessments.

Here is an area where people offering help can assist you. They can research programs and help you organize the required paperwork. A parent, social worker, church volunteer, or other person may have offered assistance to you, and having a defined task, such as researching government aid, makes it feel achievable to the helper.

Applying to programs seems overwhelming and feels like a full-time job. But think of it as a potential revenue stream. Like getting a job, you'll have to gather some documentation and fill out applications. No one is going to give you a grant, aid, or subsidy without proof of need.

6. SLIDING-SCALE PAYMENTS

"Sliding scale" refers to the pricing of services based on the consumer's ability to pay. Unlike the subsidies described in the previous section (where you apply and receive a simple "yes" or "no"), with a sliding scale you pay what you can afford. Even if your income is too high to qualify for the government subsidies mentioned previously, you can often get reduced fees via a sliding scale.

Read the fine print on services to see if they set their rates based on an ability to pay. Here are a few examples of life-enhancing services that may suddenly become affordable via a sliding scale:

- YMCA/YWCA memberships

- Private gyms

- Scouting dues and activity fees (apply through troop leader)

- Dental work (usually through a local dental school)

- Medical clinics

- Therapy

- Community adult education classes

- School field trips (talk to the principal about their subsidy fund)

- Property taxes (some towns have income-graduated property taxes)

- School lunches

- Tuition to private schools

- Fees for local activity programs for arts and sports

- Town-sponsored summer programs

7. FAMILY SUPPORT

For many, this is complicated. If you accept family support, you have to expect to receive unsolicited advice, and, for many, that comes loaded with emotional baggage.

However, for income-constrained single parents, family could be a lifeline. Those who can work with their families as a team are generally less stressed. This can be the best possible outcome for your children. It's hard work to reset your relationship as an adult with your parent. Whatever level of support you are offered and accept from family, make it a goal to put the effort into working on the relationship.

8. SIDE JOBS

Whether it's being an Uber or Lyft driver, a dog walker, or a caregiver to children or the elderly, you can generally find ways to supplement your income in the "gig economy." **Make sure this isn't another time suck that doesn't take you toward your goals.**

Pet Sitting/Childcare/Eldercare

Care.com (which matches babysitters, eldercare providers, and pet sitters to people seeking them), Rover.com (where dog walkers and pet sitters and the people who need them can find each other), and the vet's office are all good online sources for these jobs. Craigslist.org, Facebook, and Nextdoor.com can also be regular sources of clients.

Companion Care and Home Health Providers

While this is the most in-demand job, aides are poorly paid. However, the more experience and good references you get, the more you can charge. I know plenty of wealthy families that will pay big bucks for reliable care. If this is something that interests you, certifications are inexpensive and fast.

Advertising to the wealthiest segments of the population will get you hired by people who value your work ethic, experience, and education.

Childcare Workers

This job is also in high demand. An engaged, careful, competent, and reliable sitter/nanny can earn significant hourly rates. If your home is clean, organized, and safe, you can offer to sit in your own home. Preferably, though, you are willing to travel to the client's home if allowed to bring your own incredibly well-behaved children.

Pet Walking or Sitting

Working folks will pay to have dogs taken on a daily stroll.

Food Delivery and Ride Share Drivers

Several people in our online community mentioned that they drive but said it's best to work in an area with a lot of restaurants for meal delivery. The flexibility is high, but I am not convinced of the economics after subtracting for costs to operate a car for hire. However, as I write this, California is requiring gig-hire companies to treat drivers as employees and offer healthcare benefits, so my assessment may change.

Tutoring

A good college tutor in Boston can earn $80/hour. A great tutor in New Orleans can earn $80/hour. You can sign up with a national firm but will have to split your gains with them.

Advertise your services on school, campus, and community bulletin boards, Nextdoor.com, or tutoring websites such as Wyzant.com (where you choose your own hourly rate) and Tutor.com. Teachers offseason are also in high demand.

Common Side Jobs with Limited Upside

Multilevel Marketing Firms

These include Amway, Mary Kay, Arbonne, healing magnets, Tupperware, Avon, and so forth. Few people ever recoup the investment required to start. Less obvious is any firm that pays you solely on commission for soliciting friends and family to sell insurance and investments.

Surveys

I worked for a decade in market research. As far as I know, it was the only company that paid fairly for the time and knowledge of participants. I have tried out a few as a participant and found the remuneration ridiculous. I especially avoid those that offer you a "chance to be offered into a raffle."

Freelance Writing

The Internet is starved for content, but companies seem to be disconnected between demand and pay. This might explain why what we read while scrolling news feeds is so basic. You don't have to be an expert in the topic and may not need to even be an expert writer. If you value your skills as a writer, then hold out for the pay you deserve from mastering your craft. Do not pay to get access to any site aggregator to post your qualifications and get support.

Selling Your Creations

If you don't make enough to cover your costs, then this is a hobby, not an income stream.

9. SAVINGS

Try to build up an emergency fund to cover up to six month's worth of expenses and put it in savings or a short-term money market account.

You can invest any savings in excess of one year's expenses to return a steady flow of interest until their maturity. Interest is paid monthly.

10. SELLING UNWANTED GOODS

We used to call this "beer money"—quick, easy cash to fund a short-term need.

Selling unneeded items at online marketplaces (Craigslist.org, Facebook Marketplace, etc.) can be a decent source of occasional extra income. However, decide whether you would gain more from donating items or selling them. Measure that against the time and effort to sell items. If you can manage a sale without spending much time, then this can be a stream of income.

How to Make Selling Worth Your Time

In deciding whether and how to sell possessions, my guiding principle was that it be quick and effortless. I've unloaded scores of unwanted items during times of low employment. Of course, living in a densely populated area made it easier. Here are a few of my tips:

■ I priced items to move. That means about 10 percent of retail for most items, and 30 percent for electronics.

■ I used Craigslist.org for the most part. Low-value items were left on my porch for pickup with an envelope to the buyer to leave cash and push through my mail slot. (I never had anything stolen, and if it had been, I figured the person needed it more than me.)

■ I stated in my ad that I would only respond to inquiries that included a working cell phone number. Kept out the scammers.

■ I never provided my full name or personal email address.

- I met in person to exchange high-ticket photo and electronic items. Usually, this was in a centrally located, open parking lot or at the exchange spots designated at police stations.

- I used eBay for vintage and esoteric items. The selling fees came to about 25 percent of my gross.

- I sold baby and children's clothes to a consignment store where I traded for "new-to-me" items.

- I found children's (nonplush) toys and games sold well.

- I experienced variable success with furniture. Mid-century, Pottery Barn, and Crate & Barrel sell well but not much else.

- I never found having a yard sale to be worth the effort unless I was part of a community event.

11. BORROWING

If you are employed with a steady income, you can apply to borrow against the equity in your home with what is known as a home equity line of credit. Start with an institution that already has a relationship with you, such as where you have a mortgage, checking account, or retirement IRA. If you are looking to start a relationship, I recommend going with credit unions and local community banks. They are vastly easier to deal with than the mega-national banks.

Borrowing against the equity in your house can provide cash. Because this can be considered a recurring source of revenue, I have included it here. Done correctly, this *could be* a way to smooth out the swings in your income and expenses.

CUSHIONING YOUR FINANCES WITH A HOME EQUITY LINE OF CREDIT

I owned my home throughout my daughter's childhood. At one point, I could see the writing on the wall that my job would be eliminated in a pending merger. I applied for a home equity line of credit *before leaving the job*. You cannot qualify for credit unless you have a steady income. I wanted to get approved for as much as I could before getting laid off.

I did, indeed, lose my job, and because it was a time of consolidation in my industry, it was a while before I found new work. The job I did eventually find was "underemployment." The salary was never enough for me to meet expenses. Over the next decade, I dipped into that line of credit as an emergency fund—when my car died, when my roof needed replacing, for tuition, and to pay for childcare.

I would pay back the principal borrowed and then reborrow if and when another emergency arose.

A Word of Caution

These loans have to be paid back, like any debt. You should be able to foresee a repayment source (house sale, a better job, etc.) in the future. They should not be used to take vacations, cosmetic surgery, and so forth. A good use of debt is for anything that will grow in value as a result, such as education, quality childcare, and home repairs. In 2007, many people borrowed against the equity in their homes to subsidize lifestyles, rates rose, home values fell, and they couldn't keep up with the payments. Just because a bank will lend you money doesn't mean you should borrow it.

12. TEEN LABOR

I refer here to the time-honored tradition of asking your teen to get a job. This is less to support the general family coffers and more to teach the fundamentals of working. The pride a teen feels when they deposit their first paycheck is a great moment.

I have been amazed at my daughter's ingenuity in finding jobs. She didn't like to babysit but would coach youth ice hockey. In summers, she canvassed local businesses asking for work and, while at university, worked the donation call center. My proudest moment was when she volunteered in a lab whose work interested her and later asked if she could get paid. They agreed.

Lesson Learned: Income Opportunities Exist Everywhere

A teen or college student with their own money alleviates pressure on you to provide discretionary funds. It teaches life lessons under your watch so they don't become so catastrophic if things don't work out. Most of all, it teaches the fundamentals of a work ethic, which will set them in good stead for their adult life.

CHAPTER 14

Expenses:
How to Spend Your Money

Budgeting Specifically for Single Parents

How to Determine How Much You Bring In

How to Determine What You Spend

What if More Goes Out Than Comes In? Become an Expense Assassin

1. Reducing Housing Costs

2. Reducing Childcare Costs

3. Reducing Healthcare Costs

4. Reducing Transportation Costs

5. Reducing Vacation Costs

6. Reducing Education Costs

HOW YOU SPEND YOUR MONEY IS A CHOICE. Everyone wants to see their bank balance grow. Like weight loss, you know the answer: Earn more or spend less. It's "how to" that gets us stuck.

A quick search on "budgeting" returned more than sixty thousand entries. That presents a good chance that one will work for you. My suggestion is to head to your library, pick out a few books for your kid, sit in the 337 Dewey Decimal section in the stacks (are you tired of hearing that suggestion?), and leaf through a few books on money.

Unfortunately, **not much of the advice is directed specifically to single parents**. The general concepts are applicable, but some specific advice isn't. Where conventional wisdom needs to be adapted, I've made suggestions.

If your income is very low or your debts are very high, it makes more sense to focus your limited time and energy on making more money for yourself and your family. It makes little sense to shop at three grocery stores for the best deals when you work thirty-plus hours a week. Your time is better served talking to career counselors or reading up on how to upskill yourself to a better job (see chapter 12).

From personal experience, though, managing on less is doable with trade-offs. It became a necessity when I was out of work for what seemed to be an eternity.

I took up the challenge of seeing how low my expenses could go and still live a rewarding lifestyle. I had two advantages:

- I like a challenge, and

- I enjoy engaging with my money.

My goal here is to pass those advantages on to you.

But before getting into the tactical tips, let me address the biggest emotional breakthrough needed for understanding and managing your expenses: *a budget will not impede your personal freedom.*

I taught beginner money classes. The first class began with Uncle Mark's advice. "Track what we spend!" About a third of the class would check out right there. They feared what the result might be. They feared shame. They may have to change. Nobody likes change. In fact, our psyches actively resist change.

BUDGETING SPECIFICALLY FOR SINGLE PARENTS

I've developed five budgeting principles for single parents:

1. *Put your energy where it will matter the most.* We have expenses that dual-parent families can more easily absorb. In those cases, time and energy are better spent on improving our ability to earn more (see chapters 12 and 13).

2. *Tackle expenses from highest to lowest first.* Expenses get taken up primarily by housing, childcare, and healthcare costs. It's best to focus on getting

those costs as low as possible before looking to lower the other expense categories.

3. *Understand that you have to do this yourself.* No genie from a bottle will grant three wishes.

4. *Set an attainable goal like three months of savings, a vacation, or starting a college fund.* After setting a goal, then add a savings category to your budget to serve that goal.

   One savings approach is to set a general savings goal, such as 10 percent of your income. This was an easy number for me to remember. When I made $16,000/year, my savings goal was $1,600/year (or $133/month or $4/day (I've seen suggestions that start with $1/week and snowball from there). What matters is that the savings are tied to goals.

5. *Be aware of how much you spend, as that creates savings.* Almost like magic, an awareness of how and what we spend seems to lower our costs automatically. That is even before you start to do thrifty activities.

	FUTURE VALUE OF SAVING $4 EVERY DAY (OR $66 TWICE A MONTH)			
	INTEREST RATE			
YEAR	**0%**	**2%**	**4%**	**6%**
Year 1	$1,460	$1,475	$1,490	$1,505
Year 2	$2,920	$2,979	$3,040	$3,102
Year 3	$4,380	$4,514	$4,653	$4,799

OK, enough of general principles. Now let's get down to concrete tactics. In this chapter, I'm going to help you get a general idea of four major aspects of creating and managing your budget:

1. How much you're taking in currently

2. How much you're spending

3. How much you're saving

4. How to reduce your biggest expenses

HOW TO DETERMINE HOW MUCH YOU BRING IN

If you are employed, look at your paystub or bank statement. This is the amount *after* any payroll deductions for things like taxes, health insurance, and retirement savings' contributions. If you are paid biweekly, use two paychecks per month for your net income. Similarly, if you're paid weekly, base your monthly income on four checks per month.

If you are a self-employed/gig worker or otherwise have variable income, then either (1) look at the credits (pluses) to your bank account, or (2) track your income for the next few months to obtain a monthly average.

Regularly paid support such as alimony, child support, government grants, and so forth should be added to the income number. If you don't receive these regularly, don't include them. Count them as a windfall when you do get them.

Any extra paychecks and windfalls, such as a tax refund, should not be counted. These will be for catching up, covering emergencies, or paying down debts.

HOW TO DETERMINE WHAT YOU SPEND

Live Your Life and Record Its Costs: Then Figure Out How to Afford It

To understand how you spend money currently and to determine your monthly money needs, track your expenses for three months. Tracking for three months is plenty. It lets you catch quarterly bills like water or property taxes.

Record everything from rent to a Dunkin' coffee. The goal is not to judge but to find out *how* you are spending your funds. Here's how:

- Get your monthly expenses from your bank, debit, and credit card statements. These tell your every expense. Add up credit/debit card charges and rent/utility expenses also on your bank statement. If you make a lot of purchases with cash and are not sure where your money is going, track your spending using pen and paper or an online budgeting tool (such as the You Need a Budget app) for thirty days.

- Do this for three months of credit/debit card/Venmo statements and checks, online or paper.

Designate Expenses as Necessary Versus Optional

With those expenses you tracked for the past few months, designate them as "necessary" or "optional" ("nice to have"). Rent or mortgage payments are "necessary," but streaming services are "nice to have."

To some extent, what is necessary versus optional depends on your circumstance. A rideshare might be necessary for someone without transportation alternatives but optional for someone who doesn't want to drive or take public transportation. *The point is to understand how much you really have left over after necessities to play with.* If your household income is $60,000 a year after taxes and you have $55,000 in necessary expenses, then you have $5,000 a year to spend on optional expenses.

FEAR OF MONEY AFFLICTS THE WEALTHY, TOO

I developed a marketing program for money managers to the wealthy. In order to better understand why millionaires hire money managers, I interviewed very rich people. "Lisa" told me an all-too-common story.

Lisa came to my client, a financial firm, when her husband wanted a divorce. Large amounts of money were at stake. Lisa was overwhelmed not only by now having responsibility for her finances but also by the trauma of events.

Lisa described herself postdivorce as shocked, ashamed, and financially illiterate. As a result, she went into the meeting feeling fearful, overwhelmed, and clueless.

One meeting was all it took for Lisa to feel supported, calmer, and, in her words, "relieved." Advice to "live the life you want for a year" was pivotal. It dissipated the emotional pressure that could put up mental obstacles, creating inertia. It took away the fear of living with limitations long enough for Lisa to focus on calculating what those expenses really were.

As part of the divorce, Lisa had to file "purple sheets" detailing her living expenses. Lisa didn't know what she had been spending. Lisa did not find this exercise onerous. (I hear Uncle Mark cheering.)

Working through different spending scenarios helped Lisa realize that she had choices. This was giving her back that sense of control.

We experience the same feeling of relief when someone gives us a plan of action and takes away the dread of anticipation.

Some expenses are split between the two categories:

- For *food* expenses, "groceries" are a necessity but "eating out" could be either a necessity or optional. For single parents, accessing prepared meals at times is sanity saving.

- While a *vacation* may be mentally necessary, for the purpose of this exercise, consider it "optional." If you have a goal to take a vacation next year, estimate the cost, divide by twelve, and put that amount in the "optional" category.

- If you have *debt* payments, note the minimum amount owed each month in the "necessary" column. If you have a goal to pay those off early, you can add extra payments to the "optional" column.

The total of the two columns, "necessity" plus "optional" equals "total spending."

This Is Your Budget

There's no high math needed, just arithmetic.

If you are overwhelmed, reduce the scope. Track expenses for only one month, but be sure to enter expenses into either the "necessary" or "optional" columns.

Organizing Expenses

Using paper or a computer spreadsheet like Google Sheets or Excel, make three columns: "category," "necessary," and "optional." Down the left-hand side, list the major categories for spending such as rent, heat, food, debt payment, and so forth. I suggest starting with only twelve categories.

Category	Neccessary	Optional
1. **Housing** (rent/mortgage/insurance/maintenance costs/ purchases such as furniture, dishes, etc.); include utilities (gas, oil, electric, trash)		
2. **Phone, TV, Internet, cable**, etc.		
3. **Healthcare** (insurance premiums/out-of-pocket costs/ deductibles, prescriptions, drug costs, physical therapy, etc.)		
4. **Food at home**—groceries (do not include nonperishables like cleaning supplies)		
5. **Food outside the home** (everything from coffee to takeout to restaurants)		
6. **Childcare** (sitters, daycare, preschool, camp, gym nursery, etc.)		
7. **Clothing** (both for yourself and your children)		
8. **Entertainment** (subscription services, games, any Apple.com charges, cable, movies, circus, museums, etc.; I put alcohol in this category)		
9. **Transportation** (car payments and expenses, insurance, public transportation, tolls, rideshares, etc.)		
10. **Education** (tuition, supplies, school trip fees, technology, etc.)		
11. **Debt repayment** (the minimum owed is "necessary"; extra payments are "optional")		
12. **Other** (everything else)		

Go through each expense and assign it to a category, splitting between the two columns "necessary" and "optional."

Find your last statements from debt that you owe, like credit cards and student loans. Put the minimum amount due each month into the "debt repayment" category and "necessary" column.

- If the expense is an annual expense like car insurance, divide by twelve to see its monthly cost.

- If the expense is quarterly, such as oil changes or property taxes, divide by three (because three months are in a calendar quarter) for the same reason, to get the monthly cost.

This is between you and the piece of paper. We all have expenses. You aren't unique, and I can guarantee that as bad as you think your finances are, I've seen worse. Anyway, you aren't going to show me your results.

Saving for Goals

For financial goals that you want to accomplish, add to the monthly "optional" expenses the amounts for those goals. For example, if you want to pay off $3,000 in credit card debt in six months, add $500 to the "optional" column. The same would be for vacation savings. If a vacation will be in twelve months and cost $3,000, then enter $250 in the "optional" column as a monthly savings number.

Next comes the fun part. (Seriously!)

WHAT IF MORE GOES OUT THAN COMES IN? BECOME AN EXPENSE ASSASSIN

If your total income after taxes is less than your total spending, it's time to revisit the spending plan. This is where details help.

As you rework your numbers, you'll see whether you have to reduce other expenses to meet that goal (or find more income).

To rework the expenses, first assess if an entire expense is truly "necessary." For example, Internet service is "necessary," but a streaming subscription is "optional." Getting takeout once a week may be necessary for your harried single-parent life, but more than that might be "optional." Only you can decide.

Keep moving numbers around expense categories until you get to a *total spending budget that you think is realistic.*

The Big Three and How to Reduce Them

In 2012, Ameriprise Financial published a study on the three biggest impacts on a person's budget. The decisions we make in those three categories can make or break a financial future.

- Housing
- Vacations
- Education

I became so excited after reading the research. Here it was (fully vetted and grounded in good data analysis), a snackable insight into what spending actions have the biggest long-term impact. Prior to that report, financial celebrities were all about cutting out lattes from Starbucks. While

I agreed with the sentiment ("stop the little wasters of your money"), one bad decision on these big three categories can quickly wipe out any gains from forgoing Starbucks for a year.

Having gone through five recessions, I see the wisdom of choosing these categories (plus a few others, like food, childcare, healthcare, and transportation costs, which I'll also address in this chapter). For example, we saw people overextend in housing in the early 2000s, and it came crashing down in 2008. Prior to that, no one thought housing prices would decline. How wrong that concept turned out.

As a general rule, the larger the cost, the fewer strategies needed to reduce it. There are a hundred ways to reduce your food expenditures but maybe three ways to reduce the cost of housing. That's good news. It narrows the focus of our cost-cutting attention. *The impact of reducing a major expense will more than compensate for switching to store-brand cereal.*

That's why the method here is to attack the largest expenses first. Work your way down the expense categories. Reducing the largest costs will have the biggest impact on your expenses. The larger the expense, the fewer cost-saving options are available. For example, you may find yourself with a free hour to apply for a property tax rebate or housing subsidy. It'll be time well rewarded.

The good news is that as you go through your expenses, you'll find choices and options that really work. And once you become a "major budget item assassin," you can work on reducing those other expenses that add up.

Let's drill down on the six biggest expenses households face.

| 1. Housing | 3. Healthcare | 5. Vacation |
| 2. Childcare | 4. Transportation | 6. Education |

1. REDUCING HOUSING COSTS

The financial wisdom is not to overextend by taking out a mortgage so large that you can't build an emergency fund. Large houses have large expenses on top of the mortgage, like maintenance, taxes, and insurance. I've observed an inverse correlation between the size of a house and a family's financial peace.

When our kids are very young, housing size is less than an issue. I moved from a two-bedroom city apartment to a house in the next town when my daughter was born. I should have waited five years. The house was twice the price, twice the upkeep, and four times the commute. My infant/toddler daughter didn't care about the house size. While it worked out for her school-age years, I could have moved out to a town with good schools when she was five versus a newborn and saved tremendous amounts of money.

Single parents also have other considerations. We need to be close to our jobs or family to build a childcare safety net. This may or may not put you over the top in terms of housing costs. If you buy the "worst house in the best neighborhood," you may have to spend considerable time on repairs and maintenance. We need to budget our time as well as our finances. Be mindful of maintenance costs.

Where you live drives the better part of these expenses. I chose to live in an in-town Boston neighborhood on a public transit line. The town also had highly ranked schools. My housing costs were higher than elsewhere. I made this tradeoff for proximity to my job and costs:

- Travel time (only seven miles from home to work; I could get home quickly if need be)

- Transportation costs (I could use public transportation)

Regardless of what choices and trade-offs you make in deciding where to live, the cost of maintaining a home has four variable components: mortgage payment or rent, property insurance, taxes, and maintenance.

Mortgage Interest Rates or Monthly Rent

Since mortgage rates declined over the twenty years I owned my home, I refinanced my mortgage four times for lower rates. I had begun my homeownership with a thirty-year fixed rate mortgage with a monthly payment (interest and principal) of $2,700 per month at 7 percent and ended with a monthly payment of $750 at 3.5 percent by the time I sold. The payment declined through a combination of switching to adjustable rates, refinancing at lower interest rates as they fell, and using windfalls to prepay principal and melt away the mortgage amount.

In periods of rising interest rates, choices are different. Individual circumstances dictate any strategy regarding mortgage rates. The point is that there are *a lot of levers to push here*—time, rates, and prepayments. And if you're lucky, your city may have a program for first-time homebuyers who have grown up there. Mine did.

But even if you're not a homeowner, you may be able to take advantage of cost-cutting measures for *renters*. Cities and towns have subsidies that you can learn about by calling your local housing office.

A note about pets: having pets will lower your rental options or raise your housing costs as most landlords require renters with pets to pay some sort of "pet premium."

Homeowner's/Renter's Insurance

This cost rose 400 percent during the twenty years I owned my last home. Insurance premiums that started at $100/month ended at $400/month. Various claims for natural disasters and falling trees temporarily raised rates, but the real culprit was rapidly rising home values in the past ten years.

Regardless of whether you have homeowner's or renter's insurance:

- Shop the prices every year for each policy.

- Combine home/renter's insurance with car insurance if you need it, as these bundled plans tend to have lower rates.

- Go with companies with high ratings for paying claims. It's not cheap insurance if they won't pay a claim.

- Choose USAA if you are either a member of the military or family.

- Push your deductible as high as you can. If you can afford to pay $1,000 out-of-pocket for damage, then that should be your deductible. (Another reason for an emergency fund.)

- Stick with direct-to-consumer companies (e.g., Amica, USAA, Progressive) versus agent-sold policies *unless* you find one of those independent insurance agents that gives you incredible service, particularly with regard to filing claims or choosing the right type of insurance (See chapter 16, "Insurance").

- Don't overinsure your belongings. Read the policy quote and decide if you really need to cover $30,000 worth of items that might only cost you $5,000 to replace.

DO NOT SKIP RENTER'S INSURANCE

If you rent, it's imperative you get renter's insurance. As a Red Cross volunteer, I saw disasters financially wipe out families. A $40/month renter's policy could have put those families back on their feet.

Owner's Property Taxes

Whenever I was sent the next year's property tax assessment, I would look at the amount and compare it to my neighbors' amount. I found the information by going to the town or city website and clicking on the "assessor's database." There I could look at my assessment and that of similar homes around me. I found that I was consistently assessed higher on a per-square-foot basis. Three times I challenged the assessment, and twice I was granted a lower rate.

The town website will tell you how to file the paperwork, and it will ask you why your taxes should be reconsidered. The key here is to do the square-foot comparison between your house and similar houses in the neighborhood.

Step 1: Look at the assessed value of your house. Divide it by the "usable square feet." Both these numbers are available in your assessment. Note: the comparison is for the usable square feet of the building(s) on the property, *not* the property square footage.

Step 2: Do the same calculation for three to five comparable-size homes in your immediate area. If you are consistently assessed higher on a square-foot basis, then you have a case for an appeal. If you are assessed lower than the average, then count yourself lucky and stop here.

Step 3: If you think you are assessed higher than others, then fill out the appeal paperwork with your calculations and wait for a call. The assessor's office may ask for a house inspection before lowering your assessment.

I estimate having saved $12,000 in property taxes during twenty-plus years by appealing my assessments.

Maintenance Costs

Lenders don't figure in maintenance costs when calculating how much of a mortgage you can afford. You should.

Homeowners need to build a reserve for inevitable large costs. My one-hundred-year-old Victorian required constant upkeep. A new roof could cost $10,000. Putting aside money every month into a maintenance account can cover most large expenditures that come up. For me, that averaged about $400/month for the twenty years. (Sounds high? Old houses need more maintenance.) This amount varies on your location, labor costs, and age of your home. Some towns have funds to help homeowners fund repairs.

2. REDUCING CHILDCARE COSTS

The pandemic highlighted the massive childcare problems that working parents face, and while a former Washington administration tried to put the country on par with childcare options in Europe, we remain in the dark ages. Private employers are now stepping up in an attempt to attract workers, but it's driven by "the war for talent" rather than "family values."

In the meanwhile, refer to chapter 3, "Childcare," to find ways of controlling costs. You'll read about community and state-based programs designed to help you with paying for the thing you need most.

I'd like to add here *two examples of some not-so-obvious ways to reduce childcare costs*—informal child support from the other parent and moving down the cost curve.

Often, we discuss in other places about the difficulty custodial parents have with consistently receiving financial child support payments. Reasons vary, but the most common is that there isn't enough money to support two households. If you are a custodial parent not receiving the agreed-upon money, consider giving the other parent "credits" for increased childcare time. It serves both as a financial incentive and promotes a child's well-being to spend more time with another parent. It allows the custodial parent to work more. A study published in the *Annals of Political and Social Science* suggests that accepting childcare in lieu of payments actually increases the custodial parent's financial well-being.

For some, changing your childcare situation to something less expensive will have an outsized impact on your finances. If predivorce your kids were attending a private summer camp (or even a full-priced YMCA camp), check out the options offered by your town. The facilities won't be as nice, but your school-age child isn't going to care.

My own summer camp experience consisted of the town day camp at the local park and a week of church camp. Both were very basic and rustic experiences. I also made lifelong friends. Recently, I traveled to Oklahoma to visit one brother and sister with whom I had kept in touch from that sleepaway camp. We reminisced that our camp housing had been repurposed cinder block barracks and recreation was one swimming pool. The brother recently retired with the rank of vice admiral from the Special Forces as a Navy SEAL. After a career in the State Department, his sister became a professor at a big Oklahoma university. Clearly, our bare-bones experience didn't hold them back.

After losing my big job in a bank merger, I (re)embraced frugality. My daughter moved from the private camp to the bare-bones town camp. Later in middle school, she enrolled in the town science camp. She is now a graduate student in evolutionary biology. (Didn't hold her back either.) Since I was out of work, I no longer employed in-home childcare to cover all those long hours I worked. I still needed help while I networked and interviewed, but I could now employ occasional college students.

Examine your childcare situation, and using the options discussed in chapter 3, see where you can move down the cost curve. Be responsive to changing circumstances.

3. REDUCING HEALTHCARE COSTS

Insurance

While healthcare insurance can be insanely complicated, it's a major expense, so finding the right plan can have big cost-savings implications. Here are some options.

Employer-Subsidized Insurance

If you can afford the out-of-pocket costs until you hit the deductible, use the catastrophic health insurance option with very low monthly premiums. Pair that with a Health Savings Account (see below). Otherwise, select the HMO ("bronze level") option with less flexibility but lower premiums.

Health Savings Account (HSA)

I love these accounts. They are a triple-tax treat. You can fund them with pretax dollars (thus lowering your annual taxes), let them grow tax free, and withdraw the money without penalty at any time to pay health expenses. Again, the higher your taxes, the more sense this makes.

HSAs *supposedly* accompany high-deductible health insurance plans. I say "supposedly" because some health insurance plans state they are not "high-deductible plans," but their program meets the government standards as one. The easiest thing to do is ask your human resources department which health plan they offer that will trigger the qualification to get an HSA as well. If you are not buying health insurance through work, you either call your health insurance company and ask if the plan is "high deductible" or ask the bank or investment company where you open the HSA.

Affordable Care Act

Everyone is now entitled to health insurance. Start your search for a plan by going to Healthcare.gov and get directed to either your state or a federal plan. Premiums are based on your income. If your income is low enough, the programs will offer you Medicaid either for you, your children, or both.

Do not be afraid to appeal a subsidy that you feel should be higher. My daughter appealed her premium calculation and won on the second round. That reduced her policy premium by 75 percent. Worth trying.

Dental

Nothing beats brushing and flossing to reduce dental costs. You still need checkups and the occasional repair work, though.

Your cheapest plan option will be an employer-subsidized one. While premiums may feel "high," I have found that the insurance premium cost plus the deductible is a "wash" with just paying full price for general dental care. That being the case, you should take the dental plan from work. Should you end up needing extensive work, you will be insured against catastrophe and be much better off.

IS IT WORTH YOUR TIME?

Single parents need to consider whether the extra time needed for dental school appointments is worth the potential savings. Three-hour appointments are not uncommon.

Free Dental Work

You can get free or inexpensive work done at dental schools near you. I live in the Boston area. We have three dental schools. Their clinics are used to train student dentists, and the work is supervised. Get on the list now for some future maintenance work you may need, and be prepared for longer appointments since you are in a teaching clinic. See ADA.org and click on "Dental Schools" for a US directory and contact information.

The most expensive option is to ignore regular maintenance like checkups and cleaning. This will have significant cost implications later.

Braces

Rare was the child that had braces in my hometown. In fact, regular dental checkups weren't that common either. We considered ourselves lucky to have fluoridated water.

If you or your child need orthodontic work, talk to your dentist about options. This is an expensive service. However, orthodontia work is now recognized as necessary for general health. The markup is very high on this service, and as a result, you see private companies getting into the field.

THE ORTHODONTIA CHOICE

If you can, choose an orthodontist that your child can get to on their own. Regular appointments go on for years. You don't have to be there for the appointment, but you may have to drive your child if it isn't within walking distance or public transportation.

I went with the orthodontist recommended by the dentist. Each visit required that I take half a day off work to drive to each appointment. This went on for a couple of years.

The disruption to my job was such that I tried changing orthodontists, mid-treatment. This didn't work. Apparently, some orthodontists don't want to pick you up mid-treatment.

I discovered too late that there is a wide variation between orthodontists and what they charge for the same work. I went with the one recommended by my dentist. It couldn't have been more expensive. My neighbor, on the other hand, shopped prices and received price quotes varying by thousands of dollars. Recommended treatment also varied. Therefore, take your time. Straightening teeth doesn't have to be done in a rush.

No matter when and where you get braces, all that money will be wasted if the patient doesn't wear the retainer. And losing the retainer can cost $500 for a replacement, so it may make sense to hold off on doing this major work until your child is responsible enough. (Or maybe buy two retainers at once since it is a marginal cost addition.)

Out-of-Pocket Medical Costs

Miserable but not life-threatening? Then consider the pharmacy first.

Since many trips to the doctor end up with advice for over-the-counter medications, accessing the local pharmacist first could make sense. In fact, around the United States and overseas, many people don't have easy access to medical providers. They may have to travel long distances if any are even available. In some of those locations, people use the local pharmacist as the first stop for a health issue.

I once had a horrible head cold and needed to take a flight for work. I had heard scary stories about what would happen if you flew while congested. I hopped over to a nearby clinic. "Did you take any OTC (over-the-counter) cold medicines?" they asked. "No" was my reply. "Well, what do you think they exist for?" was the sarcastic comeback. Lesson learned. OTC medicines at the pharmacy are surprisingly effective.

UTILIZING OFFERED HELP FOR HEALTHCARE RESEARCH

Calling around about free or low-cost screenings is a perfect item for a person offering help. If you have someone in your life asking what they can do for you, ask them to make the calls.

Prescription Drug Cost Assistance

On the subject of pharmaceuticals, twenty-four states have State Pharmacy Assistance Programs (SPAPs). These are to help people pay for prescription drugs if their incomes are limited but too high to qualify for Medicaid.

4. REDUCING TRANSPORTATION COSTS

Cars

I talk to my twentysomething daughter that she is financially better off without a car. For now. She lives in a city.

Taking my own advice, I sold my car. It mostly sat in the driveway, going out only for grocery store trips. The rest of the time, I used public transportation. The Boston area is an extremely challenging place to drive and park, making public transit the preferred conveyance, anyway. I estimated my car was costing me $1.20 per mile each year. I sold it and took Ubers, rentals, and Zipcar. I also saved on the gym fee, which I had canceled figuring that all the additional walking would compensate.

Ironically, all that walking aggravated plantar fasciitis in both feet. I bought a car eighteen months later. *But*, I calculated that not having a car did save money and stress.

Buying a Car: Lease Versus Loan Versus Cash

This is where Internet advice of one-size-fits-all doesn't work for single parents. Typically, I see recommendations to buy used cars and pay cash. After all, cars are depreciating assets that lose value as soon as they drive off the seller's lot. One should never finance and pay interest against a depreciating asset. The interest cost would eat you alive.

But the economics of this changed radically decades ago with:

■ Declining interest rates for fifteen years (Interest rates not only drive the auto loan payment, they are also incorporated into the lease rate.)

- Escalating labor costs for repairs

As a money expert, I've changed my tune on this topic. I now contend that in the current interest rate environment, cars can be leased just as cost efficiently as if you pay cash. (This assumes that hyperinflation does not return and significantly increase lease rates.)

Leasing a car also falls within the admonition to "rent depreciating assets" like cars and "buy appreciating assets" like homes.

CONSIDER WHETHER TO BUY OR LEASE

During the Great Recession, the head gasket blew on my twelve-year-old car. That was an expensive repair, and it was likely that I would have to keep making expensive repairs. I needed reliable transportation. Used cars were scarce since folks were holding on to what they had. On the upside, dealers were willing to negotiate heavily on new cars. I bargained hard and ended up leasing since I didn't have the cash for much of a down payment much less an outright purchase, nor could I afford the payments on a five-year car loan. Three years later, the lease term ended, triggering the buy option. I bought the car for $16,000. Seven years later, I sold that car for $14,000 to embark on the aforementioned car-free experiment. My walking experiment failed, but still, the car lease/purchase worked out well, financially.

New Versus Used Car Options

Reliability is critical for single parents. What backup do you have if your car is out of commission? Is there another car or driver available to you? Do you have access to public transportation?

You will need to evaluate:

- Monthly loan or lease payment

- The time and money to maintain a used car: On the one hand, cars are better made now and break less frequently in their first eight years. On the other, labor costs have risen rapidly in the past decade, making it much more expensive to repair a car.

If you can't afford to pay cash for a new car or a monthly auto loan payment, then look at leasing. It has a lower monthly payment, and at the end of three years, you can buy the car outright or renew the lease. I've heard the argument "but then I don't own a car." My answer is "So what?" Your budget doesn't change because you are either going to have a car payment or repair bills.

During the second year into my car-free experiment, a friend asked if I wanted to buy his six-year-old car. He wasn't about to cut me any sweet deal but did offer the car at the market price.

I evaluated the buy/lease and new/used decisions and processed the decision in the following steps:

- I didn't want to invest in a new car since I only drove three thousand miles a year, well below a base lease terms mileage.

- I had public transit options if the car broke down.

- My kid was away at college.

- While I don't like buying used cars, I did know the owner and his meticulous maintenance habits.

- The car was six years old with forty-eight thousand miles, which was not terrible.

- While not offering me a discount, he did sell it to me at the Edmunds market value.

I bought that car for $16,000, drove it ten thousand miles, plus paid $4K in taxes and repairs over three years. I would not call that a great buy *except* that because of the pandemic supply chain problems, it was worth $25,000 after those three years. Despite everything, this used car accidentally worked out well.

The aforementioned analysis presumes we are talking about buying no more car than you need. This excludes high-end status cars, giant SUVs, muscle cars, or the like.

Public Transportation

If you commute regularly using public transportation, there's no doubt you know the value of a monthly (vs. daily) pass.

5. REDUCING VACATION COSTS

Chapter 22 extensively covers the topic of fun and affording it. This section deals with its impact on your household budget.

We all need/want vacations. Staycations are good once in a while. You get a chance to catch up on household management and organization. No one will be stressed by travel, and the food is familiar. But occasionally, I like to go away, disconnect, and not have my closets silently judge me, demanding organization.

Vacations can sideline your finances, though. Disney Parks are tough for single parents. For an entertainment company whose movies specialize in orphans and single-parent families, it's ironic the problems the parks present for solo parents. Also, it's really expensive. The website AllEars.net estimates that a vacation there can cost 7 percent of the average family's annual income.

You don't need a blow-out, expensive vacation for the kids. Anything new and different will thrill them. I used a concentric circle of travel for vacations. We started camping in our backyard and branched out from there. If we went overnight, the rule of thumb was a day away for every year of age (i.e., age three equals three-day vacation).

Here's the concentric circle order of trip types we did, with Boston (home) at the center:

We often stayed with friends. Some of those vacations included:

- An overnight to Block Island, Rhode Island

- A week in Oklahoma

- Travel in Oregon from Portland to Crater Lake National Park

These vacations were legendary among our friends and family. Some asked to join, and we've had some rip-roaring adventures with them.

By her teenage years, my daughter's tastes changed, and I adjusted our trips to focus on cities such as Nashville, New Orleans, and Chicago.

6. REDUCING EDUCATION COSTS

Rising college tuition and declining real salaries in the last four decades created a perfect storm, making education one of the major expenses that can wreck finances.

The good news is that it doesn't have to be expensive to be good.

A Brief History

Once upon a time, where you went to college mattered. The massive Boomer demographic made the supply-and-demand balance tilt in favor of employers. The more competitive the school, the better the job you would get. In those days, the value of a liberal arts degree assured companies that you had the soft skills they needed. The specifics they could teach you. If, postgraduation, you went to a major bank, tech, or packaged goods company, training took place in their training programs. Sadly, those went away in the era of cost rationalization. The onus for technical skills development went onto the workers.

Subsequently, the battle to enroll students heated up as the smaller population cohorts came of college age in the 1980s. Universities expanded amenities that had nothing to do with the quality of teaching. Fancy dorms and meal plans, expanded development and alumni offices, and inflated administration salaries drove costs way up and affordability way down. All of a sudden, where you went to school didn't matter because the Great Divide occurred. The wealthiest schools held on to their pole position, and everyone else grouped below. It was no longer possible to ascertain the academic chops of colleges by their name, reputation, or, especially, cost.

Then came the Great Misalignment. Those companies that abandoned in-house training? They no longer wanted generalists with prestigious liberal arts degrees. They wanted employees with specialist degrees, no matter where they came from. We are left with a handful of degrees that will deliver a positive return on the high-cost private college investment. Therefore, the less you spend on college, the more your salary will return to you over the years.

Demographics continue to shift in favor of the worker. The math now says to get skilled as cheaply as possible to get the highest return on your investment in education.

Lowering the Cost of College for Your Child

Fortunately, higher education options are plentiful. Here are ways to reduce the cost of college (and therefore reduce your cost of investment).

Transfer Anywhere

No one asks where you started college, only from where you graduated. You or your child can attend a community college for the first two years and transfer to that big-name school. Or matriculate to a low-cost college that gives you a great financial package, then transfer to the brand-name school if that is important in your field or your child's.

GRADUATION EMPLOYMENT OUTCOMES

The career outcomes rate estimates the percentage of students who are either employed, continuing their education, enlisted in military service, or performing voluntary service within six months of graduation. Any college needs to provide their students with proof of graduation career outcomes. How many graduates are employed in their chosen field one year after graduation? What is the average salary? For example, the US Department of Education tracks the employment outcomes of those holding bachelor's degrees five years after graduation. They range from a high of $78,000/year to a low of half that at $40,000/year for general liberal art degree holders. No surprise, engineering and computer science degree holders had the highest salaries. This validates the previous assertion that the closer you are to a technical specialist, the higher the rewards.

The fastest-growing professions with the lowest unemployment, however, are in the areas of healthcare and teaching. These also have financial benefits that are not included in the calculations by the Department of Education. Those benefits include terrific health insurance plans and pensions for many. Before you get dismayed that you aren't interested in a computer science degree, consider the perks of public service. My friend Paula may have had half my salary since she was a high school math teacher and I worked in a bank. But she has an amazing pension and retiree health benefits so she needs to allocate less of her salary to retirement savings.

Either way, the institution granting you (or your child) a degree is obligated to give you a copy of their recent graduate survey so you can decide how much to spend on their degree.

Commute from Home

Any college or university has commuter students. It's a different experience than living on campus if that is an option. I made lifelong friends living on campus. Some had tried commuting but eventually wanted to live in the thick of things. Ironically, they all moved back home by junior year.

Let the Military Pay Their Way

Either by attending one of the military academies like West Point or joining ROTC on campus, you can have a free education in exchange for a commitment to serve for a number of years postgraduation.

Get Good Grades in High School

Federal financial aid is limited by income status. Private funds from colleges, known as "merit aid," gets directed to the type of students the school is trying to attract. That could be for athletes, marching band trombonists, chess players, or anyone who will elevate their average acceptance test scores. To score that aid, you should be in the top 25 percent of the applicants at a school.

When my daughter applied to schools, she selected six. A "reach school," where she was in the middle of the pack in terms of high school grades; "probable schools," where she was in the top half of the test score range; and a "safety school," where she was in the top 25 percent. The probable and safety schools offered her significant scholarships. The "reach school" offered her nothing on top of federal aid. My impression is that this is a pretty typical experience.

The top 25 percent typically is measured in terms of standardized tests, but ask the school how they are measuring it now.

CHAPTER 15

Savings

CREATING A STRONG FINANCIAL AND EMOTIONAL FOUNDATION

You deserve to be at peace with your money. And it's OK if you find the topic of money daunting. I grew up in a household where it was always in short supply, and we talked about it all the time—bank accounts, allowances, rules of thumb, setbacks, and wins. It was a subject of constant conversation. We had worries and goals. My mother had no qualms communicating, in real time, her struggles to support the family as a single parent. Even though my distant father was an accountant, it was my mother who passed on the money wisdom. She just never had enough.

I realize not everyone has that advantage. For many households, discussing money holds a sense of shame, a fear of failure, and the futility of chasing a dream. But it helps to know you are not alone in making mistakes.

We've all been on the wrong side of a financial decision.

The point isn't that you make a mistake; it is how you can rebound after the consequences.

Emotionally, there is a lot of unnecessary shame attached to the idea of money.

- Shame: I screwed up, so I am a bad person.

- Guilt: I screwed up, so I am going to fix this.

Guilt is a healthy emotion, but kick shame to the curb to get going!

THE MONSTER UNDER THE BED
IS REALLY JUST THE TOY YOU LOST

When I worked with financial companies, I helped demystify their product offerings to the average customer. Companies *wanted* customers to engage with their money. I worked with Citi, Schwab, Bank of America, Hartford Insurance, and countless other financial companies to understand customers better. I went to work every day feeling I had a higher calling. Sounds arrogant? Maybe, but people would engage more with their money if companies were more relatable.

I'm here to help with simple information to give you direction and context.

THE ORDER OF SAVINGS

It's hard to create and hold on to a future vision beyond the day-to-day struggle, and the matter-of-fact approach presented here is not meant to minimize what it takes to achieve your goals.

But **my purpose here is to help you create a feeling of triumph**. No matter how small the savings amount, you will start to feel mastery over your financial position over time. More importantly, you'll begin to have a feeling of control. It won't all go smoothly. Disruptions occur, but starting on the road to financial stability can smooth out bumps.

Basic savings takes three steps. I list them in sequence and then detail how and where you put your hard-won gains. Never mind the get-rich-quick investment schemes. That's for people with money to lose. Single parents have to secure their financial future first.

Step 1: Set up an emergency fund

Step 2: Reduce debt

Step 3: Fund retirement

Each section briefly lists the why, how, and where. The chapter closes with advice on how to save for multiple goals simultaneously.

STEP 1: SET UP AN EMERGENCY FUND

Can your bank account handle a crisis? The goal here is to lessen the hills and valleys of financial life. Being able to handle a sudden car expense or broken heating system generates peace of mind. No one can plan perfectly for all the expenses that happen.

A good goal to start is to save $1,000. When that goal is achieved, move to have at least one month of expenses in savings (see chapter 15). As you get older, or if your employment is variable, you will want to increase that amount.

Don't worry about steps 2 and 3 until you get this down. A singular focus will keep you on track to meet this goal.

How to Begin

Start, Even if a Token Amount

Saving $25 per month will have you feeling better about your situation. That's less than $1/day. By starting small, you'll be surprised at how good you feel and how quickly. You deserve financial peace more than an extensive wardrobe.

Put Windfalls, Big and Small, into this Fund

If your family gives gifts, ask them instead to help you build an emergency fund. Tell them about your goal. Any bonuses, delayed child support, change found in the couch, tax refunds, and so forth should go toward building that fund. I have a clear memory of one single dad proudly shaking a jar with all his windfalls adding up in change and dollar bills.

Have Two Bank Accounts or Equivalent

Have two bank accounts, one for bills (checking) and the other for savings. If a traditional brick-and-mortar bank is not available or charges stupid fees, there are plenty of reputable online banks. You want one with no fees and no minimum balances.

Pay Yourself First Through Automated Deposits

If employed, you probably have the option for direct deposit to a bank account. Ask human resources for the form and how to fill it out. The form that authorizes them to deposit to a bank account will also allow you to split the wages between checking and savings accounts.

If you cannot direct deposit through work, or are self-employed, then you could have your bank or credit union transfer a specified amount each month from your checking account to your savings account.

Break Only in Case of Emergency (and if You Must, Replenish)

Car brake repair is an emergency. Vacation spending is not an emergency. If you do use the money, make sure it is for something you need, not want. Refilling this bucket should then be your priority.

Give Yourself a Savings Program

If you can't find a place to cut back on your expenses, then look back at chapter 13 to find other income sources. Subsidies could temporarily supplement your budget and allow you to move those savings to your emergency fund accounts.

How Much Do I Need in My Emergency Fund?

To start, give yourself a goal of $1,000 in a savings account.

Once having nailed that, you will want to be able to replace at least one month of income should you not be able to work or lose your job. Calculate this amount by dividing your annual income by twelve. If you are unsure of your annual income, you can look at your last tax return.

If you have already saved one month's income, then you will want to look at adding to that. Once you save three months' worth of income, you can keep going to six months or go to step 2.

Remember: Slow and steady is the way to go. Start with saving the token $25 amount and gradually increase it, maybe as you cut back on expenses. This has two effects. You are more likely to succeed if you start small, and if you reduce your monthly living expenses, your savings goal will shrink as well.

IF YOU HAVE ONE OF THESE, THEY CAN COUNT AS ALTERNATIVE EMERGENCY MONEY SOURCES

As I note later, build your retirement funds, and don't touch them. However, three accounts (if you have them) can be considered as emergency funds while you build an emergency savings account. Roth retirement accounts (Roth IRA), Health Savings Accounts (HSAs), and home equity line of credits (HELOC's) can all be considered interim emergency funds. (See Investopedia.com for definitions if you are new to these concepts.) It's not often discussed in financial media, but if you don't have cash sitting in the bank these accounts can be used in an emergency.

You can withdraw from them tax free and without penalties (mostly). These funds do double duty in your financial life—saving for retirement and emergency backup.

Should you have to draw on them, shuffle your budget to work to refill the HSA or Roth account. In the case of the HELOC, work to pay it down so it is available in the future for emergencies.

Important note: I am *not* including your 401(k)s from work or traditional retirement IRAs. Withdrawal from these accounts incurs taxes and, in some cases, penalties for early withdrawals. Also, you are shortchanging future growth in retirement savings.

STEP 2: REDUCE DEBT

Reducing your obligations has the same effect as saving money. The less you owe, the more you have. And not all debt is the same. Credit card debt has crushing interest rates and should be attacked first. Student loans and home mortgages have lower rates and can be seen as investments, making them less urgent to repay early.

If you are unable to pay your credit card debt and can live with a lower credit score for seven years, call each card issuer and ask to talk about a reduced payment plan. Many credit cards will write off a portion, if not all, of the debt you owe. This can stop the calls and keep the wolf from the door. At this writing, the one company less willing to work with their borrowers is Capital One. The company also has the easiest credit card to qualify for and does the most marketing.

The same goes with your mortgage company, student loan servicer, healthcare provider, local hospital, and the IRS. If you call as soon as you have problems, they might work with you. Some may require you be a few months behind in payments. *What they don't want is to be ignored.*

Getting ahead of the problem is important. Some won't talk to you if they have already sent the bill to collections.

Here's my personal feeling about companies who have customers behind in payments. It's now their problem so they need to work with you.

Good Debt Versus Bad Debt

Good debt is on assets that can grow in value, like a career, education, and a house. One has to evaluate the payback potential. Will the debt lead to a job whose salary will repay it? Is the house in a good neighborhood with good schools and the potential to appreciate? Will the job move lead to career advancement? Bad debt is high-interest-rate credit like credit cards or car loans that don't support an appreciating asset like a house or education. Bad debt is evil.

THE COMPLICATED SIDE OF DEBT

I understand the anxiety and fear that can come with crushing debt.

I graduated from college with a blown out credit card limit. I had charged my last semester's tuition and expenses on a credit card. As I embarked on my first career, I needed an interview suit, train fare to New York for interviews, and, when finally hired, a professional wardrobe.

The credit card balance had an interest rate of 24 percent, and my new salary would only cover rent and utilities, much less a credit card payment. I had only $5 a day left over for food and the subway. I was wearing out my shoes, walking the thirty blocks to Midtown Manhattan.

I understand the terror of bills in the mailbox. It happened another time when I was transferred from an employer's Miami office to Boston eight years later. I incurred large costs again for moving, a new apartment, a new (used) car, and, once more, new clothes—this time for winter. I ran up $30,000 in debt, which also included a large dental bill. It took me years to pay that off.

Sometimes debt is an investment. While I vowed never to be in that place again, I take solace in that both these debts were acquired in pursuit of improving my financial (and dental) future.

Borrowing this money was an investment in me. Education and a better job.

Financial Personalities Offering Expert Help on Debt Reduction

Massive amounts have been written on the topic of debt reduction. I recommend authors who know what they are talking about. (The list doesn't include bloggers.)

I will point out that only one of these money guides is unique to single parents. You will have to keep in mind our "successful secrets of investing in ourselves" to get ahead. That might include (reasonable) borrowing to gain skills, spending on childcare or work clothes, and driving a reliable car.

I have a preference for Dave Ramsey's Snowball Debt Reduction Plan. His book *Total Money Makeover* has been a bestseller for years, and while he is a financial celebrity with all the pluses and minuses involved, his method has helped thousands. He's been canceled in popular culture because he got too big for his britches and showed poor judgment in dealing with his employees. To be honest, I've seen that happen with a good many successful people. If you can get past that, his early books are still worthwhile.

Your Money or Your Life by Joe Dominguez and Vicki Robin has had a revival. The timeless message of prioritizing what's important to you has been rediscovered by a new generation.

Suze Orman is another financial celebrity whose advice has stood the test of time. Her ten books range from the encyclopedic *Road to Wealth* to *Young, Broke, and Fabulous.*

Emma Johnson's book, *Kickass Single Mom*, devotes a third of her book to the money topic and has the chapter "Get Out of Debt for Good."

I hope one of these suggestions click with you. Each has a distinct tone and tricks of the trade.

Debt-Reduction Methods

What all of the books mentioned previously have in common are one (or more) of the following six strategies (with thanks to Bankrate.com):

1. Pay More Than the Minimum Payment

Go through your budget and decide how much extra you can put toward your debt. Paying more than the minimum will save you money on interest and help you get out of debt faster.

Let's say you have a $15,000 balance on a credit card with 17 percent annual percentage rate and a $450 minimum payment. If you only make the minimum payment, it will take almost four years to repay the balance. You'll also pay about $5,500 in total interest.

If you paid $550 a month, or $100 more than the minimum, you could repay the debt in less than three years and pay only $4,100 in total interest. To learn more, try using a credit card payoff calculator. Bankrate.com has a good one.

Why this works: paying more than the minimum helps reduce the principal balance on your credit cards faster.

How to start: schedule the extra payment before the due date in the current billing cycle; it can also be added to the monthly minimum payment.

2. Try the Debt Snowball

You can also try the debt snowball method for debt reduction. This debt repayment method asks you to make the minimum payment on all your debts except for the smallest one, which you'll pay as much as you can. By "snowballing" payments toward your smallest debt, you'll eliminate it quickly and move on to the next smallest debt while paying minimum payments on the rest.

Let's say you have a $5,000 credit card balance, a $1,000 auto loan, and $10,000 in student loans. With the debt snowball method, you would focus on paying off the auto loan first because it has the lowest total balance.

Why this works: watching bills disappear from your mailbox is a huge psychological uplift.

THEY'RE AT IT AGAIN

You never forget your first (real) job. I was lucky enough to work in a multinational bank in one of their new expansion offices away from New York City. We were a small, plucky crew, clustered in age around ten years. We enjoyed one another's significant others, often socialized together, and had one another's backs. After about five years, we started to get transferred to other offices and one coworker, Dan, left to seek his fortune in industry. Dan ambitiously swung for the fences with the new job and his spouse, Jan, simultaneously quit hers to raise their children. He then lost his job. Loss of income and dramatically elevated costs to raise a family put them in the poor house. It could have happened to anyone. I, along with the rest of the crew, lent them money to pay bills. The next month they declared personal bankruptcy to start over.

Ashamed, embarrassed, or whatever, I didn't hear from Dan and Jan again until ten years later when they repaid the principal on my loan. They asked if I wanted the interest repaid as well, and I said "yes, please," now having my own financial needs. I never got it.

Still grateful for their early friendship and mentoring, I stopped by to see them in their new home another ten years later. Now back on their feet, they had a house with a pool in a nice neighborhood. Both were working, and the kids were grown and gone.

But comparison is the thief of joy and to rationalize what they perceived as my good luck and their poor luck, Dan and Jan continued to plead poverty. Maybe it was so I wouldn't ask for the interest on my old loan again. Or because they didn't want to throw money in the pot for dinner.

However, if you are going to try to claim a brand for yourself, make sure you are consistent. In that same visit, they mentioned their multiple family trips to Hawaii and a Christmas cruise to the Caribbean.

I guess they didn't learn their lesson to stand in their truth.

3. Commit Windfalls to Debt

This is similar to building the emergency fund. When you get a tax refund or stimulus check, add the money to your loan payments instead of splurging.

Other unexpected windfalls, like inheritances, work bonuses, and cash gifts, can also be used to pay down debts faster.

4. Reexamine Your Budget

There are two ways to pay off your debts faster: earn more or spend less. It may not be feasible to pick up a part-time job or side hustle, but you can adjust your budget.

Review the previous two chapters on earning more and spending less to make the necessary adjustments to your budget, and use the freed money to pay extra on your monthly debts.

Why this works: you can make short-term financial sacrifices to free up funds that can be used to pay down your balances faster.

5. Settle for Less Than You Owe

As mentioned previously, you can call creditors and negotiate a settlement of your debts, usually for a lot less than you owe. You will have to live with a credit score ding but such is life. You'll adapt.

How to start: Contact your creditors to offer settlements, and if they agree, get the terms in writing. Or you can hire a reputable debt settlement company to do the legwork for you.

6. Refinance to a Lower Rate at Another Lender

Whether a lower credit card interest rate or a debt consolidation loan, this to me is giving *Titanic*'s iceberg a growth opportunity. Lots of people do this, though. But it has two disadvantages. It isn't free and oftentimes sets borrowers up to expand their available credit, just what isn't needed. Bite the bullet and pursue the previous strategies.

You can do this yourself with a few uncomfortable phone calls to the lenders. And hey, we single parents do hard things all the time, don't we?

STEP 3: FUND RETIREMENT

There are multiple ways to fund your retirement using both employer-sponsored and self-selected plans.

HUMAN RESOURCES DEPARTMENTS AND RETIREMENT SAVINGS

Expertise varies. Banks I worked for obviously had this area well covered. However, my last corporate job with a start-up had less understanding of employee financial wellness. It is somewhat understandable that they would care less about retirement plans since the average employee age was twenty-six. What was disconcerting was the lack of interest by human resources in improving its game.

The human resources rep, while great at responding to management, never took the initiative on new financial developments. I explained about the then-new HSA legislation and asked that the company offer a qualifying health insurance option at annual enrollment. It was a perfect plan option for the demographic we employed. She shut me down rather than try to learn "something new."

Employer-Sponsored Plans

401(k) Plans (and the Government Thrift Savings Plan Equivalent) and the Matching "Free Money"

A retirement savings account offered by employers, a 401(k) is a plan by which you elect to have 1–4 percent of your gross pay deducted from your paycheck and put into an investment account. Many employers then offer a "match." They will generally offer a dollar-for-dollar match of money you have contributed to your retirement plan. This is up to a certain limit, such as 3 percent of your salary.

An employer's 401(k) match represents "free money" to the employee. That's why your savings plan should at least have a goal to save up to the amount you get matched.

A 401(k) is pretax money. That means the contributions get deducted from your salary each pay period before taxes are calculated and taken out. This should have the effect of lowering the income taxes you pay. *Note:* If you are in the lowest tax brackets of less than 20 percent and have a Roth 401(k) available to you, consider after-tax dollar contributions instead to get the free money match.

You pay taxes on this when you withdraw it, ostensibly for retirement. Money in this plan should *not* be considered for emergencies. Early withdrawal can carry steep costs.

Roth 401(k)

If your employer offers an option of a Roth 401(k) plan, take it. This can also double as a specific goal-focused savings fund since you can have ready access to the money after five years. I like this better for those in lower tax brackets (such as "head of household" for taxes) than the pretax 401(k).

How should this money be invested? The employer-offered account comes with a set of investment choices. Generally, they offer you ten mutual funds to invest in, plus the company stock. Choose the most broad-based stock fund with the lowest fees. (That would be the "Total Stock Fund" ETF category.)

WHEN WOULDN'T YOU TAKE THE COMPANY 401(K) PLAN?

I worked for a start-up with a lousy 401(k) plan. It had high fees, poor investment options, and no matching funds. This was during a period of higher interest rates, and I had a home mortgage. In that case, rather than contribute to my 401(k), I instead used the amount I budgeted for retirement savings and made extra payments on my mortgage.

One could argue that I was making those extra mortgage payments with after-tax money, and as a result, I would be paying higher taxes. But my low income at this start-up (a portion was paid in stock) was such that I essentially didn't pay taxes. I not only had a low wage, but I was also in the "head of household" tax bracket and had high deductions from a mortgage. There was essentially little difference between my pretax and after-tax income.

If you find yourself with any of the factors—low tax bracket, bad 401(k) plan investment options, or no matching funds from an employer—consider diverting your savings to another asset such as the home and its mortgage, an external Roth IRA, or an HSA.

But the simplest way to invest is in a "target date fund." This is a fund that automatically adjusts investments to match risk tolerance as you get older. The closer you get to retirement age, the less risk you want in your portfolio. You will be offered a selection with dates attached, such as "Target Date 2040" and "Target Date 2050." While they are not the cheapest cost of investing, they do offer an easy path to investing your retirement money. I am all for anything that makes investing easy.

Pick the fund with the target date closest to your retirement year, whether that is at age sixty-five or less.

Options for the Self-Employed

If you are self-employed or your employer doesn't offer a 401(k) retirement savings plan, the following are other tax-advantaged plans.

Traditional Individual Retirement Account (Traditional IRA)

These are more limited in the amount you can contribute (currently $7,000 per year) than for a 401(k) but are available to you if you are self-employed, if you are a nonworking parent, or if your employer doesn't offer a 401(k) retirement savings plan. Any amount you contribute under the annual limit is considered "before-tax" money. That means that in your income tax filing, you can deduct your contribution from your wages reported and pay tax on what is left over (after-tax).

You pay taxes on this when you withdraw it, ostensibly for retirement. Money in this plan should not be considered for emergencies. Early withdrawal can carry steep penalties.

Roth Individual Retirement Account (Roth IRA)

This option is also limited in the amount of total contribution allowed, currently $7,000 per year. If you are in a lower-earning tax or wage bracket, I recommend this form of retirement savings account over the traditional IRA. You have easier access to the money, it grows tax free, and when you withdraw from it, you don't pay taxes. Its two drawbacks are the limited amount you can contribute each year and qualifying income limits.

Still, I opened one of these accounts for my daughter when she turned sixteen. Since her earnings during school and over the summer didn't exceed the income limits and she was in a low tax bracket, it didn't make sense for her to have a pretax plan like a 401(k) or traditional IRA. There was no tax advantage if you didn't make enough to pay taxes. Instead, she had taxes withheld during the year, filed her tax return as soon as she could, then used the refund to fund her Roth IRA retirement savings account.

This is also a great way for grandparents (as well as parents) to contribute to grandchildren's future well-being. They can contribute to the fund up to the amount the grandchild earned that year.

Where Can You Get IRAs?

I prefer the major online brokerage firms such as Vanguard, Schwab, and T. Rowe Price. If you have access to TIAA-Cref or USAA, I like those as well. After having worked for all of these investment firms as a consultant, I got a feel for their corporate culture and customer focus. My opinion is that these firms look out for their customers. All have excellent customer service by phone with live people.

HOW TO SAVE FOR MULTIPLE GOALS AT THE SAME TIME

"Achieving your goals takes patience and time—but starting early will give you a big edge. And while it may feel unnatural, put yourself (and your retirement) first." —Kiplinger Newsletter

Kiplinger Magazine had an excellent article demonstrating why and how to start saving early. Using an example of $200/month savings, it illustrated the startling difference between starting to save early versus later.

To save simultaneously for several goals, I suggest first filling up the emergency fund bucket. Not only will you have the flexibility to meet emergencies, but the peace of mind is also priceless. That emotional energy can be redirected to more positive tasks to keep you happy.

Once you have the emergency fund established, start to work on your medium- and long-term goals, like a vacation or a comfortable retirement. Schwab.com has a good article—"How to Save for Multiple Financial Goals"—including how to separate them and keep these funds for the future.

I differ from the Schwab.com article only in its sequencing. I found it helpful to split the amount I could save equally between my goals after I funded the emergency account. Once I had the emergency funds in a savings account, I would split my savings each month between a retirement account and paying down debt.

Spend a little less, save a little more, and do it regularly. Soon, you will have a nice nest egg. Keep it in a safe place.

401(K) ACCOUNTS: ONLY USE FOR RETIREMENT!

A colleague came to me in a financial panic. In a few years her daughter would begin college and she didn't know where to begin on achieving her financial goals. I explained the "order of savings" and how to build a plan and sequence savings. Feeling much relieved, Erin gushed her thanks. Then, almost as a postscript, she gleefully informed me she decided to drain a "small" 401(k) retirement account to buy a boat. She considered it an investment in her mental health! I audibly groaned reading that email. Both for her poor financial choice (boats depreciate, 401(k) withdrawals can't be repaid) and the sense of entitlement. Sadly, she was fired six months later, never to regain her earning power.

Lesson learned: retirement accounts are for retirement, not lifestyle choices.

CHAPTER 16

Insurance: Protecting What's Yours

Minimum Insurance Needs

Other Insurance You Might Consider

Where to Buy Insurance

How to Buy Insurance

How to Lower the Cost of Insurance

Summary Table of Insurance

FOR SINGLE PARENTS, BEING ADEQUATELY PROTECTED against financial wipeout due to loss is even more imperative than for two-adult families. We have fewer resources to fall back on. Replacing a lost home or car can devastate finances. If we or our children have an expensive medical need, we could more easily end up off the financial cliff.

All the efforts to secure financial peace of mind can go out the window if we are faced with loss that we can't recover. Insurance represents the third leg of the financial well-being stool. If you can't afford to replace something, then you need to insure it.

Insurance is made needlessly complicated and turns folks off. There is also a misunderstanding that insurance is something you pay for and should get reimbursed for if you don't use it. Well, no. *The hope is that you don't have to use it.* I also have heard it explained to me that engaging with health insurance is inviting illness, life insurance makes one have to face their own mortality, and renter's insurance is too expensive (not so).

This is nonsense. It isn't about you. It's about your children and providing a chaos-free life.

I am here to cut through this for you and to talk about what is critically necessary. I'll cite the minimum insurance you need to acquire to feel safe and ways to lower the cost. If you want platinum-level coverage where you shoulder none of the risk involved and hand it all over to an insurance company, I'll explain that as well.

It is critical you secure adequate protection for your family. This makes it imperative you include insurance in your support agreement with the other parent. Don't let this slide to the back burner of negotiations.

MINIMUM INSURANCE NEEDS

At a minimum, you should have:

- Renter's or homeowner's insurance
- Auto insurance
- Health insurance
- Life insurance

Minimum Insurance Described

I've described as follows the insurance types and their importance. Other than homeowner's and auto, the coverage is voluntary. Health insurance may now be voluntary, but it is critical. It is cheaply available now. Yet I know people who forgo it. Risky indeed since one trip to the emergency room can wipe out your newly established savings account.

If some of the terms here like deductible and coverage are foreign to you, I suggest opening Investopedia.com while you read this chapter.

Renter's Insurance

It is inexpensive and can save your finances in the face of disaster. You need this policy if you rent a home, with or without roommates. This covers your possessions, not the dwelling unit. It can also cover "loss of use" should you not be able to live in your rental because of damage. If you want that covered, make sure your policy includes it.

THE APARTMENT RENTER'S INSURANCE

Three months after securing the renter's insurance policy, my daughter had to evacuate New Orleans from a category 5 hurricane. She was looking for any plane ticket out and ended up going to Chicago. It took a month to restore electricity to New Orleans. The plane ticket alone was $1,000. She was covered for airfare. She was also covered for two weeks in a hotel and any losses to her possessions in the apartment. (Luckily, the only casualty was a blender that short-circuited when the electricity was restored.)

The entire claim to Progressive was about $2,500. I had to pay $500 of it for the deductible, and they reimbursed the rest. I felt smart for buying that policy.

In New England, the number-one disaster for people is fire. We have old buildings made of wood. As a Red Cross volunteer, I saw many families lose everything in a fire. None had renter's insurance. They ended up bunking with family or friends or in shelters. Securing new quarters and replacing lost possessions cost a lot more than what a renter's policy would have been.

I have renter's insurance for my rented home. It is $30/month.

I also bought renter's insurance for my daughter's college apartment in New Orleans. It is more expensive to insure in New Orleans given they are prone to disasters. I paid $40/month for the contents and use of her two-bedroom apartment.

Homeowner's Insurance

This covers loss of contents and any damage to your physical home. Besides physical property and possessions, homeowner's insurance covers you for other losses. The aforementioned "loss of use" may be one example. If you have a home mortgage, insurance is required. The policies come in a wide variety of sizes and flavors.

The claims process rating is the most important factor to consider when looking for a home insurance company. There's no point in buying homeowner's coverage if your insurance company hassles you about approving your claim.

For a long time, I bought my policy from an insurance company that was the only one who covered full replacement costs for the antique homes we have in abundance here in Boston. I loved the great customer service for the time it saved. Sadly, things changed, and when they no longer were rated above the competition in claims-paying experience, I switched.

Both Consumer Reports and J.D. Power do independent ratings of insurance company experiences. Ask the local library's reference librarian for the latest report.

Auto Insurance

Some states regulate how and at what rates insurers can offer auto insurance in their state. I lived in New Hampshire where auto insurance wasn't required ("Live Free or Die") and in Massachusetts, where rates were standardized.

Car insurance is so important that most states require coverage by law, but not all states mandate it. If you don't want to pay for insurance, you'll likely have to show proof of financial responsibility, at any rate, by posting a bond. That feels like a lot more work that single parents don't need. Even if you aren't required to have coverage in your state, you won't escape the costs associated with a car accident.

In shopping for auto insurance:

1. Get multiple quotes online.

2. Make sure you compare apples to apples with the quotes. Are they covering the same risks?

3. Only get quotes from auto insurers with excellent claims-paying experience (refer to Consumer Reports and J.D. Power for the shortlist).

4. If you do not have access to alternate transportation, then make sure to select the coverage for *substitute transportation*. Even in high-cost Boston, it adds about $60 to the annual premium. Otherwise, if your car has to go to the shop after an accident, it will cost a lot to rent a car temporarily.

Health Insurance

If you feel solid on how this works and how to get it, feel free to skip this section. If you prefer a refresher or are a newbie to this world, read on.

Health insurance covers your costs for medical professionals and facilities. It also covers behavioral (mental) health services, physical therapy, and, for children, some dental costs. It does not cover adult dental costs. For that you need a separate plan.

Some employer plans cover drug costs. Private plans such as those through the Affordable Care Act (ACA) might not cover drug costs.

The ACA legislation was passed over a decade ago and made health insurance available to everyone. Despite this being a major leap forward for the millions of uninsured Americans, some knuckleheads decided it should be optional. Just last week an otherwise smart person told me they went without because it is "expensive." (Not so. Consider the alternative. A quick emergency room trip can cost you $5,000 without insurance, more than one year's worth of insurance premiums.) With the advent of the ACA, if you are lower income, you get subsidies for the premium. If you are really low income you get free healthcare known as Medicaid.

You buy health insurance through work, through your state program, or through the federal program, Healthcare.gov.

You also may have it negotiated in your divorce support agreement.

Life Insurance

If you weren't around, who would provide for your children either in terms of money or care?

CALCULATING HOW MUCH LIFE INSURANCE YOU NEED

Not knowing your personal situation, I don't know how much exactly you'll need. I can, however, give you a calculation method.

Consider the cost of raising a child: The US Department of Agriculture annually publishes what a child costs to raise in the United States.

Multiply the remaining number of years until your child is eighteen times the annual cost. (Add 30 percent if you live in a high cost of living area.)

Add any money you want to be available for education beyond high school.

Subtract the amount of your retirement savings like a 401(k), IRA, or equivalent.

If you have a college savings account, subtract that amount as well.

Round up to the nearest $100,000.

This takes into account any savings you might have over the long run and effectively reduces the amount of life insurance you would need.

If anyone depends on you for their well-being, then life insurance is a must buy. Even stay-at-home parents need coverage. Whatever work is done by a parent has monetary value. If that parent couldn't do it, someone would have to be hired to provide the services. So please don't undervalue your life's work, whether for monetary compensation or not.

Fortunately, this can be cheap insurance. The younger you are, the less expensive because you pay in over a longer period of time.

Again, you can buy this through work (cheapest) or privately. It is also strongly suggested you cover this topic regarding both parents if you are working out a child support agreement.

OTHER INSURANCE YOU MIGHT CONSIDER

While perhaps not essential, there are other forms of insurance that, if you can afford them, may well justify their cost somewhere down the road.

Home Warranty Plan

If you own a home with older mechanical equipment, such as a furnace, dishwasher, laundry, and so forth, more than five years old, it might be worthwhile to pay a monthly fee to have someone take care of things that break with one call.

Pet Insurance

With the skyrocketing cost of veterinary care and the coming shortages of vets, I personally am considering this one.

Umbrella Liability Coverage

This is a low-cost way to get significant extra liability coverage. It protects both you and other people that could be damaged by you or a household member's actions. If you have accumulated significant assets, this is an inexpensive way to protect them. You combine it with your home or renter's insurance.

Long-Term Care Insurance

If your employer offers a long-term care insurance plan, take a close look at it, even though it may seem a long way off to old age. The earlier you start a policy, the lower the monthly premiums. The middle class is priced out of these policies on their own. If you don't have money or assets, you could qualify for Medicaid for nursing home costs. If you have a lot of assets, self-insure a stay in a nursing home for a year or more. Otherwise, look at hybrid life insurance policies that include a long-term care option that pays for your care after a waiting period. The best time to buy this is before age fifty-nine.

WHERE TO BUY INSURANCE

While you can buy health, life, and disability insurance through an employer, you will still need to go outside work to get property and casualty (P&C) coverage for your home, apartment, car, and so forth.

Here I have broken down what you can get at work and, if that isn't an option, other places you can access insurance coverage.

At Work

Through your employer, you can generally purchase health insurance, disability insurance, pet insurance, life insurance, and accidental death insurance.

This is the least expensive and easiest way to buy a policy. If you can, load up on the best and highest policies possible *and* always ask if these policies are "portable." In other words, can you take the policy with you when you leave, or does the policy terminate when your employment ends? Health insurance has to be offered for eighteen months following your departure from a company. Disability, though, is very expensive to buy on your own so a portable policy would be of great benefit.

If buying through an employer isn't an option, these are other options.

At School

Colleges and universities sponsor group health insurance plans for employees and students (Student Health Insurance Program or SHIP). Like employer-sponsored plans, the costs are shared and are generally lower for those who are being insured by the plan.

Healthcare.gov

The advent of the ACA allowed everyone to access insurance policies. These are offered at all levels of plans, which are standardized across the states. If your state offers its own insurance program (such as the Health Connector in Massachusetts), you go through them. If your state doesn't manage its own health insurance portal, Healthcare.gov will direct you to a policy.

Independent Agents

Companies like Travelers or Chubb sell through a network of independent agents. I exclusively used this channel for twenty-five years. I had found a knowledgeable agent who could counsel me through the decision process on where my risk lay and how I could cover it. It was worth paying for slightly higher-cost insurance to have someone in my corner to advise me.

However, those agents seem to be disappearing in the face of the cheaper direct-to-consumer model (e.g., GEICO), described as follows. Now you may as well go through the direct channel and use their online agents.

Dedicated Agents

Companies such as American Family Insurance sell through their own agents.

CAUTION: FRIENDS DON'T SELL INSURANCE TO FRIENDS

At some time or another, you will be approached by an acquaintance to buy insurance. While you may trust this person, it may not be in your best interest to buy this way. In my younger days, I was talked into insurance I didn't need. It would start out with getting a policy I *did* need, such as renter's insurance, and then, naïve as I was, I'd buy life insurance. I didn't even have kids.

The expression in the industry is "insurance is sold, not bought." So, watch the sales pitches.

Friends and acquaintances have turned to insurance sales when they are starting out or starting over. None lasted more than a year. Once they had gone through their friends and family list, no more leads came in, and there wasn't any chance of commissions.

Stick with an established agent who has good reviews. Politely turn down the friend selling.

Affinity Groups

Membership has its privileges. You've seen this when you have received an offer in the mail to talk about insurance from AAA, your university, or a business association. Many insurance companies sell through groups. They provide a rate break and profit share with the organization. It offers a way to expand a pool and spread risk. You should get a cheaper policy that way.

> ## CONSIDER USAA
>
> My favorite affinity group is USAA insurance, limited to only members of the military (active, reserve, or retired) and their immediate family members. If you qualify, you should put this company at the top of your list. My father served but he never joined USAA, therefore I never could get the benefit. The same goes with the Military Officers of America (formerly Retired Officers Association).

Faith-Based Self-Insurance Circles

In all good conscience I can't say these are appropriate for single parents. Also known as healthcare cost sharing, these are very small insurance pools in which the costs of healthcare are shared among a group of like-minded people. If you want to read more about them, please do a search. There is just too much risk and no legal obligation to pay out claims. Also, with the advent of the ACA and Medicaid expansion, good alternatives exist if you are financially strapped.

Direct to Consumer

You know these companies through their extensive advertising. They include Progressive, GEICO, and Amica. They sometimes have cheaper policy premiums and offer frictionless online purchase experiences.

HOW TO BUY INSURANCE

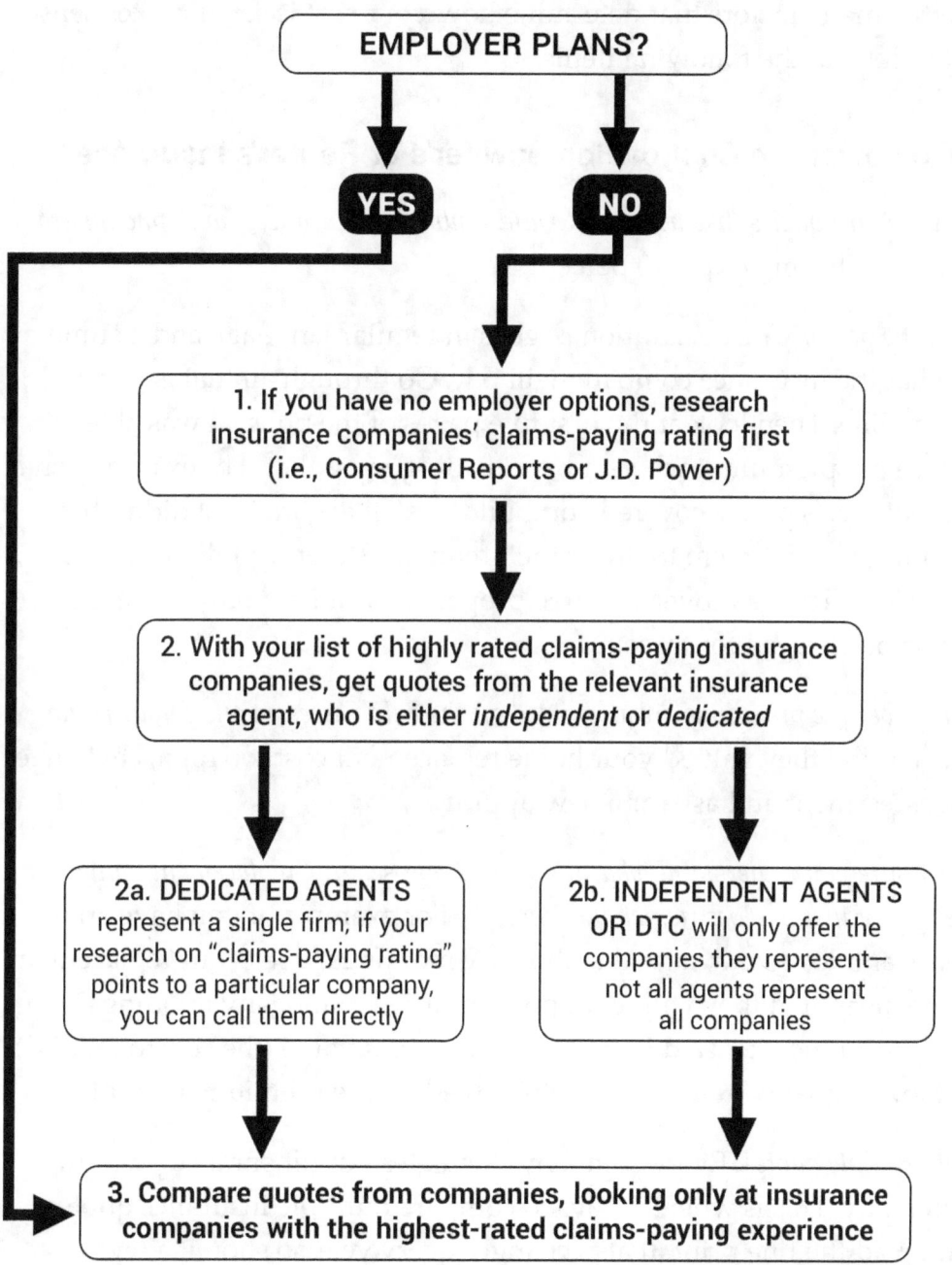

EMPLOYER PLANS?

YES

NO

1. If you have no employer options, research insurance companies' claims-paying rating first (i.e., Consumer Reports or J.D. Power)

2. With your list of highly rated claims-paying insurance companies, get quotes from the relevant insurance agent, who is either *independent* or *dedicated*

2a. DEDICATED AGENTS represent a single firm; if your research on "claims-paying rating" points to a particular company, you can call them directly

2b. INDEPENDENT AGENTS OR DTC will only offer the companies they represent— not all agents represent all companies

3. Compare quotes from companies, looking only at insurance companies with the highest-rated claims-paying experience

HOW TO LOWER THE COST OF INSURANCE

Given the many factors that determine how your cost is set, it makes sense to take a look at the following items.

How to Lower the Cost of Homeowner's or Renter's Insurance

- *Group your policies, like home, auto and umbrella insurances, with one insurance company.* This may save 10 percent.

- *Read the policy.* The declaration page is in regular language and a summary of what the insurance company will pay. Go through all that is covered line by line. Then look at the first five pages of the policy. I was able to reduce my premium each year by rereading my policy. For example, one homeowner's policy covered "outbuildings" like garages. I didn't have a garage, so I got them to lower the premium. Recently, I discovered my renter's policy was covering three properties, but I am only renting one but being charged for three.

- *Remember the premiums are also based on the value assessment of your home.* If you think they valued your home replacement cost too high, challenge the assessment and ask for a new appraisal.

- *Make sure you understand what it means if you secure "replacement value" as the type of insured loss (which you should).* For example, if you have an old house and love your carved mahogany moldings, does your replacement value mean that they will rebuild with carved mahogany moldings? Do you care? I didn't. I said I wanted replacement value (the cost to rebuild) but lower-quality items. Again, this saved on the premium amount.

- *Get multiple quotes.* Every company calculates your insurance premium differently. This is where it pays to compare multiple insurance quotes. And read the fine print. It also changes every year so shop it a few months before renewal.

- *Make your deductible as high as you can afford to cover in case of loss.* It makes a big difference.

- *Don't make a claim unless you have to.* What insurance companies won't tell you is that if you make a claim, they will raise your premiums for three years after. And those claims are public records, so any future insurance company for you or the next owner will calculate premiums based on the house's casualty experience.

How to Lower the Cost of Auto Insurance

- *Lower coverage limits.* If you don't have a lot of savings, then lower limits make sense. If you have a lot of money in savings accounts, then you'll need to protect them from liability with higher limits.

- *Get your auto and homeowner's insurance from the same company.*

- *See if there are discounts for loyal customers (more than two years with a company).*

- *Read the policy.* Did it sneak in coverage for towing, identity theft, and other things you might not need? Decline any coverage duplicated elsewhere. Towing coverage is a common duplication with your auto club membership or new car purchase.

- *Raise your deductible to what you can cover out of emergency funds.* Not only will you reduce the premium, but you will not be tempted to claim "small" losses. Like homeowner's insurance, claims can raise your premiums up to 30 percent for three years in Massachusetts.

- *Appeal accident and moving violation surcharges.* If your insurance company hits you with an at-fault premium and you think that is in error, appeal. It will be worth the savings from potentially increased premiums if you win the appeal.

CONTESTING CAR-RELATED EVENTS

I once got a ticket for running a red light. I disagreed. I went to traffic court, and the judge dismissed the ticket.

Another time, I backed into a gray car, on a gray day on a tiny street. I appealed the surcharge to my insurance. I lost.

A friend borrowed my car and got into an accident while going for coffee. She received a driver surcharge on her insurance, but my car needed many thousands of dollars in repairs. I was covered through my insurance company but had to pay the deductible because the driver of my car was deemed at fault. My friend fought the "at-fault" finding and won. Her surcharge was reversed, and I had my deductible reimbursed.

Insurance is a critical part of your family's well-being. Take the time to make sure you are adequately covered and not having to overpay.

Type of Risk Covered	Bare Bones Protection Package	Low-Cost Protection Package	Medium-Range Protection Package	Full-Coverage Insurance Package
SUMMARY TABLE OF INSURANCE				
Life insurance	Mortgage life insurance	Term insurance	Term insurance	Term or permanent insurance plus riders for long-term care
Disability	Mortgage disability or free employer long-term disability policy	Free and/or paid employer disability policy	Employer disability policy or private policy	Employer disability policy plus private policy
Home insurance	Renters/home insurance; $1,000 deductible	Renters/home insurance; $1,000 deductible	Renters/home insurance; $500 deductible	Renters/home insurance; $500 deductible + excess liability policy
Auto insurance	Auto insurance minimum limits required; $1,000 deductible	Auto insurance minimum limits; $1,000 deductible	Auto insurance limits to 300/500 levels and $1,000 deductible	Auto insurance with limits to 300/500* and $500 deductible
Excess liability	None	None	Umbrella liability coverage	Umbrella liability coverage
Health insurance	Catastrophic coverage or auto medical coverage	Employer or state-subsidized health insurance through the ACA	Employer HMO or state health HMO Bronze/Silver level insurance through the ACA	Employer PPO or state health insurance ACA Gold/Platinum plans
Travel insurance	None	None	Travel insurance bought per trip	Annual travel insurance policy
Pet insurance	None	None	Pet insurance	Pet insurance

PART 4

Relationships with Kids, Peers, and Potential Partners

CHAPTER 17

Parenting Alone or Coparenting

PUTTING YOUR FAMILY IN CONTEXT FOR YOUR CHILD

At some point, your child becomes aware that their family structure is different than others. It is heartbreaking to have to explain to a child what they are missing and finding an acceptable "why." Regardless of their age or the circumstances, this is a loss for them.

In my family, my goal was to explain it in the most neutral way possible and then take my daughter's cues. The objective was to sit with her sadness and not try to explain it away. Acknowledging her sadness and loss was the best response I could have.

There are many family configurations and many ways to explain a second parent's absence. It could be a consequence of abandonment, death, divorce, or choice. Whatever our parenting reasons, here are some fundamentals to explain this to children, no matter the age or circumstance.

Remember It's Their Loss You Are Discussing, Not Yours

It's important not to bring a parent's sadness to hijack kids' emotions. Let them have their moments. Don't overshadow it with your own feelings. Adults have many other ways to share their grief, and we can use those. Children can't. They only have us.

Keep Your Anger About the Other Parent to Yourself

Leave off judgments and personal narratives. You can tell a story now and then that might give context. Let it be neutral at worst. Origin stories are fabulous if not tinged with negativity.

Help Them Practice What to Say When Asked

Of course, I can't guarantee how it will come out when they say it. Sometimes, the stories would get back to me from other parents, and I would just smile. I really didn't care what the other parents repeated. I would just say, "She said that, did she?" and smile. One of my daughter's friends once told me that her own dad was a secret agent. "Cool!" I responded. Let accuracy go. You can't win with it, and this is really just between you and your child.

Be Attentive in the Teen Years

The teen years present a special challenge. Stories abound on the Internet, and kids pick those up to fill in the gaps in their own family chronicle. Additionally, there is a lot of acting out around emotions they can't necessarily articulate. I would make sure you have reinforcements ready, and I mean professionals. This does *not* include any school personnel. They are overwhelmed as it is and can default to generalizations. You need specifics. Talk to other parents who might be having problems. Seek out credible online resources and interviews for family therapists. (See chapter 7, "Therapists," for more on this.)

WELCOME TO CLUB FED

Matthew and his shady dealings landed him in federal prison for five years. He has remarried and India's daughter, Ava, now had a stepmother who also landed in jail. The die was cast, though, for an even rockier road for India's relationship with her daughter. While Matthew's family adored Ava, their values did not align with India's. They had a lot of that funny money floating around and showered Ava with vacations, gifts, cash, and attention well beyond what India could or would manage. Ava didn't see that the money was unclean, all her young-self saw was that she got what she wanted. Not even a prison sentence would color her attraction to the earthly rewards. It's created a major cognitive distortion in how she views her mother. Adolescence and its differentiation put India in the role of "bad cop" by having to enforce her more down-to-earth values. Adding to the fire was that the stepmother stepped over India to assume traditional mother/daughter rites of passage such as helping to set up the first college dorm room.

India's navigation of the constant stress of bad communication, loss of control, and values misalignment holds lessons for others. She looks forward to the day when she and Ava will "hug it out" but in the meanwhile she has hard lessons learned to share with the single-parent community.

Support Your Child but Prepare Them for Disappointment

I told my daughter around age five that if she wanted to talk to her father, I would try to find him. It was her sophomore year in college when she actually took me up on it. I got a number for him, made sure it was correct, and told her that I would be around the house in case she wanted to talk to me but that I didn't have a need to speak with him. I am sure he was astounded to get a message from her. It took him a while to call her back, and they set times to talk. After the second conversation, nothing. We never heard from him again. I had prepped her for the very real possibility that he wouldn't engage in a relationship. He didn't, and she has drawn her own conclusion about him.

COPARENTING

Coparenting with your child's other parent(s) can generate a lot of pain. It forces you to revisit disappointments and can arouse longing for what could have been.

As one single parent noted: "I signed up for an intact family."

Add blended and extended family, romantic interests, remarriages, and so forth into the mix, and it's a stew of complications.

It's just hard. No matter what. But it is important to your child(ren) to continuously try to negotiate visits. Research has shown that interaction with noncustodial parents is more important than financial payments. Keep that in mind the next time arrangements stress you out.

Ten "Rules of Engagement" with an Engaged Coparent

The term "rules of engagement" has its origin in military speak. These are the internal rules for military forces and individuals that define how force or other actions may be applied. The term has also morphed to business language to mean how to go about dealing with constituents such as customers, suppliers, and partners.

I've extended this concept to define the rules of engagement to coparenting.

1. Communicate with the Other Parent—Not Your Kids

I put the most complex rule first. Keep talking and leave out the anger and disappointment. No one hears when you are yelling. Maybe you have to explain things one hundred different times in one hundred different ways, but persistence is vital. Get on the same page—it no longer matters why your relationship didn't work. Leave out blame and move on to the issues at hand.

For example, you don't need to remind your ex that they were late in the past; give them the time to be there, and you can address infractions when they arise, without front-loading them. Maybe get behind the issue: "You seem to be running twenty to thirty minutes late. What would help? Do we want to change the time?"

2. Fight Fair

Life is a negotiation. I've spent my career in negotiation, learning along the way what constitutes productive negotiating to get what you need. Some conflicts resolve effortlessly. Others can't be fixed quickly and require the greatest of patience and humor, often in short supply for an overworked, stressed single parent. Experts outline how to achieve the optimum outcome for conflict resolution:

- Tackle one issue at a time.

- Don't yell.

- Avoid bombs like "you always" or "you never."

- Don't "gunny sack," a 1960's term meaning holding onto grudges and unloading later—it's better to deal in the moment.

- Don't assume; the answer may not be "no."

- Be open to learning the "why" and working around the other party's needs.

- Don't make trust an issue.

"DON'T MAKE TRUST AN ISSUE"

This statement was coined by the late Roger Fisher in his seminal book on negotiation *Getting to Yes: How to Negotiate Without Giving In.* That small book had an outsized impact on the world of negotiation by shifting prevailing opinions from "adversarial bargaining" to understanding the other party's needs to achieve a more effective outcome. Fisher's negotiation experience ranged from nuclear weapons treaties to buying a car. I had the honor to study under Fisher, and it changed my life in a world where everything I had to negotiate, including my child's college needs, resulted in better agreements for all.

The book has undergone several revisions since its publication in 1981. Fisher (along with Scott Brown) wrote related books whose titles played on the title of *Getting to Yes,* such as *Getting Together: Building a Relationship That Gets to Yes* (1988).

In terms of trust, if the other parent has a history of inconsistency, then make your agreement less reliant on trust and more reliant on verification. For example, use third-party apps and agreements to track the deal, taking blame and misdirection out of the equation. The American Bar Association published a rating of third-party custody apps to reduce conflict in families.

Agreements can include:

- Late-fee agreements if the other partner is late to pick up and you incur a penalty. You will send the bill each month to them, and they will either pay or accrue penalty fees.

- A forty-eight-hour advance confirmation from either parent to the other before the visitation. If they don't confirm, you will assume they are not coming and may make other arrangements.

- A required call from the noncustodial parent when they are on their way, so your child is not left wondering.

3. No Dumping

Another great phrase from the 1960s. It means not making the other party responsible for solving your insecurities, aggravating bureaucracies, and managing other stealers of your time. No one wants to deal with continued anger or rage.

4. Listen to the Other Person

Some people just aren't cut out to be listeners. You can model mature behavior by actively listening and holding your fire for a bit. A few "Mississippis" can head off a lot of explosive reactions. So can "I'll get back to you on that."

5. Have a Plan and Then Negotiate

Since we aren't dictators, it's not likely we can bend the world to our will. Therefore, the path forward is through collaboration and negotiation. Admittedly, this is something I have to work at. It is not a natural act for me, despite being an expert business negotiator and one of four children. It takes deep breaths and patience along with not feeling rushed all the time.

Negotiation involves some measure of understanding the other party's needs. What has the other party got going on? Do they have different pressures themselves? Do they have difficulty with planning and organization? Was empathy ever modeled for you without it being victimized?

Pick your battles. Catastrophizing a screwup and getting worked up is not going to help you. I do not advocate giving repeat offenders wholesale passes, but we all make mistakes, and saying "oh well" might get you more points.

Blended Families and Managing Mixed Messages

Sergio married a single mother. That union came with a stepdaughter and an engaged father with shared custody. As a health professional, Sergio is hyperconcerned about his fourteen-year-old stepdaughter's ballooning weight and unhealthy habits. While happy her bio-dad stays involved, Sergio feels undermined in his attempts to help the teen. We talked about getting on the same page with the other parent. If he has tactics like keeping junk food out of the house, this could be something both he and the other parents could agree on. For influencing his stepdaughter, Sergio and I discussed "leaning into likes" by mixing increased activity with her interests in fashion and music.

6. Set Goals Together

Take turns naming goals for your children. These could be activities or qualities you want your children to be working on, like patience. Be mindful not to talk over another person or let them talk over you. Articulating these goals helps each party tap into inner motivations, making them more likely to follow through.

7. Assign Responsibilities

Allocate tasks fairly and reasonably. It probably won't be fifty-fifty since everyone overestimates their contribution. The objective here is to put it in an agreement and work on that. Start small if you have to. For example, "I can handle soccer pickup if you can handle ballet." Or perhaps someone is better at getting equipment or handling registration.

WHAT'S IN THE BEST INTEREST OF THE CHILD?

I prefer a sports rehab setting for physical therapy versus a medical setting since my injuries are usually activity related. One go-around over six months was at the same day and time each week. I got to observe other patients and, in the case of high school athletes, their parents.

A red-headed young man would sit next to me in the waiting area, his face glued to his phone. This went on for months. He never acknowledged me or anyone else in the facility for that matter. After a while, I understood his affect. I saw his divorced parents take turns dropping him off or picking him up. I witnessed each parent interfere with the physical therapist's program, demanding their specific wishes be complied with—not the other parent's. The physical therapist was caught in the middle of their relationship, and the kid retreated to his inner self.

I saw this as a lost opportunity for both parents. A third-party expert can rule the day and take you out of the fight. Agree to listen to them and not make their lives more difficult.

8. Keep Meetings Short—a Half Hour at Most

Decide on a subsequent meeting to assess how coparenting is working. Agreeing to revisit the practicality of an agreement takes the urgency, therefore stress, out of the negotiation.

9. Agree About What to Do When "Things Happen"

This is tricky. Things happen, but some people just can't keep to a schedule, and giving them a pass every time validates the behavior. Preschools handle this by charging hefty late pickup fees. These can run from $3 to $15 *per minute* in the Boston area! It's not a joke. Those teachers are tired and need to go home.

This can, however, be used as a proxy to establish a fair and reasonable penalty for one party not honoring an agreed-upon schedule. Look up the late pickup fees at preschools in your area and use that fee schedule to assess fines to each other. Either can pay them by deducting or adding to support payments. It also helps if each lets their employer know what fees will be assessed if you (or they) are kept late. Ask if they are willing to reimburse the cost to have you stay late. If not, let them know another time they can have you stay late.

Keep a fair accounting of late fees assessed to each other so that you "don't make trust an issue." For example, you can rely on one of the coparenting apps mentioned previously (also known as "custody apps") to track agreements. It creates some distance between the obligation and the people, thus lessening frustration. You can assess your own fees, monetary or in-kind, for missing commitments.

Decide for yourself if you can let something slide. You know the other parent and can choose not to react or say, "No problem this time, but next time, we need to assess the penalty per minute."

IN-KIND REMUNERATION

Some people can't afford monetary penalty fees. If that is the case, you can agree to in-kind remuneration such as extra childcare time as a way to make good.

---

10. Agree on When to Revisit the Plan

Circumstances change. Kids grow. School schedules change. Give agreements trial run periods and meet again in a few months to evaluate how the plan works. If your children are school age, get their input and consider including them in deciding on arrangements.

HOPE FOR THE BEST, PREPARE FOR THE WORST

This is part of "redundant systems." If the other parent misses pickup from daycare, have you got a backup plan? Life doesn't work out the way we plan. Things happen. You have a choice here. Either let it drive you nuts or roll with it. Redundant systems help you roll with it.

As a solo parent, I feared getting that call at work. You know the one. It's when no one picked my child up from school, sports, or something else. I was susceptible to anxiety about this because I had been that kid who always got left behind. I learned to ask other parents for rides, and it felt shameful.

Guess what? It happened to my daughter, and she survived. A middle school coach forgot to let students and parents know the after-school practice was canceled. I worked ninety minutes away by street car, thirty minutes by rideshare. My daughter went to the school office and called me. I instructed her to wait there, not walk home the three miles. It was late when I finally got to school. She has no memory of the event.

Sometimes backup plans fail. We will survive 99 percent of the events.

HOW TO TALK ABOUT THE OTHER PARENT

Take the high road: Show respect to the other parent. Even if they don't have it together enough to respect your needs, don't bad-mouth them. It can backfire with your kids. They will make up their minds about their parents' character in due course.

HIGH CONFLICT, LOW RESOLUTION

Remember India, whose former partner landed in prison? She had met her ex-partner at age thirty-five. They decided to have a child and when India became pregnant, Matthew proposed. One night, partway through the engagement, they were sitting on a sofa in their cape-style house. India really looked at Matthew and thought "I cannot parent a child with this guy." She broke the engagement and while it took a while to get him out of the house, she embraced single parenting.

Problem was, Matthew was a royal jerk with money from suspicious sources. He had money to fight India in court and a family to back him for shared custody. India had some of her own savings and went back to school for a career and business that would allow her flexibility. She did receive child support but supplemented it with her budding business.

However, the court ordered shared custody and India and Matthew agreed to a "parallel parenting" plan. This differs from coparenting in that contact between the parents is kept to a minimum. Each parent has their own parenting approach when the children are with them. In parallel parenting, parents do not attend the same functions, appointments, or child-related events. This minimizes conflict between parents and, ideally, eliminates parental conflict in front of the child. For those in a high conflict relationship with the other parent, this can be a possible short-term or long-term solution.

I am giving you some tough love here. No trash-talking the other parent in front of the kids, your friends, workmates, his family, and so forth.

Your kids didn't pick the other parent, and no one wants to listen to an angry person. Once at a random bar, waiting for my take-out order, a woman went into detail about her horrible ex and how her divorce lawyer was so incompetent she felt screwed. It turned out I knew that lawyer and had always thought highly of him. I kept my mouth shut, however.

On the other hand, don't say nothing. Kids want to know about their parents. Stick to the facts, and if the absent parent isn't around, offer to help find them. It's important that you don't stand in the way of your child getting to make their own judgment about a parent. It may be they can develop a relationship without you.

As well, you may have happy or funny stories from your time together before the split. Those will go a long way toward validating a child's feelings about their parents, for better or worse.

SOLO PARENTING: NO OTHER PARENT PRESENT

"No check every month, no every-other-weekend off" is how one single mother defined solo parenting. If you see yourself here, read on.

"Solo parenting" differs from single parenting in subtle but important ways. It occurs whenever the other parent is entirely out of the picture, whether due to death, choice, or abandonment. In specifically addressing the conditions of solo parenting, I am not trying to wage a "who suffers more" contest. Instead, since there is much value in being seen, the distinction validates the particular struggles of solo parents.

Solo parenting is the opposite of having another adult in the picture. It means that you have no days to yourself while the kids are with the other parent. The outcome is that the complete mental, emotional, and financial weight falls on you alone. And when choices are facing you, there is no coparent to consult and help decide which road to follow. Nor does anyone share ownership when things go wrong or celebrate the victories when things go right.

You are the only person standing between you, your children, and whatever tempest threatens. It is a painful awareness that if you get hurt or sick, the children will be left entirely alone at any given moment.

Solo parents have to give their children twice as much, even if feeling half as capable.

But solo parenting does have positives. No one else has to be consulted, and you don't have to engage with a potentially vindictive partner. The benefits mean fewer mixed messages and stress for the child. It eliminates issues of loyalty, creating stronger bonds between parent and child. Remember these benefits on days you are feeling alone or wish for more support.

DOS AND DON'TS WHEN RELYING ON YOUR FAMILY

Immediate and extended families often serve as the first line of support for single parents. But as we all know, family relationships can be as fraught as they can be helpful. Here are a few tips to keep your family team members in the latter camp.

Do

- Recognize others have stress as well.

- Accept that support may come with boundaries and limits.

- Appreciate anything that helps, even if it is one hour of childcare.

- Agree that differing points of view have value.

- Stay away from overused terms like "controlling" and "narcissist." Instead, consider the other as "expressing an opinion," "communicating needs," and "taking care of oneself."

- Accept help as you would any gift. Be gracious.

- Work through relationship conflicts in a mature way.

Don't

- Micromanage others on how to interact with your child.

- Criticize for not helping you more.

- Complain about any gift they give.

- Act out parenting stress and frustration. It's better to admit to feeling overwhelmed than lash out at someone.

- Get annoyed at offers to help because it's not exactly how you would do it.

HOW TO HELP SOMEONE HELP YOU

Keep a list of things others can do to help you. If the goal is to get help with childcare, start with a specific need such as desiring help when you go to the dentist and someone needs to watch your child, either at home or the waiting room.

If the need is large, the first order of help could be help to break the need into smaller actions. For example, if you want to apply for subsidies to lower your costs (chapter 14), then your first action might be "help with obtaining applications." The second action might be "help with organizing financial information like taxes to apply."

CHAPTER 18

Mindful Parent, Resilient Kids

**Mindful Parenting: Less Is More, and Better Parenting
Takes Less Time**

Slow Down. Pay Attention. Affirm.

Twenty Skills to Build Resilient Kids

The Special Importance of Learning to Fail

You Blew it! Now What? Recovering from Parenting Mistakes

MINDFUL PARENTING: LESS IS MORE, AND BETTER PARENTING TAKES LESS TIME

A concept du jour, "mindfulness," pops up everywhere. Well, that may be an exaggeration. I haven't encountered "Mindfulness Margarine," but I know a few advertising types who might run with the concept.

How does mindfulness relate to single parenting? The biggest takeaway for us in this cohort is that it is yet another good practice that neatly serves our time and money challenges while removing that lack-of-time-and-money-guilty-single-parent feeling.

It costs nothing to:

- Slow down. Stroll together to take in your surroundings.

- Focus when together by thinking only about the activity, not your never-ending to-do list.

- Use your breath as an anchor, creating quiet moments.

- Learn to sit with both pleasant and unpleasant emotions.

- Listen to your child, even if you don't like what you hear.

- Pause before responding.

- Encourage quiet time.

TAYLOR AND THE SILENT MEAL

Taylor felt that she was always rushing her three-year-old. Rushing to school, rushing to work, rushing through chores. The irony is that Taylor teaches meditation alongside her restaurant job. This rushing created continuous negative interaction with a naturally curious child. Her daughter loved to take her time, such as walking to school slowly, noticing the birds and the construction workers.

Taylor tried something different. "I'm going to make your breakfast early and we can eat before school." Her daughter ate, silently, slowly, calmly for about ten minutes. Taylor sat quietly—present and calm. After finishing, her daughter announced, "That was a really great breakfast!"

This became a new part of their morning tradition. Taylor adjusted the schedule to allow time for this "slow parenting." She was rewarded with a happier child.

This took ten minutes for a significant change. It creates space to just be without intent, turning off the rational mind to allow for recharging.

Children of all ages can lead the way given they are inherently able to hyperfocus on the task at hand. Watch them take in a new experience with all their senses:

- Have fun with that bubble bath, popping bubbles and hearing sounds typically tuned out like the airplane overhead.

- Pull up a chair next to you outside and watch the "action." A robin pulling worms, delivery trucks dropping off, or people walking by. Even older kids will do this.

When you see them connecting to the moment, follow their lead and stop thinking about what you need to do for just a few minutes. The trash truck would arrive during my getting-ready-for-work time. My daughter would dash into my room, and we would pause for a while to watch the men at their work.

This is about participating and responding to what is coming in through your five senses with acceptance and curiosity. It can be fun and relaxing for you as a parent. You may come to look forward to it and may even find it the most rewarding part of your parenting day.

SLOW DOWN. PAY ATTENTION. AFFIRM.

A parenting expert tells me how she has practiced mindfulness with her child since infancy. She joins her child for a story, playtime, even a meal, with these reminders to herself:

- Put away the phone.

- Slow your breath.

- Don't rush or intervene. True for all ages.

- While your kid creates, describe and comment, but don't ask many questions so as not to take away from the child's plan.

- Show enthusiasm and a happy engagement.

You can see the brightening of the child's mood almost immediately. "I'm important." "I'm seen." A connection develops.

These are basic tenets of a parent-child interaction therapy developed explicitly for children ages two to seven who are struggling behaviorally, but they have relevance to any parent-child relationship or age. (Note that the complete parent-child interaction therapy approach should only be introduced with professional help.) However, these simple shifts—slowing down, paying attention, and affirming—can be incredibly bonding for parent and child, at any age, even teens and young adults.

Taking a page from larger therapeutic practices is a favorite technique. I see applications of trauma-informed education to treating veterans and managing people. Nutrition advice for cancer patients can also be used for otherwise healthy people. So, a few changes for fifteen minutes can make the single-parenting experience better for parents and children.

THRIVING CHILDREN IN SINGLE-PARENT HOUSEHOLDS

For many years, the conversation among researchers, advocates, policymakers, and others regarding single-parent families has focused on how this family type might negatively affect children. What if, instead, we focus on what children need to thrive?
—Annie E. Casey Foundation

A READING SUCCESS STORY

Reading was the hardest thing for me in early school days. Classmates could read pages of what looked to me like hieroglyphics. Even my first-grade teacher told me that I would never catch up to my classmates. It was frustrating as well as demoralizing, but my mom didn't quit on me. She continually brought me with her to the library and we would always stop in bookstores "just to look."

By third grade, I finally made out those crazy scratches to be the English language, but read much slower than my peers. That changed on the one vacation my mom forgot to pack my Calvin and Hobbs comic books. We stopped in a used bookstore "just to look" for a replacement. I picked up a small book, my interest peaked by a laughing rabbit on the cover. I opened those creamy pages and started to devour every word. I not only reread that book, I'd read it to younger learners.

That book (*Rabbit Hill*) unlocked new worlds. I stayed with animal-centric books, climbing a totem pole of complexity by reading increasingly advanced stories. By the time I finished my first series (Redwall), my reading speed had increased, surpassing most peers. What's more, my vocabulary soared to the top of my class!

Never give up on the slow-reading kid. They just might need the resolve of a parent to continually be around books "just to look" and build that reading confidence and resilience.

—Charlotte

TWENTY SKILLS TO BUILD RESILIENT KIDS

"It is easier to build strong children than to repair broken men."
—Frederick Douglass

Raising resilient children is a universal goal. We want our kids to be able to stand on their own two feet as best they can. I add that last phrase, "as best they can," because everyone is unique, and self-sustaining will look different for people with different abilities.

Resilience research is relatively new. It began when researchers realized that adversity and "being different" didn't doom kids. They could excel despite adversity, and we are just now beginning to understand "why" and "how." How do homeless kids rise to attend Harvard University? How did a sexual abuse survivor become the poet laureate, or an unhoused family raise a daughter to become principal ballerina at a premier ballet company?

Many skills to build resilience in our children can be modeled by us. This can also help strengthen your own resilience at the same time. That's two for one!

I'll leave the research to sociologists but summarize here the wisdom garnered from asking other parents like ourselves in my online community how to build resilience. Their direct comments appear in the following quotes:

BUILDING RESILIENCE

Encourage Curiosity
This opens them to the world of possibility.

- "Answer all their questions, even if the answer is 'I don't know.' It's fun when, as a parent, we don't need to have all the answers."

Encourage Reading

It develops empathy, interests, and creates a problem-solving resource.

- Read to your children until they are old enough to do so on their own.

- Have a regular trip to the library children's room where they can borrow as many books as they can carry.

- Encourage any reading. This builds confidence to keep going.

Support Interests and Broaden Exposure

> "Nurturing interests can help build 'islands of competence.'"
> —Robert Brooks, PhD

- Don't worry if your kid seems laser focused on a topic. Competency in that topic can serve as a launching pad to other places.

Teach Persistence

- Show them how to rebound. Single parents are a study in perseverance, so use your own examples, such as saying that you didn't get the first job you applied to but got the fifth.

- Provide some support while they tackle a new interest. This could be tossing a ball together, showing how to find credible sources, or accessing tutors online or in person.

Teach Empathy

Shifting perspective alleviates them from being a victim to their own emotions and stressing about something out of their control.

- Talk about what the book or TV characters are doing and ask, "Why did he do that?"

- Discuss why you like/dislike what they are doing.

Practice Humility

What's not to like?

- No one is right all the time. It's OK to be wrong, just don't hold on to it for a defensive reason.

- "Apologize/admit to children when you are wrong. This teaches them it's OK to do the same when they make a mistake."

- Not everything is personal. Most everything has nothing to do with us.

Teach Problem-Solving

Learning how to ask for help.

- "Let them know that when they feel broken and alone, there is always someone there for them no matter what."

- Say to them: "Try to solve this problem on your own, and if it's too difficult, ask for help. I am happy to work with you to figure this out."

- Admit your own struggle with a problem, teaching that it's not shameful to ask for help. For example, if you discuss your struggle to quit an addiction like smoking, it allows your young adult child to talk about their vaping habit. Talk about what resources you used.

Engage in Critical Thinking

- Together, look at various posts online and discuss why they might not be a good resource.

- Introduce this quip—consider the source! Does the information source have links or post ads? What do you think is their reason for posting this information?

- Ask older kids, "Who might have a self-interest in this pitch or promotion?" I am thinking particularly of "influencers" and stories about celebrities that are 99 percent made up.

Show Respect for Yourself and Others

The single-parent community suggested ways to get past conflict.

- Discuss what behavior toward them is OK and not OK. I've talked through a few difficult job moments with my daughter.

- "Talk about boundaries. Children need boundaries to protect them from harm until they are old enough to go their own way." You can talk boundaries about their bodies, time, and emotions.

- "Respect them. It's good for kids to have preferences and opinions. Don't belittle them for having emotions and encourage them to express their emotions while teaching them what is an appropriate way to express emotions. (Crying is OK. Hitting is not)."

- "Learning to hear 'no' and accepting it and listening to someone's feelings after you hurt them instead of getting defensive."

Model Adaptability

Let them learn that people can change their minds.

- "I thought about it and going to the park is a good idea after all."

- "You may borrow the car after all."

Demonstrate Tolerance

Learning to live and let live reduces a lot of stress.

- Talk about not having to agree with everything and everyone to be at peace.

- Show that your viewpoint matters but it isn't the only one.

- Discuss how people think of you less often than you would believe.

- Add that people don't notice your mistakes as much as you think.

Prioritize Truthfulness

Losing trust in another is far worse than whatever a lie may cover up.

- Be honest yourself. Don't lie to your kids or lie to others. They'll see it.

Learn How to Fail

- Don't judge your child's failings. In fact, don't judge your own. Failure creates learning opportunities.

- Use humor. If you try a new recipe and it tastes bad, make a joke, and give it a eulogy.

- Avoid futurizing. That's where you imagine catastrophic outcomes as a consequence of not succeeding. Instead, think of times that problems *didn't* happen.

Encourage Possibilities

- Brainstorm. "Always give options. [If] an adolescent [is] struggling with homework, ask what they think are options and if they don't have any, then you can jump in with your own ideas."

- "Encourage them. Don't say, 'Well, had you done it this way, you'd have succeeded.' Just say, 'I think you know what doesn't work, but I'm sure you can succeed if you try again.'"

Highlight Friendships

- Talk about friend issues you've had in the past and how you resolved or didn't resolve them and the outcomes.

A STUDY IN PERSISTENCE

My daughter wanted to play softball for social reasons. As a petite preteen, her strength was less than bigger girls who also had parents who would play catch with them. Lacking a family member who could throw a ball, I rented time in batting cages or took advantage of free clinics. I would offer to take teammates along, always a big draw.

Her interest eventually waned when swimming and ice hockey caught her eye. Our town offered competitive swimming at its pool and ice hockey with a multitown league. (Go ahead, groan. Someone did put the curse on me: "May your child play ice hockey.") The lessons from the softball interest applied here. Make every practice, attend every clinic, take coaching when offered, and have fun.

The lessons learned by persisting at an interest are what took her to college and graduate school.

THE SPECIAL IMPORTANCE OF LEARNING TO FAIL

Learning to fail gathers the most votes from the parents in an online community as an important lesson for children. Given the preponderance of business books on the topic, it would appear that adults don't have a perfect handle on this either.

The pressure to be perfect has been around for a while. Even *Mr. Rogers' Neighborhood* talked about it in the 1980s. A recent documentary replayed an old interview in which Fred Rogers talked about children feeling the pressure to excel. Mr. Rogers (in the guise of Daniel Tiger) spoke to a young boy about starting kindergarten. The child was terrified, and Daniel asked why he was scared. "Because I don't know everything," he tearfully replied.

If we can remove the terror of performance from our children, the world will be better off. While I missed the Mr. Rogers' PBS television era, I wholeheartedly recommend it for reruns, not just for preschool children but for parents' instruction for building resilient kids.

CHILD THINKING

We all make mistakes. A mistake that we've made might feel normal and inconsequential to us, but big and scary for a child—"Is this the person I can feel safe with?" By owning it, you can tell them when you are sorry and tell them you want to work to be better at a certain shortcoming (being late, losing temper, not following through). This calms a child and instills the lesson that when we do something that hurts others, we should use it as a message to work on it next time. For example:

Parent: (Yelling) "Hurry up! We have to go!"

Kid: "I don't like when you yell, Mom."

Parent: "I am sorry. You're right. I shouldn't yell. I was frustrated that you weren't moving quickly."

Kid: "It's OK. I'm sorry, too."

Parent: "It's OK."

This preschooler now always asks Mom to say "it's OK" if mom apologizes but doesn't verbalize forgiveness. The child learned the fantastic art of forgiveness from the parent. It is a simple example but often happens with our overscheduled single-parent lives.

I also quote that other comprehensive media source for life lessons, *Star Trek*.

"It is possible to commit no mistakes and still lose. That is not a weakness; that is life." —Reddit community member quoting from *Star Trek: The Next Generation*

"If Captain Picard had said that to my face when I first saw this as a teenager, I would have slowly burst into tears and hugged him, and he would have had to just deal with it. When you're suffocating under pressure to be perfect, for whatever reason, remember this, forgive yourself, BREATHE, and 'get back on the bridge.'" —Reddit community member

Consider using either of these shows as temporary stand-ins on those exhausting parenting days. Both *Mr. Rogers* and *Star Trek* endure, in part because their topics are universal throughout the ages.

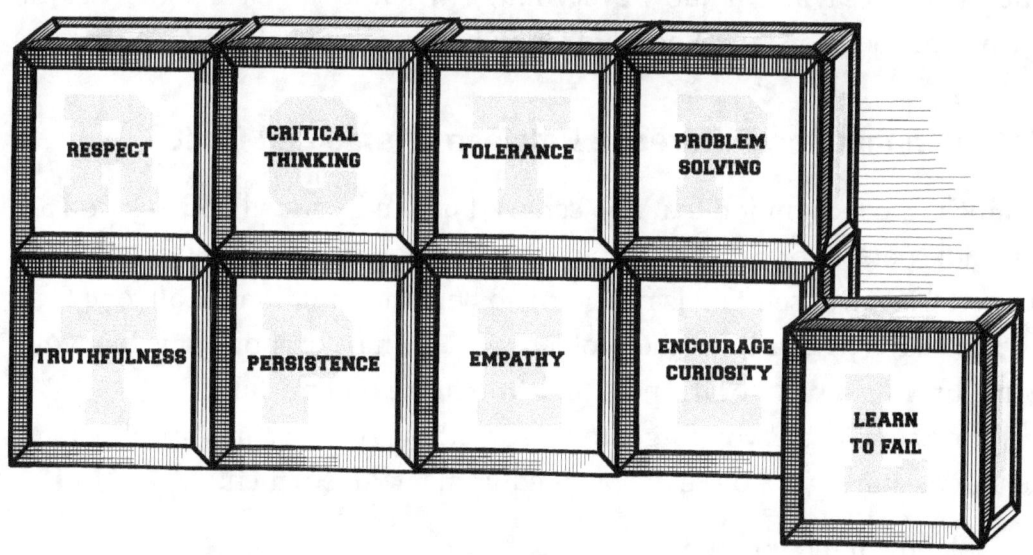

YOU BLEW IT! NOW WHAT?
RECOVERING FROM PARENTING MISTAKES

Whether recent or made long ago, do you have parenting mistakes eating away at you, corroding self-confidence? Maybe you did something to hurt your child or their other parent. It could be troubling you, creating shame or guilt. That can only exacerbate the relationship by seeping into future interactions.

For the sake of you and your child, it's time to deal with it. Showing your child (or other parent) that you recognize and can course correct for errors models healthy behavior—that is, the ability to own up to mistakes and intentions to do better. Here are some ways we can recover from parenting mistakes.

1. Recognize and Own the Mistake

We have to recognize our mistakes. We can't move forward until we acknowledge this. You can use humor here, too.

For example: I poke fun at my own arrogance by joking with my daughter and saying, "I know everything," when we all have a lot to learn. It's a family joke by now. She's old enough now to know human limitations.

2. Understand the Difference Between Shame and Guilt

Shame is the recognition that you screwed up, and you tell yourself you are a terrible person. Guilt is the recognition that you screwed up but will work to fix it. Negative self-talk is not going to help the situation for anyone.

Instead, try ways to fix the problem. What's most important is that you come up with a plan for the next time you make that mistake.

For example, did you forget to do something (pick a child up, attend a school meeting, get a piece of sports equipment)? If so, then:

Ask how it felt for them.

Talk about how you will correct it now and for the next time.

Ask if they have ever forgotten something. The understanding goes both ways.

3. Determine Why

Once we recognize our mistakes, we have to search ourselves and discover why we did what we did. It avoids repeating the error.

For example, what events lead up to complete frustration devolving into yelling? What tripped you up? Were you sleep-deprived, hungry, anxious over a pending deadline?

How can you avoid this for the future? Eat regularly, go to bed earlier, renegotiate a deadline? (More possible than you think.)

4. Apologize

This is the big one. The most mature thing we can do for our kids is apologize and ask for forgiveness when we mess up.

For example, name it and talk about how you will work on the issue. "I am really sorry I yelled. I was frustrated/scared/etc. That is no excuse but if I talk about it with you it'll help me to do better next time."

5. Discuss It

Once we apologize, we don't just move on. Now is the time to talk. Find out how it affected your kids and openly and honestly share your feelings. Resist the urge to talk over them. A lot of "Mississippis" go into listening to your children. It's also important to stay neutral no matter how much you disagree. A parent who always reacts negatively just tells a kid to shut down.

"Would you rather be right, or would you rather understand?"
—Warren Berger

For example, say, "I am sorry if I hurt you. I'd like to hear how you think about it. I'd like to understand. I am not always right."

6. Learn from It

We are all a work in progress. Understanding what you did and its impact presents a growth opportunity.

7. Respond with Tangible Action

Discuss what you will do with those affected if faced with a similar situation in the future. Is there something that needs to be done now, beyond an apology, to fix or reconcile the situation or relationship? Be thoughtful, as the more you understand this, the less you will face it. If appropriate, ask your child to hold you accountable and point out if you start to repeat the same mistake.

For example, say, "I overreacted when you [broke curfew, didn't clean your room, etc.]. Next time I'm not going to approve [borrowing the car for a week, turning on the TV] until your room is clean. But if you think it is unreasonable, let's discuss why from both our points of view."

8. Move On

Now it is time to move on. Don't let the guilt of your mistake hold you hostage. The narrative spinning in your head can be changed.

CHAPTER 19

Understanding Child Development (in Brief) for the Early Years

Seven Types of Intelligence

Get to Know Your Child: Ten Aspects of Temperament

Why Should You Care?

Early Childhood Single-Parent Challenge: When You Are the Only Playmate Available

Concerns? Early Intervention Can't Hurt

PARENTING IS ANXIETY-PROVOKING ENOUGH EVEN WHEN there's a partner in the picture. But whether we're single or coupled parents, we all worry at times about our child's cognitive and emotional development. Are they "on schedule?" "Normal?" "Keeping up with the other kids?"

My goal in this chapter is to preempt some of those worries to give you some theories and frameworks that will help you take a curious and hopefully more relaxed approach to understanding your children's strengths and challenges.

SEVEN TYPES OF INTELLIGENCE

In the 1980s, a developmental psychologist, Howard Gardner, theorized that people have multiple intelligences, not just a singular "general intelligence." He identified seven distinct types of intelligence:

1. Word Smart (linguistic intelligence)

2. Math Smart (numerical/reasoning/logic intelligence)

3. Physically Smart (kinesthetic intelligence)

4. Music Smart (musical intelligence)

5. People Smart (interpersonal intelligence)

6. Self-Smart (intrapersonal intelligence)

7. Visually Smart (spatial intelligence)

Gardner argued that each child evolves based on their own strengths. Thus, a child who does not show interest in language, for example, might have extraordinary abilities in the field of mathematics and spatial intelligence.

Later, researchers expanded this to eight and then nine categories. The number doesn't matter. What matters is that we understand that children develop at different speeds with different skills. Because they aren't the quickest, fastest, or "est" at anything doesn't matter. It isn't a bad omen for their adulthood.

Not only do kids feel relieved to know they have their own kind of smarts, but for parents, it can be a lifeline. I remember hearing a school administrator describe the Gardner theory and feeling relief come over me. At age five, it was apparent that my daughter had at least one learning disability. My family was inundated with learning differences. Eventually, like her aunts, uncles, cousins, and grandparents, my daughter overcame them and went to college.

I took great comfort in understanding these concepts while raising my daughter. Knowing anything could be managed with help took away any catastrophizing. Keep in mind that there are a hundred different ways to get to the same goal. In the case of children, that goal is self-sufficiency and a chance at happiness. In a child's younger years, the joy is to expose them to all that you can in a safe environment and make it possible to explore with fun.

TRYING NEW ACTIVITIES WITH YOUR CHILD

As far as I know, no one in my family tree possesses an art gene. Nevertheless, my daughter and I took art classes. Who knows, maybe there is recessive artistic DNA in there. So, I threw clay and drew lines with her at the local art center, silently congratulating myself for letting her explore activities outside my comfort zone.

Now and forever, remember: "We all develop our intelligences at different rates."

GET TO KNOW YOUR CHILD: TEN ASPECTS OF TEMPERAMENT

By the time they're ready to start school, we've developed some sense of our children's temperament. Starting in the 1950s, researchers began to categorize temperament into multiple traits.

Alexander Thomas and Stella Chess, researchers, identified nine traits that combined to make up children's temperament. Others expanded the traits to an even ten. For example, is the child easygoing or intense? It frustrates me that articles and books on the topic skirt adolescence and early adulthood, but we can adapt these findings to all ages.

These aspects of temperament may help you assess where and why your child may be struggling and help you change your home environment and parenting strategies accordingly. By leaning into the unique traits of your children versus trying to change them, you will be able to have a powerful influence on their development.

Here are the ten aspects of temperament and more about how you can navigate them with your child.

1. Intensity

How does your child show happiness or frustration? Strongly and dramatically? Or does your child express those feelings mildly?

As the saying goes, parent the child you have. Set up boisterous children in spaces so as to not overrun quieter areas. Let them be loud or quiet.

2. Activity Level

Is it hard to read a book with your child because they are always on the go? Or does your child prefer quiet, sedentary activities?

Allow children time for movement throughout the day. If you have a greyhound, let them run. Encourage physically challenging activities throughout their time. And you can also train them to wait for the race to start.

For more sedentary types, choose less strenuous activity that also keeps them moving, such as walks versus runs, activities versus sports.

3. Regularity

Does your child eat and sleep at predictable times? Or is your child unpredictable in terms of eating and sleeping schedules? Routines make for good self-regulation but allow flexibility within the boundaries of an activity's times.

For example, set the boundaries of an activity such as having a lunch hour but allow for self-service within that time.

4. Quality of Mood

Is your child generally in a happy mood? Or does your child seem more serious?

Teens especially can go negative. In that case, break the mood by calling on favorites to lead a moment. Agree to watch their favorite show after doing the dishes. Ask about the "best part of the day/worst part of the day" to give equal airtime.

5. Emotional Sensitivity

Does your child react strongly to their own or others' feelings and emotions? Or does your child seem unaware of how they or others are feeling? This is a biggie, and as a parent, there will be many teachable moments.

For example, while reading a book together or watching a TV show, you can pause and ask their observations of how a character is feeling. Or if they are highly sensitive, give some perspective on how a character might get out of danger.

6. Sensory Sensitivity

Does your child react positively or negatively to sounds, tastes, and textures?

You can lean into this by responding to their sensitivities. Some hate
the feeling of sock seams or wiggly food texture. Take those away while
they learn to desensitize. Sensory overload can be managed. But do
set boundaries on how to react when they dislike something, since not
everyone feels the same way.

7. Adaptability

Does your child have difficulty with changes or transitions from one activity
to another? Or does your child handle them smoothly?

This is a tough one if your child has difficulty with change, but it does get
better as they age. You shouldn't take away change but instead add small
steps. Practice an event ahead of time. If they fear medical appointments,
go sit in a waiting room without a visit and then go home. I once had the
pediatrician come out, say "hi," and then leave.

Desensitization therapy is another technique. Have them ease into
interacting with dogs or other things they fear rather than expecting them to
start romping with them.

8. Approach/Withdrawal

Does your child easily approach new situations or people? Or does your
child seem to hold back when faced with new situations, people, or things?

Caution is a valuable trait. But if their reticence concerns you, again take it
slow. Start with familiar and contained situations like small family dinners.
If you can, talk about how they felt meeting a new situation/people.

9. Distractibility

Is your child easily sidetracked when trying to do chores or homework? Or
does your child stay on task?

There are whole websites and books on distractibility. Universally, they start with shortening the time required to stay in one place or one topic. Once they master the first five minutes of focus, start ratcheting up time.

10. Persistence

Does your child react strongly when told "no" to something? Does your child have a hard time letting ideas go? Or does your child seem to give up without trying their hardest?

If your child isn't persistent, you can talk to them about it. For example, share that this is an important skill and something that can be strengthened, like a muscle. As usual, start small. Have them work on a project with your help and encourage them to stick with it. Praise any small gains.

You can work with the child you have at any age, by enhancing strengths and supporting lagging traits. Think "balance."

WHY SHOULD YOU CARE?

Seven types of intelligence. Ten traits of temperament. So what? After all, at its worst, categorizing can become stereotyping, leading to negative judgments. Examples include: "bossy girls" (vs. future leaders) and "feminine boys" (vs. empathetic). The same characteristics that make raising children difficult are the same qualities that serve them well as adults.

It may feel like a lot of work to understand the implications of temperaments, especially when you already have so much on the parenting plate. But this isn't a test; there's no quiz at the end of the chapter. Instead, I offer this information because:

■ It helps to know how your children respond so you and your children can more successfully handle difficult situations. Too often, comments will be made about a child's temperament negatively instead of seeing how it is a strength. For example, children considered "stubborn" could be viewed as persistent. Children labeled "negative" may be thought of as serious.

- It is comforting to know the many paths to success for single parents and their offspring.

- It is good to know people study these topics and have suggestions.

- It is good we don't feel alone in our worries.

- It helps us evaluate where our child might need more support and tailor our parenting strategies to meet their needs better. Supporting them now will be helpful later. Intelligence and temperament aren't uniform. In the face of pressure for conformity, it helps to understand the many different paths to success.

EARLY CHILDHOOD SINGLE-PARENT CHALLENGE: WHEN YOU ARE THE ONLY PLAYMATE AVAILABLE

"I don't want to f*ing play anymore. I'm done with Barbies and dolls and hair salons. From the time she wakes up until she goes to bed. I'm balancing working and playing. 24/7. I'm going crazy."
—Reddit single-parent community member

This parent seems to have struck a nerve on Reddit. Within one day, fifty-plus single parents posted supporting this universal parenting complaint. How long can one stand to play at the three-year-old level? Then you feel guilty because you need to stop playing either to do other things or because, as an adult, you need a different level of activity. After receiving sympathetic "amens," the community proffered suggestions:

"Dude. My son gets so mad at me if I don't play with his tractors the way he says. I'm like 'ya know what, dude. Do it yourself cuz I'm not gonna get yelled at by a four-year-old about TRACTOR NOISES.'"
—Reddit single-parent community member

"What you're feeling is normal :) especially if you work all day and come home and immediately have your child. You need a short bit to at least come down and decompress. Instead of DADDY, YOU BE KEN!" —Reddit single-parent community member

I howled with laughter recognizing these situations from my own life. Take a deep breath and remember that the days can be long, but the years are short. Set the boundaries to maintain your sanity, or call in reinforcements. Kids do need playmates. It just doesn't have to be you.

How to Play with Your Child, Suggested by Other Single Parents

"Explain you'll play Hot Wheels but first you need to do 'x, y, or z.' Ask if they want to wait."

"Set a boundary of 'quiet, alone time,' in which you don't interrupt each other until a fifteen-to-thirty-minute alarm goes off."

"Hire a teenager to come in and play for a few hours."

CONCERNS? EARLY INTERVENTION CAN'T HURT

If you are concerned about development in an area, keep asking professionals. No one has a lock on all the information. Even the "experts" are continually learning and customizing strategies.

SOFIA'S STORY

Sofia put aside marriage and family until she was through medical school and had established her pediatric practice in Florida. Sofia adored children, one of five herself, including two much younger brothers. She had the temperament and joy to enjoy them personally and professionally. Predictably, she had four children: two sets of twins—two boys and then two girls.

Given her training, it's not surprising that she identified the lagging development in one of the boys early on. She got him into early intervention for autism, and since he was a twin, the other brother was allowed to join him by state law. The son lagging in development made great strides with the one-to-one focused development work. As for his twin brother? "It made him a genius!" proclaimed Sofia when I asked her. Hyperbole aside, it demonstrated the value of focused attention available to compensate for developmental delays.

Your pediatrician may not be as astute as Sofia or as well versed in nuances of other childhood development. Listen to your gut. My first pediatrician kept telling me, "You have a winner." Yes, that's what I wanted to hear, but, no, something wasn't developing in my child at the same rate as her peers: her reading.

Since the school wouldn't test for learning disabilities until third grade, I arranged with my insurance for neuropsyche testing. I wanted it done as soon as possible, given my family history of learning differences. Yes, she did indeed have the family gift of dyslexia.

Still, knowing what I was dealing with allowed me to target early intervention. She did learn to read, even reading for pleasure; has incredible perseverance; and graduated from a competitive university science program.

CHAPTER 20

School Age Through Young Adulthood

Elementary School

Middle School

High School

Parenting Young Adults

Boomerang Kids: Coping with Adult Children Living at Home

ELEMENTARY SCHOOL

So as not to duplicate all the infant and toddler parenting books out there, we pick up child development at around age five. When our kids enter elementary school, we enter the golden era of single parenting. And there we stay until they are seventeen or eighteen and ready to leave high school. It is between six and seventeen years old that children learn to become independent and form their own opinions.

Now you have sounding boards in teachers, and you even socialize with other children's parents. Often those parents will talk about their children's development. It's understandable if that causes you to fall into the comparison trap. This is where knowing the seven types of intelligence described earlier can be helpful. Rather than worry about your child's development or your skills as a parent, you can take comfort in the relative growth of your children and their skills.

THE GIFT OF SPECIAL ED

I understand some parents' trepidation about having their child "labeled" as early as grade school. But this fear of stereotyping stems more from what other parents might think than from other children's opinions.

Beginning in second grade, the literacy teacher would come to get my daughter from her classroom for a devoted hour together learning with the Orton-Gillingham method. At the spring parent-teacher conference, I asked how my daughter responded to having someone come and take her from the classroom. I didn't expect the teachers' answer. They described the joyous look on my daughter's face when the special ed teacher came to get her. She would jump out of her seat and rush happily to the door. I imagine she was feeling just lost in whatever subject was being taught. The stress of losing the thread of a lecture can be very discouraging.

As far as feeling "singled out" or "different," she never expressed a concern to me. Instead, getting to leave was a gift, not a burden. It turns out many kids were coming and going from the classroom all the time—for English language instruction, occupational therapy, literacy, and other specialized instruction. It was familiar enough that kids didn't give it much thought.

Her success with special ed continued through middle school, where, ultimately, she was an *A* student. The lesson here is to embrace whatever individualized or small group learning you can get.

As a parent, I channeled my late mother, who, as a single parent with four children, learned to chill out about differences. It also helped that I had an older brother and sister who academically struggled yet made it out the other side of childhood intact. They both went on to have careers that comfortably sustained them. It could be that my well-read mother kept up with child development current research or she instinctively understood the seven types of intelligence.

Eventually, my daughter learned all those skills. Her superpower turned out to be perseverance. She keeps at a skill until she gets it. It helped that she had a parent willing to seek out experts and coaches, keeping at it while they got it right.

It took a while for me to realize life's truths about child comparison:

- People aren't always honest.

- Bragging about yourself or your kids is equally insufferable.

- We make our own insecurities: *"No one can make us feel inferior without our consent"* (ascribed to Eleanor Roosevelt, a former First Lady).

- Children develop different skills at different speeds (Seven Types of Intelligence).

The Elephant in the Room

I put this section between elementary and middle school since some time in there kids get on social media. It could have been a gift for single parents as an electronic child minder, except it isn't vetted as safe for kids like PBS Kids television. While I want to blame a lot of social ills on this, we have to avoid the temptation to think "it was better then." Every generation has its freak-out about a new trend. This one, though, does require more action on a parent's part to minimize the downside.

Here are some ways I think you can navigate social media and your child:

- Insist on full access to a child's phone and all social media apps. Be aware that kids can have more than one account.

- Follow their social media accounts, and using a calm tone, explain why a particular post might not be safe.

- Instruct all children to keep their social media settings on "private." Explain why and also explain that their friends posting about them could also create a risk. It would be nice if friends were as careful as you and your kids, but they aren't.

- Have them turn off location services when home.

- If your child has been approached in any way, contact law enforcement first versus the platform. You want the evidence to remain available for prosecution.

- Above all, be present. Give love and attention and maybe they won't look for it online.

MIDDLE SCHOOL

Middle schoolers get a bad rap. In prepuberty, most are still open to suggestions. They take pride in having home jobs and maybe earning an allowance as a result.

Single parents, this is your time. Our children have a leg up on learning to take responsibility. We need them to do things themselves. Since children this age can envision independence from the family, they can take on a more significant role in family participation and even achieve satisfaction in their responsibilities.

BETHANY'S STORY

Beth became a parent during college. It was a tremendous amount of work to score that degree while parenting. Richard was a bright, academically astute young child. In the competitive scene of suburban New York, he excelled and gained early admission to an Ivy League college at age seventeen.

Understandably, Beth crowed about her son's achievement. Herself competitive by nature, Beth went to business school when less than 10 percent of classes were women. She worked at a big NY bank, but she and her husband divorced while their son was in school. When Richard matriculated to university, she transferred to her employer's nearby office.

Unfortunately, Richard hit a wall in college. He was young, the classes were a big step up in challenge, and everyone there had also been top of their high school class. Emotionally, he had difficulty adjusting, and academically, he started sliding. He moved back with Beth, commuted to classes, but failed every class. It turns out he was leaving home ostensibly to attend class but instead sat in a coffee shop. Richard felt too ashamed to confide in Beth. He dropped out and had yet to finish college twenty years later.

The lesson here isn't about setting high standards; it's about leaving the door open for failure and building resilience. Let the process and effort, not competition, define the person. Richard's story is not uncommon. College administrators frequently talk about "readiness," especially in four-year programs.

Seize the moment. It's important to push their increased family role at this stage. Make it part of their daily/weekly habits. Let go of perfect for your children and embrace the mess as they learn responsibility. Besides instilling pride, having a family role generates emotional growth and self-confidence.

School-age children can learn to instill pride in themselves. "You must be proud of yourself" versus "I am so proud of you." Praise the effort instead of the outcome. Ultimately, we are going for balance here. The balance of being a good person, a productive member of society, self-supporting to their best ability, and self-sustaining.

But don't offer praise automatically. "Everyone gets a trophy" may be tongue in cheek, but overpraising can lead to negative consequences later on. Following middle school, academic and activity expectations rise overwhelmingly fast. Supports start to fall away. The brightest, fastest, and strongest peers begin to meet others who are just as good academically or better. The same in sports, art, and other activities. All of a sudden, if they've been praised for meeting minimum expectations, those kids get a crisis of confidence.

HIGH SCHOOL

As single parents, we look forward to a time of greater independence so we can catch a break about always "having to be on." I've read comments in single parents' columns asking if "it gets easier."

Yes and no. Yes, you can be less "available," but no, high schoolers need you just as much, if not more, than younger ages. The difference is how you fulfill that need.

The search for a separate identity characterizes this time for children. It requires that they separate (known as "differentiate" in psych speak) from their parents and get for themselves a sense of self.

While I am so very sorry to be the bearer of bad news that adolescence needs more time from you, not less, I can offer consolation that it doesn't have to consume all your mental energy.

GIVE YOUR CHILD BREATHING ROOM

I once arranged a panel discussion on the current state of college admissions. My cohort, whose children were in high school and on the college track, packed the room. Panelists hailed from both college and private high school admissions departments. Their message to parents primarily was to "back off" on the college pressure and let kids find their own motivations.

One panelist vividly described his at-home experience where he would be in the living room after dinner, reading. His child might cruise by him several times. This fellow never interrogated his kid as to what was up. Instead, he kept reading, and at about the fifth walk-through, the son asked his question.

Honestly, I don't remember the question, but I do remember the picture painted. "Give 'em space," but not too much.

Being Present: The Joy of Potted Plant Parenting

Read the sidebar story of the school administrator who counseled parents to be present, not pushy? A *New York Times* article also picked up on that with an article titled "What Teens Want? Potted Plant Parents." I laughed at the alliterative title. Beyond the funny vegetation reference, it reinforced that sidebar story from the school administrator who told how he sat in the living room after dinner reading, should his teen decide to open a dialogue. And from the *New York Times*: "So, here's a complaint one might not expect to hear from teenagers: They wish their parents were around more often."

The research behind this was with several thousand adolescents who had a parent who was gone outside traditional work hours.

As single parents, chances are we indeed are gone weekends and evenings. The experts advised staying connected during absences by regularly checking in by social media, texts, and FaceTime—letting their kids know that even though they were away, they were still watching. If physical presence isn't possible, these proxies can substitute.

Being present, not pushy, is an unnatural act for single parents. Always running against the clock, we have limited time to wait out considered responses, make something a teachable moment, or drop everything when the rare moment arrives that our teen wants a chat.

Think of this suggestion as a time-saver versus a time user. It's the theory that an ounce of prevention is worth more than a pound of a cure (Benjamin Franklin). It is being present now. Listening when it suits your child and generally moving on their time frame can save time down the road.

That's the "Why," Here's the "How"

While being physically present, it's also important to be laid back. One high octane (single parent) friend is constantly advancing an agenda with her son. She is competitive herself and terrified her children won't succeed in adulthood. They react by escaping into their rooms or using cannabis.

Here are some concrete suggestions for managing both the routine conversations and the difficult ones with your teenager.

Exercise Patience

Being wiser and older, parents are more inclined to talk over their children, who are slower to formulate thoughts.

Check Your Reaction

Save your horror for something terrifying and life-threatening. And if you catch yourself overreacting, own it. They'll learn that Mom or Dad can make mistakes.

Wait on Your Wisdom

Sometimes our teens don't communicate because they don't trust our reactions. They question our empathy. That's why it's critical to keep quiet and listen instead of jumping to a solution. If you think you've reacted strongly in the past to something like failing a test, then you could ask your teen if they are quiet because they worry you'll have an adverse reaction.

Even aware kids do dumb things like get into a fender bender. Let them get out the whole story of what is wrong before passing judgment. I've gotten very Zen about things like the car. *Every* first-time driver has an accident their first year. I call it obligatory. No doubt your kid is worried about the consequences. It's not to say that there won't be any, but you can calmly deliver them later.

Let Natural Consequences Play Out

If they forget their homework and get an *F*, that is a natural consequence. If it happens repeatedly, the first step is to note the pattern and talk with the schoolteachers. Your child's forgetfulness may be part of a more significant attention problem, and strategies can be employed.

If they get caught shoplifting, the first time they may get off with a court diversion program. But more than court diversion could be life altering, so you'll need an advocate that the child pays for, not you (See chapter 4, "Legal Help").

Pace Yourself

Things are going to happen during the teen years—a lot. Moderate your reactions because chances are you don't have the whole story, and it may be more of a case of faulty thinking than evil motivations. We learn through our mistakes, and teens are no less prone to them than we are.

Use Third-Party Validators

In the quest to differentiate from their parents, a lot of kids get downright nasty. Combine that with adolescent narcissism, and you can cut the tension with a knife. Single parents bear the full brunt of the backlash. There is no other parent present to tag team the situation. This can have serious mental health consequences for you, the parent.

If you had another parent around, they could point out the great things about you. Your child would have a more balanced view of you as a person, not just their own limited experience. Get someone to tell your child nice things about you. This needs to happen. It can be a relative or friend. Prep them to do this and explain why. This is to present a complete picture that the child of a single parent might not otherwise get.

Kids get more messages and conflicting signals at this time than ever before. As adults in their lives, we should be available to help filter the flow of information. As one pediatrician says, all high schoolers should wear an emblazoned sign warning "Faulty Thinking!"

PARENTING YOUNG ADULTS

Graduating from high school doesn't automatically confer the title "adult." Brain development undergoes a "rewiring" process that is not complete until approximately twenty-six years of age. Adolescence (and its accompanying faulty thinking) technically ends at that point. But many of the supports needed by teens might need to continue past this stage.

The single parents' challenge is to keep moving their kids *toward* independence, reclaiming more of themselves in the process.

Parenting never really stops. The goal should be to reduce your direct involvement in tasks and move to a more supportive role. Again, you may get them to self-sufficiency, ready to kick back, and then a pandemic happens, or they have children themselves. Without sufficient funds, they need help with childcare, monetary contributions, navigating social services, and so forth.

Dismantling the Scaffold

Scaffolding is a term used in learning circles where students are provided with specific support while developing skills. For example, a teacher may break work into chunks for a student while they learn a topic, allowing for focused study. Hopefully, the student will learn "chunking it" as they progress.

The concept of scaffolding can expand beyond education. Life skills may also require scaffolding while a child learns mastery. Some life skills are so complex that they can overwhelm the sturdiest of people. Healthcare and related insurance is one topic that comes to mind.

A close friend once defined adulthood for her children as when they pay for their health insurance and process their own claims. The Affordable Care Act allowed children to stay on parent insurance plans until age twenty-six. Even Congress recognized that young adults need scaffolding.

The supports should be coming down in stages. If you despair at your child's progress to independence, look back to one year ago and see what tasks they do now with confidence that they couldn't do before. And if they need your help with insurance claims, sit side by side with them at the computer. Be in the same room when they call the billing departments for clarification. Give them the cookbook and let them make the grocery run.

BOOMERANG KIDS: COPING WITH ADULT CHILDREN LIVING AT HOME

Even before the pandemic forced an additional 2.6 million young adults back home in 2020, they were increasingly staying with their families. Student debt, cost and complexity of housing, the disappearance of well-paid entry-level jobs, and healthcare costs had households joining together. While it was typical for my age group to establish financial independence after high school or college, the reverse is true for our children. They mostly come home again. Some temporarily, some permanently. Some come home after college. Some never left.

The share of eighteen-to-twenty-nine-year-olds living with their parents has become a majority since US coronavirus cases began spreading, surpassing the previous peak during the Great Depression 1930s era. And most of the 2020 increase in adults living with parents was among the younger adults, who are eighteen-to-twenty-four-year-olds.

Given the cost to acquire and afford a home, it's not surprising that families would move back to living in multigenerational households. Even without a pandemic, there are several reasons why young adults continue living with their parents or move back home—some for a short time and some forever. These include the following:

Working Toward Self-Support

■ Attending school or higher education

■ Saving money to afford the setup of an independent lifestyle

■ Identifying and working toward career options

Sheltering

■ Experiencing illness

■ Dealing with unemployment or being underemployed

■ Being unmotivated or unguided

■ Experiencing delayed development

■ Living with disabilities, physical and mental

■ Coping with mental illness

And, of course, sometimes young adults move back home to help parents with living expenses and family caregiving.

Some parents have found it a gift to reconnect with their young adults (and sometimes grandchildren). For others, having an adult child at home involves parenting someone who isn't in a good place emotionally and requires reparenting.

A parent's prime directive—protect their child, even at the expense of their own needs—makes it easier for young adults to stay home. The challenge, therefore, is to continue moving children toward self-sufficiency while increasingly regaining one's sense of self.

Here are some ways to do that.

Be Supportive, Not Enabling

A narrow line exists between enabling and being supportive. After high school, children should support themselves or work on getting there. That includes getting work while they look for something to help themselves. (Assuming no insurmountable developmental or physical disabilities.)

Work Together to Set Mutual Expectations

Taking the lessons from our chapter on managing conflict (chapter 18), have an honest conversation about your expectations of each other. Collaborative problem-solving will bring in your adult child's voice and have a greater likelihood of success. Author Laurence Steinberg (a professor at Temple University) discusses in detail the mental pivots both we parents and our adult children need to do to peacefully coexist. The disagreements with a visiting college student differ from those moving back in with parents. "A visit home from college often feels like a vacation; moving back in often feels like a . . . step backward."

Treating a Grown Child as an Adult Means Establishing an Adult Role

It's crucial that your child contribute to the household, either financially or by equally participating in the activities in managing a home. This should include cooking, cleaning, laundry, shoveling snow—and any major projects. Letting them just do their own laundry doesn't cut it. You need to include common needs and common spaces.

Have an Explicit Agreement on How They Should Be Spending Their Time

Whether attending school or looking for work, they should be taking the steps to do so. If taking a job as a barista to get cash, this should mean they save the money as well as do career-focused activities.

Some young adults didn't care enough in high school and therefore aren't ready for a better-than-minimum-wage job. They may resent this and avoid working, thinking they're better than that. You don't have to accept that as a parent.

Treat Adult Children as Adult Guests

It's hard for parents to know how to treat an adult child. Should they be allowed to stay out all night? Ask yourself if you would be happy if a visiting guest stayed out all night. If they are staying in your house, they have to let you know they are OK. This means calling in if they decide to stay at a friend's house. You have a right to expect this.

If you feel taken advantage of by an older child, realize the child is an adult now, even if they don't act like one. If they won't respect you or contribute in a meaningful way, you can ask them to leave.

After all, you agreed to the living arrangement, jointly.

Write Out a Living Arrangement Agreement

Take some time to write down your values and how living together will honor that. Ask your adult child to do the same. This could include your feelings about drugs and alcohol, arrival times, overnight guests, and communication.

What are your thoughts on expense sharing? One friend charged her daughter a nominal rent when she returned after college. It was a way to accustom her to the real world and responsibilities. When the daughter was ready to move out, her mother surprised her with a check representing all the rent she had paid during the time back home. This may not be realistic for all, but you get the idea.

Consequences for Noncompliance Are Tricky: Separate the Mundane from the Serious

Bickering over chores is mundane but undone chores can drive you nuts. Have a regular family meeting when you review your plan and brainstorm ways to help get back on track with a fair allocation of duties. If moving back was to save money and job hunt and it's not getting done, this is serious. Time to set a timetable together for them to move out if they can't engage.

As a matter of course, mutual agreement should contain consequences if it isn't honored. One parent I know required her daughter to renew and pay the auto club (AAA) membership. When that didn't happen, she couldn't borrow the car.

Manageable consequences should reflect how you would expect a guest to behave. If they are drunk or high, they'll have to stay somewhere else for a night. If they don't come home by 11 p.m. on a work night or check in if they decide to stay with a friend, you ask them to leave for three days. Where they go doesn't concern you. The fact is that their behavior can't compromise your well-being.

The goal here is to move your child along the path to adulthood and not stunt their growth.

Communicate Goals with the Other Parent

Mixed messages won't help anyone. If the other parent doesn't share your values, you'll need to acknowledge that difference to your child and explain that sometimes reasonable people can disagree reasonably. You and your adult child put together a living arrangement, and your child needs to abide by the arrangement or live someplace where they feel free to go on their own.

CHAPTER 21

Parenting Through Troubling Behavior

Addressing Troubling or Difficult Behaviors

Parenting Adult Childrent Through Mental Illness and Substance Abuse

Where to Find Help

THE TOPIC OF TROUBLE GETS SCANT attention in mass-market parenting books. (If you have a diagnosis, it is easier to find specialized books and websites.) The dearth of parenting materials is surprising given that managing problems takes vastly more time than managing a steady state. As single parents, there is no one to pinch hit when we are at our wits' end. Layer on that the social myth of single parents as inadequate parents, and we become ashamed to admit we're out of our depth.

But we are most certainly not alone.

ADDRESSING TROUBLING OR DIFFICULT BEHAVIORS

Not all challenging behavior is a product of mental illness, and it doesn't always take the form of substance abuse or addiction. There is a spectrum of troubling and difficult behavior that some parents must learn how to handle:

- Abusive and violent behavior
- Adult-child conflicts

- Anger or explosive temper
- Disrespect
- Disregard for family rules
- Laziness/lack of motivation
- Risky behavior
- Schoolwork refusal
- Self-harm
- Stealing

Even the best parent can have children who make bad choices. Whether they get into trouble, violate our values, or make poor choices, a tendency can be to blame single parenting. The questioning of our parenting abilities can come from others but more often we turn our doubts inward such as:

- *What did I do?*

- Would this have happened if two parents were present?

- Could I have been a better person?

- Would this have happened if I had chosen a different partner/worked harder at my marriage/argued so much?

Fill in the blanks with your torment.

While some degree of introspection is healthy, beating yourself up erodes confidence as parents.

It's heartbreaking to watch a child waste his life and potential with poor choices. And the older a child gets, the bigger the problem. Grown-up problems can disrupt your child's life, but their choices don't have to break you. Nor do they make you a bad parent.

But we are all imperfect beings, and as stated early on in the book, thankfully there can be multiple paths to living with another's choices.

Save Yourself First

This section deals with the two people involved—the child and you. It will focus on your need to be the best self you can be and resources to help your child's needs.

Start with a Healthy Dose of Self-Interest

It's important not to lose yourself in the management of this problem. Double down on your job, take an art class, start a walking program, or sign up for a short volunteering event. Do what you want, with or without your child in tow. However this problem may play out, in the end, it will be you with yourself, *so you must practice how to make space for your own needs.*

Find a Neutral Third Party

In an effort to avoid the contagion effect of bad behavior, it's important to have a safety valve. This can be a therapist, educator, online group, or support group. Friends whose children have similar behavioral issues can be the best companions, but be prepared to have them drop out when one of you successfully solves the problem or concern.

Dilute the Negative Effects of Troubling Behavior

If you have more than one child, make a conscious effort to balance your focus between them. Oftentimes, the bad behavior gets all the attention, and the child presenting fewer issues gets left out. Balance takes a conscious effort.

If you have a job, or are looking for a job, double down on your focus there and take it away from the situation. It's important to not focus every moment on the problem to avoid spiraling down the rabbit hole of anxiety.

Stop Basing Your Self-Worth on the Unattainable Goal of Perfect Children

If your child's development is a self-reflection of your own worth, this is going to be a tough row to hoe. So many factors affect development— temperament, environment, behavior, genetics, and personality. It won't work to assign blame to yourself (or others) if your child has a problem. Yes, you are in the mix, but believing that you can control the situation 100 percent is not realistic and is bound to disappoint you.

Ignore Your Kids More

Cut yourself a break and reframe the situation to what you can control: yourself.

If They Are Adults, Keep Your Mouth Shut but Support a Process of Restoration

Any change needs to come from within. It's better when your child acknowledges they are stuck in a bad spot. Then you can support a process to improve rather than trying to control the process.

PARENTING ADULT CHILDREN THROUGH MENTAL ILLNESS AND SUBSTANCE ABUSE

More than 8 million Americans care for "an adult with an emotional or mental health issue." About half of those caring for adult children are single. Most of the caregivers are women over sixty. (A substantial number of men also care for adult children, and the book by Judith Smith, *Difficult: Mothering Challenging Adult Children*, should have a more inclusive title.)

Judith R. Smith, an associate professor at the Graduate School of Social Service at Fordham University, looks to define and explore a form of parenting that never stops. If you recognize yourself in the title of her book, you know firsthand the pain and exhaustion of having nonfunctioning, grown children in the house. You may be taking care of family members at the cost of your own physical and mental health. Many parents taking care of adult children do so with limited incomes and need all the support available.

These caregivers keep many nonfunctioning adults off the streets, out of institutions and hospitals. They deserve all the help we can give them.

The author states it is essential to deal with your ambivalence here. Who wouldn't feel the siren call to protect their young versus pushing them toward independence and finally getting a respite for yourself? Smith states the obvious in her assessment of patchworked social services. One has to be a master organizer to work through all the support available. Help is out there in one way or another, but it's not integrated (see the next section Where to Find Help).

WHERE TO FIND HELP

Pediatricians: Maybe and Only Before Age Eighteen

Self-help and parenting literature address your concerns with a fairly limited suggestion: "Talk to your pediatrician."

Pity the pediatricians. They get fifteen minutes allocated per appointment and have to divide that time between the patient and the parent. In a world gone crazy for performance, parents have higher anxiety and more questions than ever.

For the best chance at getting your pediatrician at their most engaged, make a separate appointment and maybe a follow-up one with the child as well. Before the appointment, make a list of your concerns and their evidence. Your goal here is to present your concerns quickly, get referrals, and determine a plan for a baseline evaluation. Some specialist follow-ups may include:

■ A neuropsych exam to assess for learning disabilities

- Personality tests to indicate any underlying disorders

- Specialists to assess for issues such as attention deficit hyperactivity disorder (ADHD), autism spectrum disorder (ASD), and obsessive-compulsive disorder (OCD)

Educators

Another overworked profession, but they do have eyes on your child. Ask for time and listen. This isn't about you; it's about your child. A single mom wrote on the single-parent community about her anxiety concerning a school meeting. It was a private school. She was nervous because she had attended this school herself and had negative associations from her time there. We talked about separating her issues from what her child needed.

The behavior she described sounded like a young child's frustration with schoolwork and acting out because of frustration from a learning disability. I suggested that this private school might not have qualified resources to assess and support her child. She should go in, listen, take notes, and then move on to discuss this with her public school district. It may be that assessments would show her child needed learning or development intervention.

Educators can provide good input. If they have years of experience, they may have a good assessment of some troubling behavior. But this is one data point.

Consider any input as one data point of several. Continue to gather others.

Behavioral Specialists

Neuroscience research has made great strides in the past decade. Pharmaceuticals combined with talk therapy have had remarkable results for people suffering from neurological misfires.

The best treatment consists of mingling art with science, and it takes several iterations to find the right combination of help that is effective. For instance, learning disabilities are a specialty, and medical doctors get a half hour of training on the topic of ADHD, and many therapists won't have the latest research.

Like any topic, it is important to educate yourself as much as possible about a problem. The Internet is a great place to start, but realize the limits to its quality. Stick with known institutions and specialists and take other information with a grain of salt. At the risk of being redundant, books give more in-depth information and, if put out by a major publisher, will have had a good degree of fact-checking. Try to find recent publications (within the last ten years) to get the most up-to-date information.

See chapter 6 for more information on finding specialists.

Dial 211

The phone number 211 is a nonemergency referral service for statewide, nationwide, and community services. Unlike 911, 211 has information you can utilize in your everyday life. The call bank is staffed with volunteers from nonprofits and social services. They have lists of resources available for healthcare and essential services.

The 211 call centers have comprehensive health and human services information and resources. The most common requests 211 specialists receive are from people looking for help paying for housing and utility bills. However, 211 handles referrals for many different issues:

- *Children and youth services* include childcare, after-school programs, educational assistance, summer camps, and tutoring

- *Mental health and suicide prevention*, such as regional or national hotlines, community clinics, and other community mental health resources

- *Financial needs*, such as food, clothing, shelter, rent, and utility assistance

- *Health resources*, such as information on health insurance programs, Medicaid, Medicare, medical intervention hotlines, children and maternal healthcare, counseling, drug and alcohol programs, and crisis intervention services

- *Support for people with disabilities*, such as community meal services, respite care, home healthcare, and transportation to medical appointments

- *Employment services*, such as job training, applying for unemployment, education programs, and transportation assistance to job interviews

When you call 211, you might receive a mixture of national and local/community resources. Specialists have an extensive inclusive database to research resources and nonprofits that best fit your situation. Local resources can include food banks, homeless shelters, financial assistance programs, medical clinics, agencies with individual grants for energy bills, rental assistance, and help with clothing.

The number works similarly to 911 in that wherever you are when you call, the number is routed to your local call center with local information. You should be linked with a knowledgeable person. If not, try what I do with any customer service call center. Thank the unhelpful person for their time and call back later. You'll probably get a different individual.

I realize urban areas concentrate their services and the rural regions are more spread out. Nevertheless, the 211 calls should provide information on local services.

Online Resources

For many behavior issues, I've reviewed multiple sites online. What follows are ones that I think are helpful and may direct you further.

EmpoweringParents.com

This is a website with articles, online parent coaching, and a program you can order called "Total Transformation." The team is a group of therapists who employ the principles of cognitive behavior therapy in a tough love format to parents. The goal is to support parents through the difficult behavior of their children through adulthood. It is one of the few programs I reviewed that was practical, detailed, and used real-life examples.

TheShulmanCenter.com

This is the Shulman Center for Compulsive Theft, Spending, and Hoarding. It focuses on the addictive behavior of these disorders and is one of the few organizations that I found on the topic. It estimates these behaviors are hidden epidemics, with 10 percent of the population shoplifting and another 9–10 percent compulsively spending. The site offers online ebooks and links to support groups and articles. It lacks a lot of functionality, but if you can get beyond that, you may find useful resources. One therapist I know recommends it.

Caregiving.org

This is for the National Alliance for Caregiving. This website provides information on the population caregiving for adults with mental illness. A study provides new data on family caregivers of persons with moderate-to-severe mental illness, including people caring for a loved one affected by bipolar disorder, schizophrenia, major depression, or another mental illness. The most helpful aspects of the site are that it gives you community if you self-identify with it and suggests resources.

ADDitude.com

This focuses on the field of ADHD and its comorbidities, which is a fancy term for accompanying conditions. The number of conditions described as concurring with ADHD is legion and includes not only behavior disorders but also learning disabilities. Owned by WebMD, the site vets articles from specialists as well as sponsors a multitude of webinars.

CHADD.org

This is another online resource for attention-deficit support. It provides information along with resources for those already diagnosed with ADHD.

AARP.org

AARP.org devotes significant space to parenting and kids in crises as part of their mission. The newsletter provides tips and resources. It does independent, credible research on many topics related to social well-being. It publishes some of the best articles on parenting that I have read. Go figure. Check the website and search for "teen crises."

As of this writing, they currently have professional resources and guidance for helping teens in your life. Stories include cell phone addiction, ways parents can fight back again teen cyberbullying, and keeping teens safe from cyber predators and online scams.

CHAPTER 22

Fun: How to Laugh and Enjoy Each Other

Going Places, Indoors and Out

Community: How to Find Playmates for Your Child (and Yourself)

Birthday Parties

Travel

Managing the Cost of Fun

MAKING REMARKABLE MEMORIES AND BREAKING UP daily care tasks provide needed respite from the demands of single parenting. It's important that we don't run ourselves ragged in the process.

To find fun, go the minimalist route and look to accomplish two goals:

- What's good for you (distraction, a break, positive interaction with children) *and*

- What your child might want (positive interaction with a parent, unscripted time, a new experience)

No matter what the age, you can achieve these two goals in as little as an hour or with a longer vacation.

Repetition reduces stress. Kids like sameness and knowing what to expect, even when expecting fun activities. We had Sunday traditions. I didn't do paperwork. We left the house.

> ### REMEMBER THE DEFINITION OF ENTERTAINMENT: A DIVERSION, DISTRACTION, AND AMUSEMENT
>
> Note that this definition doesn't include adjectives like expensive or exhausting. It can be an hour or a day.

GOING PLACES, INDOORS AND OUT

Out and About in Town: All Ages

If the weather is good, go outdoors. Start with the local parks. Then walk the town trails and let kids get dirty. The walks can get longer as they get older. Children love to explore the grounds around them. Pack bag lunches and protein snacks for rest stops. Even urban areas have natural attractions such as food forests, town forests, and walking tours.

> ### RULE OF THUMB
>
> Keep the outing length age appropriate. Kids get overloaded and tired, leading to meltdowns. Pretoddler, I would stroller to train stations with a snack and watch the trolley cars for an hour. That was enough stimulation at my daughter's age. You could easily substitute a fire station, a construction site, crop harvesting, or the local dump.

In bad weather (generally all winter in New England), plan indoor activities. If you have a car or take a rideshare, most likely there are exhibits within thirty minutes of your home. Rather than pricey name-brand museums, we would take in the smaller exhibits, the odder the better. These included:

- An antiquated museum of natural history

- A trailside exhibit at a state park with a few local otters

- A toilet museum

- A private collection of WWII memorabilia

- A stamp museum at a college

WAYS TO FIND LOCAL, LOW-COST ENTERTAINMENT

The various hilarities of *oddball collections* can be found in your area at RoadsideAmerica.com. Or search for a list of the "small but mighty" museums. Call ahead and see if they are open (or even still in existence). If your tastes run sophisticated, then *Atlas Obscura* may be more to your liking. Again, using Boston as an example, *Atlas Obscura* lists:

- A scavenger hunt in a Victorian-era cemetery

- An enormous 1935 stained-glass globe you can walk through

- A medical museum

- An authentic Italian café

- The Old North Church and all things American Revolution

Admission is usually free or very low. These entertainments appeal to a variety of ages. Even the most disaffected teen can be distracted from their phone if there are anatomical medical exhibits like Phineas Gage. (He was the railroad worker who had a thirteen-pound tamping iron blown through his head and lived to tell the tale.) Who can resist selfies with the World's Largest Ball of Twine roadside?

Go Outside

If the weather is nice and you want to get out for something different, check out some of the following sources for ideas:

■ Use your humble library card and browse the library's recreation section for books on local walks.

■ Search a town or city's website using terms like "trails," "parks," "forests," or "things to do."

Some areas have multiple books published on local walks. Others are guide deserts. That's where you will have to use an online search engine to explore your area. In our travels to the fifty states, my daughter and I have found fun, popular, and obscure events to entertain us in every area.

Again, this works for all ages. An out-of-town single dad friend came to visit his grown son. They took the time to walk a mile around Walden Pond for some nature-bathing, fresh air, and conversation.

COMMUNITY: HOW TO FIND PLAYMATES FOR YOUR CHILD (AND YOURSELF)

"Anyone else struggle . . . trying to make friends with people in general?" —Reddit single-parent community member

When taking your child out, invite others to join. As an extroverted, only child, my daughter delighted in having friends along on our outings. No doubt their parents appreciated our taking their child with us for an afternoon. (It had to be balanced, though. If I found child-minding not reciprocated, I changed families.) Around age three, when kids start playing in groups, group family excursions (aka other families whose adults I enjoyed) became the norm.

Having more adults around diffused drama and peer pressure and made the children behave better. My daughter's high energy could be directed toward a peer rather than always with me. I didn't have to be "always on."

Friends appeared early for us. I met another single parent in a mothers' group when my daughter was an infant. She liked our get-up-and-go attitude, and her child was also energetic. At preschool, I found several two-parent families who loved palling around. Generally, these were folks without family in the area, similar to us, hence also looking for community. Many times, this meant immigrant professionals who had come to Boston to work in the medical lab facilities.

Including those other detached families in our holiday celebrations made it more festive for all. And because our friends were not caught up in American consumerism, no one felt bankrupted by expensive gifts. We also shared similar long-term goals to educate our children, and everyone understood one another's financial priorities.

FINDING YOUR PEOPLE

Look around. Like-minded folks can be found to form a community in many places. These include:

- School parents
- Parks
- Houses of worship
- Affinity groups
- Scouts
- Extracurricular activities

This lasted mostly through middle school. High schoolers are more discerning about who can be in their "tribe." After-school sports and activities also chewed up vast amounts of time, especially during the weekend. My daughter discovered ice hockey in middle school. By high school, it became an all-weekend commitment, leaving little time for me to host anyone. We still managed the holidays with other families, but Sunday outings fell by the wayside.

> *"It takes practice and honestly if very young, they . . . mostly just 'play adjacent' rather than really engage. Get over your fear, say hi to other same-age parents and start yourself a 'park bag.' Fill a tote with bubbles, chalk (enough to share and lose), a blow-up beach ball, and age-friendly racecar toys—no matter the gender. If there is a park water feature/sprinkler then have a bucket or watering can. Your kid will make friends in a heartbeat."*
> —Reddit single-parent community member

> *"This year, I decided to visit a local church, and honestly, it has been great! Although I'm not religious at the moment for other reasons, just to have the connection and support network is totally worth it. I have met some amazing people, and my kid joins the Sunday activities with the other children and she looks so happy!"*
> —Reddit single-parent community member

> *"I found my 'mom friends' by taking my son to extracurricular activities."* —Reddit single-parent community member

> *"Oh, I know I'm not alone in this . . . I met a few single dads but we all work. I just find it funny people think [like] Hollywood movies that incompetent go hand in hand with single dads. In reality, we put our kids as a priority."* —Reddit single-parent community member

Check neediness at the door, though. It can overwhelm a new acquaintance. Some otherwise nice people have left me in balls of flames with their outpouring of trauma and needs. I never knew what the right response was since I had just met them.

BIRTHDAY PARTIES

We turned the planning for celebrations into a tradition of a monthlong family project. My daughter's birthday is in September, so starting in the summer, we'd brainstorm the Big Event. It remains among her most pleasurable memories. (The only downside is that she now considers her birthday to be a national holiday.)

Party Planning Ground Rules

The first task would be to choose a theme. I allowed a $100 budget, and we had to source decorations and props from within the house or from yard sales or thrift shops. The planning became the event. We would invite the whole class in elementary school, which could be twenty-five kids.

For the most part, we succeeded in staying within our budget. Some years I had less time and would grab a cake from the supermarket or do a swimming afternoon at the YMCA using their party room for cake and ice cream. Other years were blowouts with adventures, games, and party favors.

Preschool Through Elementary Age

Theme ideas were pretty easy to come by. Google was in its infancy, but the web had "bulletin boards" listing ideas on topics. I am not particularly creative when it comes to parties for five-year-olds, but I can "borrow" ideas and follow directions. I found a bulletin board on birthday party ideas where people would describe, in detail, *exactly how* they pulled off a themed party. For example, someone described their jungle-themed event where they used old spray paint to color camouflage a plastic play tent, used a drill to slowly twist crepe paper into long vines, and used a bundt pan to bake a birthday cake that when cut into fours could be reassembled as a snake. Green food coloring was the "icing on top."

Backyard jungle party

These were much more useful than the over-the-top events now pictured on Pinterest. I feel exhausted looking at those carefully curated social media exhibitions. The full-colored pictures of parties that only Martha Stewart could pull off intimidate me. The parties look expensive and time-consuming. Those bare-bones bulletin boards more suited my needs. "Homemade" appeals because it isn't perfect.

Here are some pre-K and elementary school parties that my daughter and I pulled off. Feel free to poach.

"Under the Sea"

Oceans always fascinated my daughter. We would watch the same fish swim in circles at the New England Aquarium giant tank from the time she was in a baby carriage. This would have to be a party theme. A friend had given us a big net to keep blueberry bushes safe from birds. This formed the basis of the party. Hanging above our tiny backyard and tied to four trees, it canopied the twenty-foot-by-twenty-foot area. Before hoisting, we tied crepe paper strands that an electric drill had twisted at a slow speed. These represented strands of seaweed the children ran through.

Giant inflatable pool creatures, picked up at yard sales, dotted the yard.

We played backyard games that included "Sea Hunt." Kids went fishing off the back porch, and a hidden adult tied Beanie Baby toys to their lines. A homemade sheet cake with blue-tinted frosting and a dusting of graham cracker crust for sand was made to look like a beach. Complete with Fruit Roll-Ups rolled out as beach blankets.

"Jungle Jaunt"

The aforementioned netting was again pressed into service. This time before it was raised, we filled it with leaves to form a tree canopy. Jungle-dwelling stuffed animals were included among the leaves, and the whole thing was again pulled up into the trees. I used up the small amounts of remaining old spray paints to create a camouflaged tent where the party girl could sit and open presents with her friends. That tent was a hit. For the weeks prior, we made fake binoculars from toilet paper rolls and used the camouflaged spray-painting technique again. I added colored plastic wrap (really hard to find) for the lenses. If I had to do it again, I would have bought them for a buck apiece. It is hard to determine whether you make something a craft project or just buy some cheap, planet-destroying item instead.

Again, with backyard games included, we had a scavenger hunt and prizes for all did double duty as party favors.

"Arctic Adventure"

Appropriately themed because it snowed that day in September. I resigned myself to having the house trashed by fifteen nine-year-olds. I removed furniture and breakables and let them have at it. Invitations were sent out with stamps of arctic explorers and an invitation to celebrate the anniversary of McMurdo Station in Antarctica. At a rummage sale, I bought scores of white socks. I washed and dried them, then rolled them into balls for a "snowball fight." The igloo on the porch was that former camouflage tent, now spray-painted white. I froze plastic bowls of water so the kids could carve igloos, but the plastic knives didn't "cut it." The snow globes made from empty jars and little plastic toys were more satisfactory.

It took weeks to set the house right again.

"Rock Party"

This was a day in a local park. I brought a picnic and a lot of geodes, goggles, and small hammers. The kids hunted "gems" and got to smash rocks with their hammers to find crystal geodes inside. They raced "mine cars" (wagons) and played other games, rolling around in the grass and clambering on playground equipment.

"Afternoon at the Movies"

By the cusp of middle school, the kids could be trusted to sit in a movie theater. The next town over had an indie theater that rented daytime viewing rooms. We rented one for a Saturday afternoon and brought in our own DVD, *The Cat from Outer Space*. The room was large enough to accommodate my daughter's whole fifth-grade class and a few older siblings who could help keep order. Everyone got popcorn and water.

I hope all the parents appreciated that I would take their kids for hours and send them home tired.

MY DAUGHTER'S REFLECTIONS ON HER BIRTHDAY PARTIES

"My birthday not only became a national holiday for me, but for my friends as well, knowing we would have some clever theme and crafty activities. I may have been young, but I'll never forget that tent that went from sea cave to jungle cave to igloo or the streamers hanging from the net tied between the trees. As a kid, it truly felt magical running through what felt like fields of kelp or vines. I remember my friends always asking what my theme would be that year and trying my best to keep it a surprise. I remember the Beanie Baby fishing game was a huge hit. We brought it back all through elementary school due to popular demand. My friends and I agreed that it was way better than a goodie bag; the surprise element makes it extra fun! For $100 or less, I had the most memorable birthday parties of my peers. We still talk about them."

—Charlotte

Middle School

Middle school requires a step up from cake and balloons. It's about kids being kids but wanting to feel grown-up.

"Just Desserts"

I booked the party room at a local patisserie. No games or activities this time, but there was a lot of focus on exotic desserts such as chocolate mousse, key lime pie, cherry tart, and so forth. I only had to be present and make sure the kids didn't wander off. They entertained one another fairly well and ignored me. I read a magazine and other parents got a free Saturday night.

Corn Maze

Fall birthdays work perfectly with fall traditions. I recruited a few other parents to help drive the group to a corn maze outside the city at a farm. The kids exhausted themselves in the labyrinth, and I didn't lose a one. The farm provided outdoor tables, and I provided picnic food consisting of sandwiches, side dishes, and, of course, birthday cake from the supermarket. By then I was done making fancy ones myself.

"City-Wide Scavenger Hunt"

This also required the help of another parent since we broke into two teams and were going to race point-to-point in the city using public transportation. In Boston, we have an unusual set of sculptures presenting nine planets of our solar system. Most are accessible via the MBTA (Boston's train service). Starting with the sun at the center of the solar system, we began in the Museum of Science after first watching a planetarium show. This was before smartphones, so we gave clues to the next station. Even though Pluto had been kicked out of the solar system planet club, kids remained incredibly loyal, so it was included, and the winning team got there first. Thankfully, Pluto was located at an MBTA stop in our town, so all the parents could pick up the kids there.

Chances are you are not in Boston, but your own town may have a collection of something that could be scouted on foot. Geocaching or letterboxing can do the trick. Check out the web pages for your area and design a scavenger hunt around those.

High School

This is a whole other realm. Kids want to hang out but still will gravitate to a structured event. I held one pizza party at home and a sweet sixteen at a local restaurant. I would call the latter less than successful. Her diverse group of friends didn't mix well. The introverts didn't have anyone to talk to except my daughter, and she was engaged with other guests. That was the last party I orchestrated. I had fun with the parents, though.

TRAVEL

Having to be "always on" exhausts single parents. (Probably exhausts all parents.) We just never get a break. If you have a rambunctious kid who gets into everything and anything, queue the worry machine. Take these factors into account when planning a trip. If you have to focus on getting from point A to point B, how will you keep an eye on your child? What's happened before? How can a situation be contained?

Rules of the Road

Keep Trip Length One Day for Every Year of Age

I'll never forget a friend's advice. Kids savor predictability, and travel puts that off. Generally, limit overnight travel to their age, gradually increasing as they get older. If your child is three, only go away for three days to an unfamiliar place. Sage advice, it turns out. Every time I tried to push it past the "day for every year rule," I regretted it.

Plan and Pack Your Patience

I always have a first-night plan. I know where we are going to stay and limit the activity that first day. Don't try to wing it when you get to your destination. It introduces too many variables. Know when a park opens, what documentation you need to travel, and what activity options are there.

Expect disruption. That's why traveling is a growth experience.

Leave a Day Between Your Return and Back to Work/School

That day not only serves as a time to organize for the week ahead but also serves as a buffer travel day. We've been bumped from flights and were glad to have an extra day to get back home.

Get to the Departure City the Day Before Your Flight Home

You don't want to be rushing back to an airport from out in the hinterlands. Things happen when you are traveling. That's the joy of travel, experiencing the unexpected. But do you really like racing for a flight or missing it and having to rebook travel?

Don't Overschedule

Remember that sometimes everyone just needs a day to sleep in and play at the pool.

Differentiate Your Needs Versus the Kids' Needs

Don't be dismayed if kids aren't into historic battlefields. Long car rides bore everyone. Keep everyone's needs in mind when planning.

Have Redundant Systems

By redundant, I mean "backups." Cell phones don't always work in remote areas, so you should have a Garmin GPS or be able to read a paper map. This is a great skill to teach your kids. It will take a while for some to learn.

I despaired for years that my daughter wouldn't be able to fluently read a map. She now not only proficiently reads maps but can keep a direction in her head, getting us back on track if lost.

Check Your Energy Level When Venturing Out

My daughter was a toddler when I wanted to get out of town for the Fourth of July. I rented a room on Cape Cod, an hour away. What I hadn't realized was how exhausting it would make me to mind a toddler in an unfamiliar place. At one point, I wanted to take a break from driving and pulled over to a beach. We sat down to play. I tied a "leash" from my hand to hers so her movements would be limited. Thank goodness I did because I promptly fell into a deep sleep. She had managed to stay occupied playing with the sand, but if she had undone the rope, the outcome could have been very different.

Finally, Ease into Travel

Start small and work your way up. Affordable, though exotic, cities like Mexico City are not "starter locations."

I started in our backyard and progressed to a local park, Cape Cod, and so forth. My friends Tom and Gail are avid outdoors people. They adopted an elementary-age brother and sister who had never traveled or camped. The first camping trip was an hour away at a state park. If anyone got nervous, it was an easy ride home. Everyone made it through that first trip quite well.

Travel the Fifty States

By the time my daughter started college, she had been to forty-seven of the fifty states. It began with a primary school project. In fifth grade, the class had to choose a US state, research it, and create a presentation for the class. My daughter and her friend chose Oklahoma. They made diagrams and dioramas. Truthfully, I knew little about the state beforehand.

LIST LOVERS

Lists inspire and motivate. They represent an organizing principle for years of fun to come. A laid-out plan sitting at the ready for execution takes away decision stress. You no longer have to decide *what* to do but rather *how* to do it. Nothing beats the feeling of accomplishment when you cross something off that list.

Lists can drive your family adventures. The kids can color in states they have visited and check off parks they've seen or peaks they've climbed. Your list will be different from my list, but here are a few of our lists:

- Sixty US national parks
- Forty-eight peaks over four thousand feet in the White Mountains
- Fifty states in the United States
- Thirty local museums
- Forty local trails
- Fifteen friends/relatives out of town
- Ten city parks
- Eleven local professional ballparks—one major, three AAA, and seven Cape Cod League

We haven't completed any of the lists but still have ready-made options that take off the stress of "what should we do."

The late travel writer Anthony Bourdain gave an interview once where he described his childhood travels as taking place in the form of ethnic restaurants in New York City circa the 1970s. Your list could include amusement parks, arcades, restaurants, or donut shops.

Fast-forward to middle school. We had thoroughly explored New England and other states within driving distances in the Northeast. Primarily, these trips landed us with friends and family as springboards to sightsee and lots of downtime to visit and play. Now we were ready to branch out.

I vaguely remembered a church camp friend who had moved to Oklahoma. An online search revealed she still maintained a home there. I dashed off a letter and received a reply! Yes, she remembered me. Suzette had settled back in Oklahoma after a ten-plus-year career overseas. And she was a single mom, too, having a son a few years older than my daughter. "Consider yourself invited!" she closed her note to me.

Thus began a series of trips each spring and summer that would take us much farther afield to reconnect with long-ago friends. In Oklahoma, we also visited Suzette's father, an eighty-year-old storm chaser. In Oregon, we traveled from Portland to Crater Lake with a retired biologist. Custer State Park found us staying on top of a mountain, meeting a Hollywood makeup artist and her creative director husband.

Our hosts have been unfailingly generous. Some lent us a car. Some joined our day trips, and all had fabulous suggestions that only locals would know. Think about your far-flung network and use them as an anchor for a trip. It may not be possible to bunk with them, but it feels easier to know someone local.

National Parks

These are made for single parents. After working through our list of friends, we realized we had visited a fair number of national parks. The United States has sixty national parks in the fifty states. We established our second travel list for national parks. All have family activities, and you can manage excursions with "contained" environments that a single parent has to love. My residual memories include feeling "safe" with my daughter and having the ability to enjoy the experience for myself as well.

To date, we have experienced twenty national parks plus a good number of state parks like the aforementioned Custer State Park in South Dakota and the Adirondacks in New York.

It takes planning, but you can visit national parks on a budget. Books and blogs give advice about traveling cheaply. It's an investment in time but also a great teaching moment if you do this together. The major cost variable is the travel season.

With school-age children, you are forced to visit these attractions in the high season. You and everyone else are traveling during spring and summer vacations. This makes for higher airfares, car rentals, and hotel rates. The parks are far-flung and not served by hub airports to where flights are the cheapest. I've saved credit card points for tickets and loyalty points for hotel rooms (usually Best Western). Upon arrival, we would always stop at a big-box store to pick up a cooler and groceries.

For the long car rides, I borrowed audiobooks from the library. It was also a bonus in the teen years that cell service was spotty in most park locations, forcing us to communicate.

The Teen Years: Urban Romps

It was around age fifteen that enthusiasm for destination vacations at national parks held less appeal. A new city, though, could provide different stimulation. Different buildings, food, and culture (country/western music isn't commonly heard in Boston) all provide enjoyable, multigenerational experiences.

I added gateway cities to the national parks.

We amped the adventure in Nashville, Chicago, Detroit, Ann Arbor, Houston, New Orleans, Kansas City, and Omaha (yes, Omaha). These cities were a triple play with friends, an urban atmosphere, and jumping off places to nearby nature preserves like Mammoth Caves, Jean Lafitte Bayou, and the Indiana Dunes. Because my daughter had college in mind, we started adding college tours.

Happy Trails > Inspired Envy > Happy Companions

Our travels became the envy of friends and family. When others heard that we welcomed fellow adventurers, I got requests asking to come along.

One rule of the "friends and family tour" was that everyone had a planning job. To spread out trip planning, everyone picked an off-the-beaten-path oddity and researched how to get there. This rule has resulted in some terrifically fun adventures. These included:

■ A house on stilts in the Louisiana Bayou

■ A ten-thousand-acre animal sanctuary in Colorado

■ A two-story Chihuly glass sculpture installation in Omaha

■ The Cornhuskers' marching band exhibition in Lincoln, Nebraska

■ An Indian nation in Oklahoma

■ Congaree National Park in South Carolina

We have those memories of our times together that still bring us joy.

Travel represented an integral part of our parent/child time. If you have more than one child, I still recommend it. Even with a teen that only wanted to be with friends, travel forced us to be with one another, and those memories survive up to the present day. It also helped to have a "friendly" along. A "friendly" is another adult who genuinely likes your child and can help so you don't always have to be on.

MANAGING THE COST OF FUN

The enjoyment of something is inversely correlated to its cost. We got far more out of camping in Yellowstone National Park than staying at Hilton Head Resort in North Carolina. I once drove all night to Shelburne Farms in Vermont with a three-year-old so she could pet a cow for her birthday. It was a lovely resort, but I was the only singleton sitting at the dinner table, and most of them looked askance at a preschooler scribbling at her place. The farm was great, but I could have had the same experience staying at a motel down the road and eating at Denny's.

In my defense, I was still trying to pretend I had my old carefree life back.

After similar missteps, I learned to apply the cost multiplier ratio. Did the swanky Shelburne Farms Inn, which cost three times the cost of a Best Western, return three times the fun? Not really. I was uncomfortable. The food was three times better than Denny's, but I couldn't really enjoy it. The same happened when we went to Hilton Head Island for Thanksgiving. We wanted to get out of Boston for some warmth. I didn't realize that North Carolina is actually cold in November, and unless you play golf, it is boring since much of the area attractions were shut in the offseason.

Feel free of guilt in choosing a budget for fun and sticking with it. I promise the kids won't notice. Anything new and different is fun, and cost is a relative factor, anyway.

Low Key, Free Entertainment

You may have to be the cruise director. In our friend group, each had particular strengths. Denise enjoyed finding new restaurants or spending a day at a pool. Heidi liked hiking. I could uncover obscure (and usually free) museums. To make friends with other families, you may have to organize the first few outings.

Go Retro

Card games and board games at home—canasta, spades, hearts, or poker. Head to the library! Many have a section for board/card games. Add a potluck, and no one ends up with all the cooking and cleaning.

Fresh Air

The activity level is age dependent. All that visual stimulation makes for worn-out kids. The modern definition of walking in the woods is "forest bathing." Start locally and work your way to farther destinations. I've never had another family turn me down to join on a nature outing.

Free Outdoor Events

Concerts in the park, Fourth of July parades, and fire department open houses. Keep an eye out for notices or go to your town's website and look under "calendar" or "activities." Or go old school and check the paper.

Stargazing

If you can get away from light pollution, head to a hilltop and watch an astronomical event. The Pleiades Meteor Shower comes every August. Just make sure to load up on bug spray and bring comfy blankets to spread out.

Museum Free Days

Some banks and merchants may sponsor free admission days if you are a customer. These tend to be fairly crowded days, so either plan to go very early or check out the lesser-known museums. The museums themselves might have a free day once a month.

Library Passes

Our library lends passes for two to four people to museums, aquariums, historic properties, and parks. Reserve online.

Seasonal activities

Think pumpkin carving in fall, cookie baking/decorating in winter, or swimming in the summer.

Beach Days

Depending on where you live, these could be year-round options or just in the warmer months up north.

Outside Dining

Consider BBQ, park picnics, or something else alfresco.

Geocaching

So fun and easy to do anywhere there is a cache, and you get to be active in nature. Just get the app to see what is in your area. It's a scavenger hunt for kids and adults alike.

Pokémon Go!

Kids of all ages get enthused with the hunt and never realize they're exercising. It's also a great way for adults to relate to kids. My best friend never had kids, but he enjoyed chasing the creatures with my teen.

Volunteer

Pitch in as a family or group; join a beach or community cleanup day.

The goal for these activities is to change up your surroundings, enjoy adventures together, and provide new experiences for your child.

CHAPTER 23

Friends, Enemies, and Peripherals

Finding Your Tribe

Maintaining Friendships

Ignoring Judgers and Haters

Managing Immediate and Extended Family

Handling Coworkers

Telling Your Story and Diverting the "Just Curious"

FINDING YOUR TRIBE

Companionship ranks third as a major challenge for single parents, after time and money. It can be hard to find community. A lack of time, the prioritization of children, and a singular focus to get through a day makes it hard to find new friends or even be someone's friend.

Sometimes we are in a strange social place. Couples don't invite us to hang out with their crowd, and single, child-free friends don't have the same time constraints. Other single parents may have many demands on their free time, such as large extended families, and they aren't available for close friendships.

CONNECT WITH AFFINITY GROUPS

If you have a special needs child, isolation can compound. Empathy in the general public is hard to come by; the child or children need monumentally more attention, so it is hard to consistently connect with another adult. If the people you meet are in the mindset of the perfection-raising of their children, they aren't going to be in your tribe.

Luckily, there is nothing like a shared challenge to create a community. Affinity groups offer excellent opportunities to connect. I've seen online groups devoted to parenting children with special needs and websites specific to nonprofits like New England Asperger's and Autism and National Center for Learning Disabilities (NCLD). Many have connection events and programs you can join. Take a brief look at their websites to see their support services and events.

While I don't regularly recommend Facebook as a place to connect, it (and other social media sites) do offer special interest groups. Limit contact to online interactions and use safe social media practices. I've read too many stories of creeps and catfishing to say that social media platforms are good places to meet people without taking the most basic precautions.

How Many Friends Is Enough?

The good news is that you don't need many close friendships. The rule of thumb for emotional health is that you need five people in your life to know you well. It seems to be a just-right magic number to manage friendship closeness. The researcher Suzanne Degges-White writes, "Research suggests that the number of close friends we need to feel that we have enough is somewhere between three and five. Not only that, but adults with four or five friends enjoy the highest levels of life satisfaction, and those with three close friends are not far behind."

For a sense of satisfaction about the smaller or larger number of people you count among your friends, the *Atlantic* magazine wrote a fun article about the concentric circles of friendships. The circles range from 1.5 for intimate friends to 5 for close, shoulders-to-cry-on friend, to 15 best friends with whom you feel comfortable exchanging childcare. Lest you fret you don't meet those numbers, they get sized up or down depending on your age, family situation, and personality (introverted vs. extroverted).

Meeting and Socializing with Adults

In 2002, a start-up formed, creating affinity groups organized around common interests. This became known as Meetup.com. They earn money by charging organizers of events a small fee. It's not hugely profit driven, which may explain why megacompanies don't want to buy it. It also explains why it still works for people.

BEWARE OF TECH GIANTS AND SOCIAL MEDIA COMPANIES' AGENDAS

If, at the time you read this, Meetup.com has been acquired by a tech giant or social media company, ignore my recommendation. This platform worked because it wasn't driven by ad revenue.

Local Meetup.com groups organize around just about any interest. Go to Meetup.com and search in your area for groups. If you live in an urban metro area, you may have to put in search terms for what you seek. Try a few outings. If you don't find your community, try five more times.

"Be the Change"

If you don't find an existing community of like-minded folks, then start your own group. You can create a group to be as broad or specific as you want. Remember that the broader the criteria for your Meetup.com group, the wider the net.

Persistence is key here. Adult companionship keeps us sane. It's important to be balanced, and what you need changes over time. Your mental availability will also change as the kids grow up and need less from you.

Infants and Toddlers: Finding Friends in the Loneliest Phase

Infancy and toddlerhood is this high-need phase of childhood where children compete for all our attention, and it's especially tough. Outside of close friends and family, it's hard for others to break through our singular focus on the children. We are distracted and may be inattentive to our friends, possibly making them feel that they are neglected and that the relationship is unbalanced.

On the upside, this is the easiest kid age to manage. At first, babies will stay where you put them, you control the schedule, and you can pick up and move them when and where you want. Hopefully, they sleep a lot. Toddlers require more supervision and are everywhere at once. But they are easily engaged and easily redirected, facilitating change.

New parent groups, religious institutions, and community centers present good places to meet folks. New mothers' groups exist from rural to urban environments and everywhere in-between. You can also find groups sponsored by La Leche League, which are commonly sponsored by local regional hospitals and family service leagues. I have also seen babywearing walking groups on Meetup.com.

I made a great friend—another mother with an infant daughter—through a mom's group. Both single working moms from the get-go, we were able to relate to each other as well as engage in same-age activities. In those lonely days of early parenting, these types of connections can be a lifeline.

Consider houses of worship and their related activities. Services might have childcare. Volunteer events may provide an extra set of hands for childminding. Whatever is available, don't overthink it. Sign up before you talk yourself out of it.

The local library may conduct toddler story hours during the day. You can take your child and meet other parents of young children. These often occur during weekday working hours. If you'd like weekend or evening times, then email the head librarian. Often, librarians just don't know what demand is out there for their services until someone requests it.

School-Age: The Golden Stage

If I could freeze time in a bottle, this would be the era I would capture. It was a time to be seen and heard. Both my daughter and I experienced new friendships and new horizons. As a social child, my daughter's name for any another child was "Friend!"

Other parents were eager to socialize their children, and I was happy to reciprocate. For several of those years, I was unemployed and able to share rides, host activities and playdates, and so forth. When working full-time out of the house, I had sitters that were happy to take on a friend with my daughter. "Two are easier than one" goes the expression.

Everyone felt so amenable. Even though I lived in a city with a high-income component, the financial differentials between families didn't show up in their attitudes until years later.

Children start to engage in after-school activities and weekend sports clubs. It's hysterically funny to sit on the sidelines and watch a scrum of seven-year-olds chase one soccer ball. You can choose to sit with other parents (or sit in your car to go through emails). Either way, it gets you out and provides you a chance to interact with others.

Middle School: Exploring Sports, Arts, Nature

In my opinion, middle school gets a bad rap. In fact, it's a time for personal exploration and opens the friend universe both for you and your child.

Activities may take up your time now, but think of them as an opportunity for you and your child to hone executive function skills. Advance planning is needed to organize transportation and schedules. Food is the social lubricant here. I would cart snacks for the sideline parent contingent. It seemed to make the world happier, and we could chat for the hour or so during the activity.

Not sporty? My daughter and I tried all sorts of activities, such as art and pottery classes and hiking and camping adventures. We'd join other groups and, if none were established, set up group events with other families from school. This worked because we are both extroverts. I viewed our effort here as an investment in adult time.

Landed in the Community of Duds? Switch tactics. It can happen that other parents have social circles and don't want to expand.

High School: Making Friends Independently of Your Kids

As noted at the start of this chapter, we need to have five people who we feel know us well. Perhaps you fill that quota with your immediate family, and other relationships stay on the periphery. But it's important to have your own stable of close relationships, be they family or friends. And while some of your closest friends may be people you've met in your capacity as a parent, it's good to find friends independent of your kids, particularly once they get older and enter high school. At this point, they'll be much more independent.

Here are some ways to get out among the living:

- *Introduce yourself.* If in a new city, ask whoever you know for introductions to others, and say yes to meeting other people.

- *Build relationships in the workplace.* Workplaces are the closest thing we have to the school setting that we had as kids. So when you're at work, ask yourself: Who can I go to lunch with?

- *Volunteer events.* Take on a role, even a small one. I didn't want to lead the PTA, but I could manage a before-work hour at the bake sale.

- *Book clubs.* The pandemic and moving to Zoom constrained opportunities to meet people. Many book clubs went virtual, and as limiting as that is to form friendships, it did provide a boon to single parents in that they could still participate without having to get a sitter.

- *Houses of worship.* If you didn't make it to one in prior kid stages, it can present another ready-made community as you have more time to cultivate your own friends and interests.

- *YMCAs and recreation centers.* If the thought of starting an exercise or sports program terrifies you, consider attending one of the fifty-five-plus programs. You are less inclined to get hurt, you ease into moving more, and you could gain a "council of elders" as a support group.

- *Meetup.com/Facebook groups.* In-person gatherings will be more abundant in urban than rural areas, but consider checking into events and groups on social media from time to time. They come and go, and your needs will change as well.

- *Support groups.* Affinity groups exist for every challenge, including parenting, addiction, medical conditions, seniors with ADHD, stock market gamblers, new mothers, and so forth. I've seen these groups sponsored by local hospitals, senior centers, libraries, special interest groups, and others.

MAINTAINING FRIENDSHIPS

I've just offered suggestions for how to find friends. Now on to keeping them.

Maintaining friendships requires care and nurturing. But how can you manage them when your emotional gas tank runs empty and social expectations include conventions like birthday cards, thank-you notes, and the like? Often, check-ins are moved from today's to-do list to tomorrow's list until they become delayed for days, weeks, or months.

Friends may interpret long silences as a lack of interest. After a gap in communication, some parents feel guilty about their silence and fearful of its consequences, so they let the friendship slip away rather than try to explain their silence.

DIFFERENT FRIENDS FOR DIFFERENT PURPOSES

Shasta Nelson runs a website, shastanelson.com, and wrote the book "Friendships Don't Just Happen." She makes an excellent point. While we may all be searching for that new BFF, as adults our friends have different lives. They can fill separate roles in our lives and when aggregated, they form a complete circle. One or two may be very close; others may be more peripheral. Expect that they may come and go, but while some may last only for the duration of your children's time in school together, others will last a lifetime.

For single parents, keeping friends means we have to show up, be consistent, respond to calls and texts, and be vulnerable. All of these are hard given the demands on our time, and they require both organization and some amount of *in*sensitivity to rejection.

Make Time

The key to connection is making the time. Before you fall into peals of laughter, hear me out. *It's about time.* You must spend time together to be friends. Even though we are all so busy with work, driving our kids to various therapies, maintaining a home, helping with schoolwork, and so forth, both parties need to find the time to be in the relationship.

You can't neglect the other person and maintain a relationship. Everyone is busy. The world is too damn fast, but if you can't find fifteen minutes to talk to a friend, then that relationship is going to be unbalanced and die from neglect.

That goes double for romantic relationships. You need time for the two of you as well as time together with the children as well. If either of you works to the extreme or keeps so busy that you are neglecting the other person and can't even find fifteen minutes to talk every day, you may have some past personal issues you need to take care of first. Make sure you do that.

If you feel that time is an elusive concept, refer to part two: Time: How to Make More When You Have None, earlier in this book.

Reciprocate and Recognize Reciprocation

You can ask all the questions you want, be super polite, and say all the right things, and sometimes people still won't be having it. If every time you approach Sarah she miraculously gets a phone call, take the hint. Spend your resources elsewhere. This will happen—there's no pleasing everyone. While it's very important to put in the effort, put it in where it's likely to be rewarded.

Relationships are a give-and-take. If you're constantly the one making the effort, sending the texts, and going out of your way to be nice and friendly, take a look at the situation. If there's an explanation (the person is going through a hard time, they work sixty hours a week, etc.), then you may have to take the initiative. But if they're responsive to other people yet don't seem to have the time for you, move on.

Remember That Friends Aren't Therapists

You have good reason to feel badly about the world. It's really hard for single parents, and loneliness compounds it. Venting to a friend makes you feel good for a short period. Maybe. But often the bad feeling doesn't go away, and you come across as a bitter, disappointed, and angry person. Generally, that's not a quality that attracts people.

Being on the receiving end of your anger won't cause someone to establish a relationship. Yes, you have a valid reason to be angry. And, most likely, so does the other person. But no one likes an angry person. It's really hard to handle blowback.

Positivity takes practice. A friend once told me that confidence and happiness attract. Luckily, a little preparation goes a long way. This doesn't have to require a weeklong meditation retreat. Like anything, start small:

- *Get sleep.* It's hard to manage negative self-talk when you are exhausted. Every new parent can tell you this. If you put energy into resolving any problem, let it be finding ways to get some sleep. Try an occasional sitter so you can go to a hotel nearby, a night nurse (paid or family) during infancy, naps when the baby naps, and letting go of perfect. If you battle medical or psychological conditions, insist that your medical team works with you to solve this. Nothing can get done on a few hours of sleep.

- *Recognize your own negativity.* One year, I lost a brother and father in the same month. A few months later, I had to go public with a long-term skin cancer battle. My supervisor gave me great feedback: I had become angry. With this observation, I was able to take action on my external affect. (However, I did change supervisors shortly thereafter. Criticism in place of compassion is a no-go in my book.)

- *Get perspective.* Recognizing that you have a choice and autonomy can take away a lot of the time and soul-sucking blame games. It gives you agency to know your awesomeness and that some things work out and others don't.

IGNORING JUDGERS AND HATERS

Many single parents report being ostracized by married couples. They hear about game nights, walking groups, and other activities where they are not included. This happened to me—I got excluded from events, mostly in the evenings. It didn't feel great.

This exclusionary behavior happens for a few reasons:

- *Lack of understanding.* Our empathy tends to be constrained by our own life experiences. Lacking complete knowledge of a situation, people will fill in information from their own point of view. So, for example, if the last thing I want to do is socialize with other adults on a Friday night, it might not occur to me that you might be looking for an invitation to an activity.

- *Discomfort around single people.* Maybe some think it's contagious, or they feel inferior to our awesome self-sufficiency.

- *Affinity or "like me" bias.* As people, this is an unconscious bias we have to surround ourselves with people just like us. That's kind of lazy if anyone asks me, but no one is asking.

- *Unjustified sense of superiority.* Sometimes people feel smug about being in a relationship and don't want to be around single people.

- *Desire not to be brought down.* If you talk about the pain of single parenting in social situations, it's pretty hard for people to sit with that.

- *Dislike, whether outright or subconscious.* Remember, not everyone is going to like you (or me).

At any rate, you can't do anything about someone else's emotional reaction to you, so smile and move on. Brooding is not worth the energy.

How to Counteract Single-Parent Bias

Most literature focuses on confronting our own biases versus dealing with *being* stereotyped. But single parents face a lot of prejudice and microaggressions, and we need strategies to deal with them.

The term microaggression originated in the 1960s but came into vogue during the pandemic-era time of active social movements. It describes little verbal jabs and injustices that are almost too small to identify but accumulate over time to make the recipient feel judged, undermined, and demoralized. Sound familiar? For many single parents, it will.

Personally, I am clueless enough to really never recognize when microaggressions are happening. I just know that I feel "less than" when someone acts in certain ways toward me. Later I may realize what happened. I have heard from others that when comments come their way it compounds fears of inadequacy. Your sense of self and confidence erode.

What can you do when you're on the receiving end of such behavior? You can counter it directly in conversation, if possible, with a statement like "That's not my experience, and it's not the experience of many other single mothers." However, you have to decide right then and there if you want to put the other person on the defensive (you will) and negatively impact the relationship.

Most of the time, I don't think quickly enough to do that. Instead, I:

- *Ask for clarification.* "Can you explain what you mean by that?" ("Tone is important: Go for curious, not antagonistic." —Warren Berger)

- *Debrief with a friend.* It helps to find a few friends to share everyday experiences with. If, like me, you can't readily identify why an interaction leaves you feeling down, talking it through with friends or a group is an easy way to share stories and clarify what you feel.

- *Clear a pathway to yourself.* Make it easier for people to draw closer to you. Adopt characteristics that generally make people likable:
  - Quiet confidence (vs. arrogance/sarcasm, etc.)
  - Humor (vs. "Doomsday Denny")
  - Showing interest (vs. being interesting)

It's Them, Not You

In an era when advertising and social media encourage constant comparison, people's self-esteem is incredibly vulnerable. They can feel insecure, inferior, and/or jealous, and judging and hating can be self-protective responses to these feelings. Judging or disdaining someone else is an unfortunate but common way to raise their own self-esteem.

This isn't something you have control over. Other people can get to know you better, and that may help. But if their experience with you is a carefully curated projection of your life, then it's bound to raise the green-eyed monster. I advocate authenticity rather than a composed Instagram presentation of your situation.

It's You, Not Them

Sometimes, our actions brush others aside. They feel mistrusted, ignored, not heard, and so forth. Every parent feels exhausted, unfulfilled, entitled, incompetent, and any other number of negative feelings. Double that for single parents, and we could have a lot to answer for in our own dealings with others. Our eyes are on the next task, next drama, next challenge—not another's feelings.

We need to slow down, count our blessings, and realize (absent evilness) that everyone is doing the best they can.

MANAGING IMMEDIATE AND EXTENDED FAMILY

Parents have forever looked to their families for support in the journey: A word from the more experienced grandparents. A spell of babysitting. A check to defray costs. Some family members will have outsized influence; others will be more peripheral. Alternatively, there are those just not present at all, consumed by their own lives. They can ebb and flow and fit better into your life at different times.

If your family feels the strong pull of obligation to those who share their bloodlines, then consider it a blessing, warts and all. Even the most self-centered relative can provide a moment of entertainment or respite during your life. Try to be on the plus side of the relationship ledger, where you give as much or more than you receive. Especially consider older relatives who also may be feeling the isolation of their life circumstances.

When she was an infant, I would take my daughter to visit a disagreeable great-aunt in a nursing home. Even in her earlier years, this relative spoke ad nauseum about her interests, indifferent to those in her company. I visited because her daughter asked me. I suspect my cousin sought distraction for her demented mother. Babies elicit joy, and it's difficult for even the most entrenched, self-centered elder to resist. I also figured the other residents of the facility would get a kick out of a visiting baby and welcome the chance to cuddle. It would serve multiple objectives by also giving me a baby-free hour.

Some relatives require more boundaries than others. If you feel negative about yourself after an interaction, then keep a distance and limit time together. Everyone has a favorite age for children so your relative may respond better at an older age.

Similarly, as time goes on, some lives become less complicated, and others can be more open to helping you either with companionship or emotional support. If the relationship doesn't work now, it may work later. Instead of ditching the relationship, keep it simmering until your interests and needs sync up and a connection is mutually agreeable.

Of course, if the family member consistently engages in negative, off-putting behavior, there isn't much you can do except draw your boundaries. The line not to cross with me is lying. That equals a big "NOPE." After adolescence, this shouldn't be around. I can understand kids lying not to get in trouble, but not an adult. If they lie to avoid responsibility or create an advantageous position, that signals more significant problems that probably won't change.

Relationships are hard work. No relationship is perfect. Our objective, therefore, in dealing with those to whom we are bound as a family should be to find what works and when, reciprocate as with friendships, and keep relationships on an even keel.

"Helpful" (AKA Critical) Family Members

Of course, there have to be some. They have opinions on your singleness—they'd raise their kids differently and keep house better. It's not helpful to get criticism in the guise of advice.

Agree with them that things could be better for you, and this is a plan you are working on. Then give them a task. "What would help me right now is _____." Don't be stoic for two reasons. First, we can all use a measure of help, and second, it's important that others can see your needs. It makes you more approachable and more authentic.

Living with Family

This can be a lifesaver, emotionally and financially. Living costs shared among multiple adults reduces the cost of raising a child. It also provides children the opportunity to bond with other adults, assuming it's a healthy relationship. Young parents, in particular, find cohabitating in a multifamily household helps them get on their feet and work toward independence. This could be working a job, saving, and building a financial nest egg. Other circumstances help the parent go back to school by providing childcare and a financial cushion.

When Living with Family Becomes a Problem

At times, young parents find multigenerational living untenable and the tension palpable. It's the tug between wanting independence and financial wherewithal. Setting up a household is expensive, but so is a bad living situation.

A goal could be to work toward independence and self-support. As discussed elsewhere in this book, that means having a household income (support, salary, subsidies, etc.) of at least $100,000 (2023 dollars) in Boston Metro to afford housing, living expenses, and childcare (for one child without subsidies). Your area may have a lower cost of living.

My daughter is on the cusp of adulthood. She has learned life skills from living apart from me and with a variety of roommates. She found it scary to engage with her money. However, she has started putting the pieces together for her job to be the source of support.

My plan is to help her develop a budget. "This is all the money you get for a month from your job. Let's build a budget and look at trade-offs. It may be that you will have to take a job in Boston and live at home for a while to save up the key money."

Since she wants her independence, that should be motivating. Maybe.

A common budgeting suggestion is to create two mini budgets—one for your goal to live independently and another on saving money to get there.

HANDLING COWORKERS

Coworkers, past and present, represent the lion's share of my friendships. Since we worked in a high-stress profession, regular collegial support was critical to success. If your work environment is healthy (i.e., not toxic), these relationships can be a great source of adult company.

Coworking relationships don't have to be with contemporaries. During my daughter's childhood, I managed teams of entry-level employees, often twenty years my junior. Closer to my daughter's middle school age than to my middle age, they kept me grounded with their less-distant memories. I saved myself a lot of freak-outs by consulting their opinions about boys, sports, schoolwork, and other adolescent issues. I can safely give them credit for helping to raise my daughter.

I am not a fan of starting relationships with your (or my) problems, as you no doubt realize by now. This is a personal preference. Another manager at my last corporate job led with her single parenthood, a critically ill sibling, and the stress of managing it all. I think it made her seem approachable and relatable to the senior staff. I had a different orientation. My values call for me to check personal issues at the door before entering. Also, I didn't trust management's empathy and therefore wasn't comfortable changing my approach. We each have to gauge how much to tell.

Workmates are sources of strong and lasting friendships (at least until you retire). It's a good friendship starting place if you miss adult interaction. At the outset, you have topics in common, challenges to share, and, in normal times, a shared workspace. More friends make you happier at work. We'd all like a raise, but research shows that feeling supported and valued on the job contributes more to our happiness and mental and physical health. Having friends at work makes tasks seem less onerous. One feels hopeful and more likely to take on challenges. When we have more friends at work, we feel less lonely in our entire life.

To strengthen those relationships, eat your sandwich with a few colleagues now and then. Listen to their stories and opinions. If you feel comfortable, share your own, but it's not required. Listening is a great starting point.

TELLING YOUR STORY AND DIVERTING THE "JUST CURIOUS"

On Reddit, someone in the single-parent community asked: "How do you quickly explain your status?" He was tired of people presuming his marital status. Those in the Reddit single-parent community replied:

"I just say I'm not married because I want to make it normal that people aren't married and have kids. If I say it like it's nothing then hopefully people are realized that it's not a big deal."

"Same. Or I say no husband. Inside I'm screaming 'I do this myself and I deserve all the credit!'"

"Sometimes I feel I'm the only not-married one at whatever event. Even if I'm alone, people assume I'm married. I'll even always refer to my kid's mom as 'my kid's mom,' and they'll come back with 'so your wife . . .'"

"I just say 'We're not married anymore.'"

The original poster finds curiosity perturbing. It feels more like voyeurism than authentic interest in him as a person. Also, I suspect that as a single father, he evokes a good amount of curiosity at social events. It's tough being an outlier.

For single parents who never had an involved coparent, this feels even trickier. Where is he/she? What's the backstory? How can I relate to this person? These might all be in the questioner's mind.

Projecting Openness Without Inviting Voyeurism

Some people assumed I got a check every month and every other weekend off. (Wrong!) Most never asked how I managed financially or emotionally. Maybe I came across as supercompetent, always together. (Again, not so.) More likely, they just didn't care to think about it.

But when someone does ask how I manage, I reply, "Not well. I sure could use any tips you might want to share."

This creates a partnership with the questioner *and* makes them feel visible.

KIDS NEED NARRATIVES

Case in point: I never felt that how I came to be a single parent was the business of anyone peripheral to my life. But they were curious because our human tendency is to make a complete story.

One mother told me what she heard from her kid, who heard it from my kid. My daughter had gotten it right, but I didn't want to talk with someone I barely knew. I laughed. "That's what she said?" And I just left it at that. (Lesson learned: expect family details to get repeated.)

I had told my daughter the details she needed to know at her age along with facts. The story was filled in as she matured and therefore had more context.

I realized that children need a narrative to relate to. Kids are curious and are going to ask. I always felt my daughter's family structure was her story to tell. I just wasn't fast enough on my feet.

Be prepared for this earlier than you think. You can keep it fact based and add details as they get older. Practice with a child development professional if you want. If you are in an online single-parent community, ask them how they managed the information. I've read through community members' situations involving the other parent with mental illness, addiction, and incarceration along with amicable separations and divorce. The goal here is to counter feelings of loss and abandonment.

I didn't feel that I owed an explanation to anyone. Honestly, I know two people who can keep personal matters to themselves. Decide for yourself how much to say and what you don't mind having repeated.

Where Does Your Issue End and Theirs Begin?

It's hard, if not impossible, for traditional parents to calculate the impact of a missing second parent. At times, I have witnessed the community coming together for a widow/widower. I think it is easier for someone to envision what life would be like with a sudden loss. However, imagining the loss by divorce, abandonment, or choice is probably too hard to fathom. This next story is a perfect example of the contrasting ability to size up a loss.

One year, during seventy-two hours, more than fifteen inches of rain fell onto the still-frozen New England ground. Metro Boston declared a natural disaster. Water seeks the path of least resistance, and without natural drainage, flows into basements. Many homes flooded, furnaces and water tanks were ruined, and a foot of water needed to be pumped out of basements. Schools closed. I had to take the day off work. My daughter wanted to boogie board in eighteen inches of water in the basement.

Others, though, were less affected and could go to their jobs. I had my eleven-year-old at home. Her close friend Mia had two working parents who asked if their daughter could spend the day with us since I was home. "Of course," I said, thinking two was easier to mind than one.

Mia's father, Mack, brought her over. Standing on my sodden porch, he related how he and the other guys on their block got together to bail out the basement of a widow on their street by buying the last available portable pump.

That he made a distinction between my crisis situation and another single parent's wasn't lost on me. I lost a day's work to stay home, pump out my basement, and take care of my daughter. Mack and his wife went to work because I could take their daughter. Yet, here he was, virtue signaling while standing on my porch. In the pouring rain. Talking to a single parent who was also managing this all on her own but without helpful neighbors.

I like Mack and his wife very much. They're good, down-to-earth folk. He just didn't read the room. (Or maybe they imagined that I had a secret plumber hiding in my basement.)

Moral of the story?

It's hard for outsiders to tap into every single parent's struggles. This is especially true if you are reluctant to ask for help or appear vulnerable.

Not being able to express needs can come from any number of reasons. You were failed continuously in the past and every disappointing adult run-in since then reinforces feelings of disappointment, or you may come from a culture of individualism (self-sufficiency and pull-up-your-own-bootstraps mentality) versus collectivism ("we're all in this together").

It's OK to ask for help, directly or indirectly, from your community. In fact, "asking for help" is the adult response to a problem.

One single-parent friend, Janna, embraces her wider community and has no problem verbalizing what she needs. She communicates her needs in terms of what her child lacks: be it support, tuition money, childcare, job help, or something else. Since most people need specification for how they can help, her narrative is effective in appealing to people who are, by nature, generous and willing to help.

If you are not comfortable letting people know you could use a hand, make it a goal. And like any goal, it's best to have some small steps you can take. Start small. Make a list of what you need. See if you can break it into more manageable items. For example, if you lack childcare to go out once in a while, ask a family member. Start with once every other week. Or offer to trade childcare with a neighbor or friend. Similarly, if you feel financially under pressure, make a simple budget and ask a financially savvy friend to look where you can make changes. Earlier we discussed the time-consuming tasks to apply for cost subsidies like utilities, recreation centers, and free lunches. This is a task that can be broken into bite-size pieces and therefore be made more manageable for someone to help you. Actions such as gathering documents needed, calling an organization, and filling out an application can all be separately managed. Finally, ask for help. If you get Mack standing on your wet porch virtue signaling, ask if he knows how you can get the same help.

Tone is everything. How you ask will affect how people feel about jumping in.

CHAPTER 24

Pests, Pervs, Annoyances, and Other Distractions

Pests

Pervs

The Clueless

Annoyances

Scammers

Social Media

OPPORTUNITIES TAKE YOU IN THE DIRECTION of your goals. Threats take you away. Single parents experience a unique host of threats and annoyances that get in the way of living their best lives. We need to call them out and neutralize their impact.

PESTS

These are soul-sucking, selfish people who prey on single parents. They make assumptions that we are desperate, lonely, incompetent, and so needy we'll believe their BS. I've listed types here:

- Vendors who assume we are too busy to realize they jacked up prices

- Shrinks still believing in Freud and his curse of the mother

- Married people looking for a hookup

- People who use your energy/skills rather than building a sincere friendship

- Judgmental healthcare professionals

- Anyone stereotyping you as a single parent

- Grown-ups with parent issues themselves

- Scammers

Pests don't take the time to know you for who you are and make assumptions about what you need.

PERVS

This is the number-one reason single mothers avoid dating. The risk of introducing a potential predator into your life is a widespread fear. And it doesn't just have to be a romantic interest.

The movie *Spotlight* retells the story of how the *Boston Globe* broke the child sex abuse scandal of the Boston Catholic Archdiocese. At its heart was a corrupt system that knew about priests taking advantage of children in single-parent homes and exploiting them. Those of us here in Boston didn't understand why it was headline news. We all knew about pervy priests and ministers (so as not to pick on one group).

Pedos troll online dating sites looking for single women with kids. Yes, it's a real thing to watch for. Sometimes parents want an adult relationship and want it to happen so badly that they miss warning signs. Other pedos are just really good at subterfuge and wriggle their way into schools, camps, and church youth groups. I don't have to go much into this, given media attention on the topic.

If it concerns you, arm yourself. Do a search on how to recognize warning signs. We don't have to be paranoid, just cautious (refer to chapter 25, "Romance").

THE CLUELESS

One situation may be more commonly experienced by single female parents. Without a male adult present in a family, people with poor personal boundaries feel they can ignore social norms. The rule is that another adult does not directly contact your child without your permission.

While texts to confirm logistics with your kids might be expedient, you need to give permission. Not going through you first is out of line as is discussing personal matters with your child.

If this happens, contact the other parent and explain your preference. If they don't knock it off, block them on your kid's phone.

ANNOYANCES

These are minor exasperations. Sometimes they can be redirected to focus on a more balanced attitude toward single parents. Sometimes it only takes a little education. Annoyances in my life have included:

- *Teachers who are unaware that their language might not be inclusive.* After September 11, my daughter's nursery schoolteacher asked the children, "How do your daddies keep you safe?" She knew my daughter didn't have a "dad." I asked for time to go in and speak with her. A gifted teacher, she said she had immediately regretted her phrasing and would be more conscientious.

- *Bosses who would call early morning meetings.* I would passive-aggressively just not show. I couldn't get my child off to school and get to work at 7:30 or even 8:00 a.m. I understand that has changed since the pandemic, and that is a good thing, too.

- *Colleagues who think you are antisocial for turning down lunches/after-work events/Christmas parties, and so forth.* The worst are "off-site, team-building" activities. They generally bled into my parenting time, and only child-free or two-parent colleagues could attend.

- *Online daters already in a relationship.* A 2023 research paper estimates that 65 percent of online daters were either married or in a relationship and scrolling for entertainment.

- *Any organization promoting a "father/daughter" or "mother/son" dance.* How not to be inclusive.

SCAMMERS

These jerks could just be annoyances, but given the potential for financial loss, I've given them a dedicated category. Scammers on the Internet have progressed beyond the "Nigerian prince" level and moved on to more sophisticated techniques. I've listed a few that follow (edited for brevity) from the posts of single parents from our online community. They may sound ludicrous here, but, obviously, enough people have fallen for them that they are still around.

The Deployed Serviceman Fake

"I replied to one of the many random messages I got from a man because this one had a real pic, and within a few conversations, he was asking for money for his son's video game cards and then for his own food [saying] he was a deployed serviceman.

"The photoshop job on his pics was really good. I have military family and thought they were legit 'til I . . . realized the emblem on his hat was plastic, not sewn on. Do not believe their sob stories—they are fake and they are predators. . . . I shudder to think I talked to him on Google Hangouts so he has my email, which has my first and last name." —Reddit single-parent community member

Friend of a Friend

"Watch it from your acquaintances too. Had a single dad friend ask me to lend him £20 'to get his daughter some stuff'—problem is he started it by saying 'can this stay between us?' Just don't lend anyone money." —Reddit single-parent community member

A little research goes a long way in fending off scammers.

"I run the pics through Google Image."
—Reddit single-parent community member

"This is what blows my mind. They're GOOD. Like where are you practicing these skills because it seems as soon as they start targeting people, they're already pros. And the level of effort and work they put in. Like, hey jerk, if you applied this tenacity to real life, you still might do pretty well." —Reddit single parent community member

"Anyone who randomly messages you on Reddit is a scammer. It's that simple." —Reddit single-parent community member

And remember, single dads get scammed, too.

"As the mod[erator] of [a single dad community], I'll attest that this isn't limited to single moms and men scamming at all. (Well, to be fair, one never knows the actual gender of the scammer. . . .) The attempts to prey on lonely men are certainly there as well." —Reddit single-parent community member

SOCIAL MEDIA

It may seem disingenuous for me to cite social media as a threat when I quote threads from discussion boards here. I look at social media for clues into the voice and needs of a community. Some sites provide information. While "the Internet" receives much-deserved derision for the land of scams and crackpots, some communities of like-minded folks can be helpful. I continued to be impressed by the money skills on some of Reddit's financial subs and the kindness of strangers during times of disaster. That said . . .

Facebook and Metaverse are *not* your friends and especially are not your children's friends. They spend millions (billions?) employing consumer behavior experts to find ways to hook you on their products, including Facebook, Instagram, and WhatsApp.

Thankfully, I don't have to make the case for dropping social media as a form of connection to others. The inauthentic nature and negative side effects of Facebook and friends are well documented. It's been impossible to escape headlines surrounding concerns about social media (ab)use.

It's not just problems with teens and young adults. The "highlights reel" people post online eats away subconsciously at readers, and they understandably fall into comparison traps and "fear of missing out" (FOMO). Here are some of the mental health problems documented:

- Body image dysmorphia
- Poor self-image
- Low self-esteem
- Loneliness
- Depression
- Anxiety
- Poor sleep, which is associated with depression, memory loss, and poor academic performance

Try to power down. Social media use can affect users' physical health even more directly.

SOCIAL MEDIA AND BIG TOBACCO: BOTH KNOWN HARMS

"Facebook executives have long boasted that its platforms are safe, even as they invested in ways to keep teenagers hooked and hid what they knew about the side effects.

"Sound familiar? Critics say Big Tobacco once used the same playbook, and it is fueling a whole new level of outrage against the social media giant.

"Facebook consistently played down its own research that showed how photo-sharing app Instagram can harm the mental wellbeing of its youngest users, according to a report in the *Wall Street Journal*. Almost a third of young teen girls told Facebook they feel worse about their bodies after scrolling through the site, documents reviewed by the newspaper showed.

"Despite that knowledge, Facebook is dedicating more resources to reaching even younger consumers, including developing a children's version of Instagram." —Business Live.com

I watched as the carefully curated lives of friends and celebrities ate away at teens' self-esteem. I witnessed firsthand as younger employees remained continuously distracted by their Facebook feeds (a thing in those days). I also lost serious points at a job where the CEO extolled the joys of Facebook et al. to her employees, and I refused to sign on with what would become the social media giant.

While LinkedIn.com became the currency of my career, even there, I saw contributors begin to bleed their personal life into this business platform— probably dooming it to irrelevance, the way teens abandoned Facebook. Maybe. Hopefully.

While Congress and the executive branch may never succeed in breaking up social media giants, the recent revelation that Facebook has known through its own research about their ill effects on teens' mental health now makes the company a public health problem. Finally!

As I write this, Facebook is having its Big Tobacco moment. This reference is to when the CEOs of the major tobacco companies in the United States were confronted over internal memos acknowledging the damaging effects of smoking on the health of consumers. This was after spending billions on fake research and lobbying to refute claims of the dangers of smoking to avoid regulation. As a result of the public knowledge of their arrogance, those companies had to pay major damages to states that, in effect, funded smoking cessation programs. It also reconfigured the entire industry.

Sound familiar?

CHAPTER 25

Romance

Dating Mindsets

Challenges

Introducing a Relationship

Should Your Romantic Partner Spend the Night?

Your Future Has Yet to Be Written

EVEN WITHOUT CHILDREN, MODERN DATING IS COMPLICATED. Add in the children, prospective minefields with online dating methods, and fear of recommitment, and for single parents, dating and relationships often take a back seat. Yet most parents would want to find a soulmate—someone to share the joys and burdens of parenthood.

Since circumstances vary, I relied on the collective experience of single parents to write this section. I absorbed discussions among the single-parent members of my online community on the topic (books are notoriously silent on the subject), and common themes arose.

As a preface, here is the good news:

■ You are not alone.

■ Your feelings are perfectly normal and shared by many.

■ There is hope for a future healthy relationship if you want one.

■ No one can predict your future.

DATING MINDSETS

Dating as a single parent presents all kinds of practical challenges that I'll address shortly. But I think it's important to first examine the mindsets—some of them despairing, some hopeful—that influence our approach to romance.

- At one end of the spectrum, among the dating averse, some people just need time out from relationships, having had a rough go with the child's other parent.

- Many parents of young children say, "Not now; later, when they are older." As a result, some single parents forgo romantic relationships for the children, saying that "Being lonely sucks, but I hope it means my kids will be happier in the long run."

- And for some, dating feels simply unmanageable, as in this post: "I've been thinking a lot about dating, but the logistics break my brain." In contrast, some people use their history as grounds for optimism: "Dates were always fun for me because it's someone new who wants to get to know you. None went anywhere, but it gave me a shred of hope for being happier."

- Among those more open to dating, most hold on to the notion of dating at any age. Dating offers hope and the chance to be seen as someone more than a parent: "Dating would inject normalcy into feeling like a whole person, not a parenting automaton."

- And many people distinguish between dating and a more durable and committed relationship: "Companionship is nice, but marriage or moving in is off the table."

CHALLENGES

There is no one "right" mindset to have, and you may be all of these people at different points in time, depending on what's happening in your life and that of your children's lives. But despite the differences in attitudes and beliefs among single parents (and within ourselves), the challenges we face are pretty universal.

The following table shares challenges and suggestions as brought up in the online Reddit community I moderated:

CHALLENGES	SUGGESTIONS
Time	Lunch dates may be more manageable given that children are in school/daycare.
Unpredictable schedules	Even one dinner date can be enough socializing to refuel you.
Syncing schedules	Give yourself time to socialize. It doesn't have to be only dating. It could be play groups.
Effort required	You can flirt online and stay in that stage for a while. You don't have to act on it.
Predators	Do your research.
	Don't advertise that you are a single parent.
	Don't offer up much info on *why* you are so busy. Don't volunteer that your ex isn't very involved. Unfortunately, perverts do target single moms. When a prospective date asks if the other parent is involved, say "yes." Predators won't pursue a relationship with another parent around.
Complication with children and confusion about parent dating	Some parents advise passing on dating until the kids are older. Focus on self and child in the meanwhile.
	Choosing not to date allows you to become close to your kids while they are still young.
	See "connections" challenge/suggestions that follow.
Childcare	Childcare may be easier to secure midday.
	If you have family who will watch your kid, take them up on it to go on a date. Similarly, if you have the resources for a sitter, find one for a consistent time that you will take for yourself, to date or otherwise.
Connections between child and parent's date	Take it slow. Get to know the person.
	Anyone you date should be respectful of prioritizing the child. Be careful whom you have around your child because even women with or without kids can act out.
	Avoid complications by drawing boundaries at the start and sticking with them. This may be no introductions until dating for a specified period of time, defined times when you are not available, etc.

CHALLENGES	SUGGESTIONS
Finding a match	Other single parents with 50/50 custody or older kids may be more approachable.
	Date people with careers, hobbies, and interests outside of dating. Some people are very reliant on being in a relationship. That can be messy to untangle.
Vagaries of online dating	There are "dating coaches" who can expertly guide one through the unique language and online etiquette. Community education centers online also offer classes. This may be a safe way to check out the process.
Fear of another disappointment	Keep your expectations in check, given all the complications.
	Date in moderation, and it can be a good time.
	Enjoy dating but don't get upset when it doesn't work out.

Close friendships can satisfy the craving for intimacy in a different way. Those friends can be the ones that know you inside and out, drop everything for you, and be there when needed. It may be that is enough for now.

INTRODUCING A RELATIONSHIP

Everyone's situation is different. An infant isn't going to connect with a casual introduction, but school-age children can get confused. When a parent begins dating, negative feelings surrounding lack of a mother or father in the house can intensify for the child. Other factors influencing your decision might depend on children's previous experience with forming and losing attachments, their relationship with you, and how the household energy is affected.

My toddler daughter was thrilled with every male visitor—whether they were an uncle, friend, or neighbor. She saw them as wonderful and new. As a preschooler, each became a potential mate for me so she could fill in the missing picture she saw in books, movies, and friends.

By high school, a romantic partner for me would have been a train wreck on top of everything else she had going on. She stopped mentioning it. Other single-parent friends had no qualms about bringing around dates, new or old. It all had to do with their individual children's temperament, relationships between parents, and household stability.

REAL-LIFE STORIES

This section on romantic relationships focuses on tips and cautions from the voices of online single parents. The topic is universal to single parents, but the execution is unique. I witnessed as many individual dating styles as I had single-parent friends. Some approaches were successful, others not so.

Rebecca was twenty when she got pregnant. The father has some but limited involvement with her and the child. Rebecca went home to live with her mother. She still had connections with high school friends and dated frequently. While it did cause friction with her mother (also a single mom), the available childcare gave her flexibility to work and date. Rebecca married, moved out of state, and had two more children with her new husband.

Liza had her son in college and married young. The marriage didn't last due to affairs by both parties. Liza continued with her married paramour, who dumped her soon after becoming available himself. Later, Liza again took up with another married man who left his wife and then carried on a second affair with another woman while dating her. Last I heard, she was still single.

MORE TALES OF SINGLE-PARENT ROMANCE

Lavonna had untreated ADHD and anxiety, managed through exercise and diet. After a rocky career start, her professional success accelerated following a cross-country move, but her husband's job plateaued, much to her disappointment. A son had learning disabilities and behavior problems that exacerbated the difficulties in her home life. Her marriage came apart when her kids were in middle school. Once divorced, Lavonna was determined to hack the online dating algorithms and find a new mate. She invested hundreds of hours and thousands of dollars in profile writers, dating coaches, and life coaches. She has had several long-term relationships, including one that currently appears to meet her expectations.

Sam lost his wife to suicide. The children were eighteen and twenty-three. The marriage had long suffered the effects of mental illness parading as alcoholism. Years before, Sam had psychologically made the mental relationship break and wasn't caught in complicated grief when his wife died. He waited a respectable one year, then went online, found another widow, and remarried shortly after that.

Carlyne grew up in Kentucky. Her intelligence was evident from a young age but of no importance to parents who lived on the edge and didn't see futures for girls. Carlyne looked out for herself, and in her adolescence, impulsiveness ruled her decisions. Pregnant at sixteen, she married, divorced, and became the noncustodial parent. One day, the school called and said she should come to get her daughter because they wouldn't release the girl to her father's custody. As a reluctant parent and unable to support herself, her survival tactic was to take up a new boyfriend, this time a married man who left his wife for her. He became Carlyne's second husband. While he made good money, its sources were suspect. This second husband died. More mature and wise, Carlyne is now a wealthy woman having successfully parlayed her late second husband's money into real estate. She married a retired accountant.

How to Talk About Your Love Interest with Your Child

Here are a few simple but crucial guidelines for having that talk:

- *Take it slow.* Wait until you are a year into dating. The emotional safety of your child trumps your desire for companionship.

- *Communicate.* Talk, listen, and talk some more long before you introduce a potential third party. If you have trouble putting the topic into words or fear what reaction you might get, practice with someone.

- *Set expectations.* Don't spring someone on your kids without warning. Warm up to it and talk about it as the relationship evolves.

- *Don't "elope" and leave the other parent to explain it.*

SHOULD YOUR ROMANTIC PARTNER SPEND THE NIGHT?

My answer is a hard "no."

Sorry to burst your bubble. You may be entitled to have a life, but it's risky enough even without kids. The risk of traumatizing your children is too high. Here are some ways single parents note that this plan could go sideways:

- What if you think you're being quiet, but your kid hears you (best case scenario)?

- What if your kid wakes up in the middle of the night and walks in on you?

- What if the sex is great, and you both fall asleep, and then your kid finds you in the morning?

- What if your kid decides it's the night to get sick and throws up . . . or it comes out the other end?

Get a sitter and go out.

WOULD YOU HAVE SOMEONE SPEND THE NIGHT?

"Only after I've known them for a while. Having someone over is giving them access to your safe space and your child whether your child is awake or not." —Reddit single-parent community member

"I don't think I could ever do it. My mom was a single mom and would do this. I hated it. I used to lay in my bed and cry and felt trapped in my own room." —Reddit single-parent community member

"I have been doing this with a guy recently, and I regret it."
—Reddit single-parent community member

"Look for a sitter and find somewhere else to hook up."
—Reddit single-parent community member

YOUR FUTURE HAS YET TO BE WRITTEN

We glimpse a few of the multiple permutations of finding romantic relationships as a single parent from these stories. As a single parent, the future for you has not been written and can have one of many outcomes. The process can be daunting, but you have the collective wisdom of your singles cohort here.

Take advantage of hearing others' experiences. Listen, absorb, and weigh the applicability to your own life.

CHAPTER 26

Start Living the Life You Want

Creating a Vision of the Life You Want

Matching Actions to Goals

Sample Action Plans for Single Parents

Treat Yourself Right for the Life You Want to Live

The Past Is Not the Future

WE ADOPT GOALS TO CHANGE OUR lives. Your best life differs from my best life and everyone else's. It's important to imagine what you can make out of your unique gifts amid your specific challenges.

It starts with knowing what you want.

"Single mothers might set goals such as completing a degree, attaining a better job, or developing a strong support group, and then they work toward achieving those goals."
(Kjellstrand and Harper, *Yes, She Can*)

CREATING A VISION OF THE LIFE YOU WANT

1. Think About What You Want

I do my best thinking lying outside at a park on a picnic table while children play on the nearby playground equipment. I allow myself to free associate.

To stimulate your creative juices, ask yourself three questions:

1. *What activities make you want to get out of bed in the morning, and why?* Here are possible answers:

   Exercise, because I like the results

   Anything involving people, because I draw strength from them

   Playing with my kids, because we can play make-believe

   Housework, because I think better in a clean place

   Making money, because I like the peace it brings

2. *Who do you want to hang out with?* Are some answers:

   Other single parents

   People my age

   Older, wiser people

   People with the same interests

3. *How do you want to spend your time?* For example:

   Raising my children

   Working for profit

   Having fun

2. Write Down Your Answers and Then Prioritize Them

That imprints it on your brain. Saying it out loud has the same effect.

> *"Write down 25 things you want to accomplish. Put them in order of importance. Take the top 5 and those are your goals. Throw out the remaining 20. They aren't worth your time if you can't prioritize them."* —Warren Buffet, nonagenarian venture capitalist

3. Articulate the "Why" Behind the "What"

Life improvement programs ask that you seek your own "why." Inner motivations are the most powerful motivation tools to make a change. They work to counteract the psyche's resistance to change.

That's enough for now. Picnic table time over. Everyone is probably waiting.

MATCHING ACTIONS TO GOALS

Did you enjoy your break? Good, because we're getting back to work with a new set of steps. Having created a high-level set of goals, here are the steps for bringing them into focus and turning them into reality.

1. Pause for a Self-Check on Your Life Fantasies

> *"Often, it's hard for us to think about what we want to do because we are terrified of failing, of looking stupid, or of what sacrifices we might have to make if we actually follow our dreams."*
> —Taryn Watts, certified life coach, Ottawa, Canada

Did you "self-censor" what you want? Did you rule it out for your own reasons or for reasons someone told you? It may be that something isn't achievable in the short term, but with time and resources, it may be possible later on.

Her whole childhood, my daughter felt math was impossible. All because she couldn't memorize times tables. She wanted a career in conservation science that necessitated high-level math classes. Relentless, she found a talented tutor during college who could coach her through her learning disabilities and approach problem-solving in new ways.

That said, it is a quicker path to success to do a reality check about your goal and consider whether you have an aptitude for it.

2. Give Yourself a Timeline

For a while, happiness self-improvement books were all the rage. Each was structured about taking one year to make changes. Think of Shonda Rimes's *My Year of Saying Yes*, Gretchen Rubin's *The Happiness Project*, and so forth. Observers mocked these books as "stunt journalism." While I am always ready to call out copycat behavior, this didn't bother me. Forcing behavior changes with time-bound pressure makes a lot of sense. We mark the beginning and end of months and a year with all sorts of rituals. It helps us feel time and forward momentum.

Many years ago, I gave myself a year of goals—eating better, getting more energy, moving. I designated each month as the initiation for that goal. These were all in service of my vision of creating a better life for myself and my young daughter.

Here's how I began my year:

- In January, I committed to upgrading my work situation. It's usually the time companies look for help with new business plans.

- In February, I initiated a new exercise program. It was low key, I didn't get hurt, the community was welcoming, and I had more energy.

- In March, I started decluttering and, once momentum was established, continued all year. Exactly one year later I found my next house and had a lot less stuff to move.

3. Write *One* Action Step

The action step should be the smallest amount of time to dedicate to this goal. Five minutes is fine. (It could be looking up a phone number of the YMCA and putting it next to your phone or computer.)

No home runs are necessary; singles and doubles will do just fine.

Walk, don't run.

4. Engage in Positive Self-Talk

We all need encouragement, and who better to encourage you than you? Tell yourself:

"I can do hard things!"

"Every time I say, I 'don't feel like it,' I postpone my goal-getting."

"How good will I feel when this is done?"

FIRST, TAKE OUT THE TRASH

At the end of her first college year, my daughter had to pack up the dorm room. It was time sensitive because the company storing her belongings for the summer would arrive at a specific time, and she had to vacate the dorm. Overwhelmed, she called the night before.

We started small. "Do you have any trash bags or an empty box?" She had bags. "OK, empty the trash cans. Put the bag into the hall." That was all it took. A nudge toward starting, and momentum was established. The approach to any overwhelming task is to break it down to small bits.

---

5. Work It Backward

This is my go-to for planning a project. With the end goal in mind, I think in reverse, identifying each step that would have to happen in order to make the next one happen. Keep stepping back to break down the action items until you are at the first essential step, such as "lookup phone number [. . .]."

My career BC (before child) involved extensive travel. I couldn't envision continuing that postchild, not having any family support. I embarked on a career change, stepping back in intensity, travel, and money (no surprise). It took a false start and a couple of years, but I did make the change to everyone's benefit.

6. Make Action Items Specific and Time Bound

"Run a marathon" is unrealistic if you don't work up to it. "Walk fifteen minutes a day, increasing by five minutes each day" would be a good start toward a goal to get more energy through exercise.

SAMPLE ACTION PLANS FOR SINGLE PARENTS

While everyone's "best living" is unique, they generally involve gaining more time, money, companionship, and child resources.

Here are a few action steps for the most common goals. These are examples only and are meant to serve as thought starters. But before diving in, remember to ask yourself *why* you're setting a specific goal. Is it for the right reason or because someone else wants it? Does it serve any of your needs?

GOAL 1   INCREASE INCOME WITH A NEW JOB

Why

To make a better life.

Action Plan

I can find the time to look for a new job by investing in some help at home and more childcare for a limited period.

On my next library visit with my child, I'll talk to the reference librarian.

I will search online for "strength inventories" and print out a list to reference.

Example Action Plans in Fifteen-Minute Steps

If the sample action plans still feel overwhelming, here are some ways to break them down into even smaller increments.

Goal 1: Increase income

Time period: Six to twelve months

How: Gain new skills or new job for the skills I have

- Identify potential employers in the field of interest (information technology, healthcare, finance, etc.).

- Check their skills requirements by looking at job postings or people who have the job I want.

- Call the human resources departments there and ask what skills they want and the salary range.

- Find a certificate program (note: the new potential salary must make the certificate investment worthwhile).

- Research nonprofit certificate programs either online or in-person with childcare.

- Email programs for more information.

- Call and talk to programs.

- Look for funding available (employer, school, the state department of education).

- Apply for funding (if necessary).

- Enroll in program.

- Attend (OK, this is more than fifteen minutes).

GOAL 2 FIND MORE TIME IN THE DAY

Why

To reduce my stress and focus on my goals

Action Plan

I will accept that no to-do list is ever completed. The point is to have a list, not finish it.

I will identify the little wasters of my time, like mindless phone use or social media.

I will track my cell phone use for a few days to identify usage.

I will schedule social media use only from 8 p.m. to 9 p.m. at night.

I will hire out my worst household task

I will drop a nonessential, nonenjoyable activity

I will double the amount prepared for dinner and then have an extra dinner for the next day (or use leftovers for lunches).

GOAL 3 GET MORE ENERGY

Why

To increase resiliency

Action Plan:

I will increase my physical activity by fifteen minutes/day, and here's how:

Move fifteen minutes a day cleaning with music (with/without kids).

Walk my child to school by getting up fifteen minutes earlier.

Sign up for the activity app with my health plan.

WHEN YOU CAN'T WALK ALONE OUTSIDE

Most books on well-being prescribe taking a walk and getting out in nature. But what if that isn't an option for you? You feel unsafe or vulnerable when walking alone or with a child. My daughter lived in a violent city where gangs of teen thugs roam about looking for easy cash (or cars).

If that is the case for you, here are possible options to choose from:

- No equipment-needed-exercise videos on YouTube.

- A buddy app that lets someone know the time you leave, the time you expect to get home, and your route.

- A walking club that provides safety in numbers. And if it meets at a regular time, you'll be more obligated to follow through. A girlfriend in Gaborone, Botswana (Africa), does this with her friends. Historically a peaceful city, food shortages created desperation and increased violence as a result.

- Local college outdoor tracks where more people are likely around.

GOAL 4 SKILL UP FOR A HIGHER-PAYING CAREER

Why

Live less paycheck to paycheck.

Action Plan

Earn a new skills certificate or degree to earn more:

Make a list of people who have the job I want.

Talk to those people about how they got to that job.

Look up tuition reimbursement programs from employer or the state.

Identify schools with childcare.

Talk to human resources at work about paid time off for studying.

TREAT YOURSELF RIGHT
FOR THE LIFE YOU WANT TO LIVE

As we head into the final section of this book, I want to recap some of the key takeaways that I hope you'll not just remember but turn into mantras in your daily life.

Make the Right Friends

If you look at your five closest people and see traits you admire, such as relationships, career, financial stability, or parenting, then you have a positive support group.

If you only hang out with people who like to get hammered at bars and spend money, you will likely do the same. These friendships sap your money and probably your energy and happiness as well.

Upgrade your life by upgrading your friends. My friend Howie likens it to playing tennis with someone better. It ups your game, so to speak. Instead of being jealous of someone with money, study their habits. Are they the first to work? Do they ask to learn new skills?

Don't Compare Yourself to the Joneses: They Aren't Real

I get how it is so compelling to look at others and say, "I deserve that." In fact, you probably do. But here are some of the things you don't see behind someone else's "success":

- *They were born luckier.* There is luck in timing. A lot of people who should have gone broke didn't because of the artificially low-interest rates between 2008 and 2021. Their houses gained equity, employment was high, and the cost of borrowing made it a no-brainer to use excess funds to invest in the stock market instead of paying down debt. I wouldn't count on that as a strategy going forward.

- *There is a direct correlation between the stuff people have and their financial stress.* Car payments, mortgages, expensive towns, and vacations promoted by a certain lifestyle weighed heavily on the family breadwinners who have confided in me.

- *Conversely, you don't see the choices people made to go without things to instead build a nest egg.* One (married) colleague asked me after I retired early from our firm, "You made your money before you worked here, right?" I just nodded. I had made a lot of hard choices to get back on my feet.

- *You don't know what strife exists behind closed doors.* People don't know how close I came to losing my home after a long unemployment period or the lifestyle adjustments I had to make. I didn't talk about money.

The upshot is that you can't know or have in your control the circumstances surrounding the Joneses. Ignore them.

Get More Out of the Day You Have

In 1908, a grumpy old guy wrote a tongue-in-cheek book about the economy of time: *How to Live on 24 Hours a Day*. He poked fun at those who complained about lack of time but idled for hours in the evening. His solution? Get up earlier, even before the servant.

So not us, right? But we can recognize the sentiment of idling hours away. In modern-day meaning, we refer to the Internet and social media that have spent billions of dollars on the best way to hijack our attention so it can be sold to advertisers.

We can't manufacture a thirty-hour day (and it sounds exhausting anyway). However, I can give away techniques and tips that helped me get more out of the day. Here are my top five.

Pay Attention to How You Spend Your Time

Here's a lucky break I got. I am old enough not to have grown up with endless television programming, streaming, social media, and Google. In fact, I disliked automated technology even before it came around. Toaster ovens are a stretch for me. My daughter, however, was born the day Google came online. Facebook came about while she was in elementary school. "Oh, this isn't going to end well," I thought to myself.

I did my best to limit electronic exposure. We didn't get cable until the Federal Communications Commission's change to digital forced me. On June 12, 2009, the Federal Communications Commission required all high-power analog US television stations to turn off their signals and move to a digital-only transmission. They gave us "conversion boxes" that didn't work so I got cable rather than buy a new television. The downside was that my daughter reports not understanding certain cultural references from her childhood. She is also not as much a "digital native" as her peers. She'll live.

Limit Your "Scrolling Time"

It's probably not a successful strategy to swear off all social media. Digital detoxes don't work. But awareness of how much time distracts you might help. Apple sends me a "screen time" summary each week. When it shocks me, it serves as a reminder to "step away from the phone."

Put Together Routines for Recurring Activities

Why reinvent the wheel? Make morning, work, and nighttime routines. I write every day and was constantly interrupted. I finally set a writing schedule and will return calls in the afternoon after I finish my daily writing task.

MAKE IT A DAILY ROUTINE

Eat right, sleep well, take medication correctly, move, and take time in nature. These are things within your control and can be done in the context of parenting. No extra time required. Here are others:

Get fifteen minutes of sunshine each day.

Eat lunch outside.

Take a walk.

Move fifteen minutes more each day.

Get off a stop earlier from the bus and walk.

Take in an elderly neighbor's trash cans for them.

Do one vigorous household task.

Drink more water.

Substitute one coffee or soft drink with water.

Purchase a very cute reusable water bottle.

Do Important Activities in Your Prime Operating Time

Certain tasks take tremendous concentration. I schedule those for the morning. Other tasks like cleaning and laundry are no-brainers and I do those in the evening. My eyesight is better in the daylight, so I do close work like reading during the day.

Outsource Your Most Annoying, Time-Consuming Task

Whether this involves ordering takeout, hiring in vacuuming, or sending out laundry, this will depend on your personal return on time calculation, explained in chapter 10 ("What Is the Value of Your Time?").

Build connections

Call a long-lost friend for fifteen minutes (no texting/email).

Sign up for a parent/child class at the library.

Look at classes at the YMCA and its childcare.

Take your teen on a long walk (a nearby pond or lake, a bus to a city park).

Call an elderly relative.

Read the friendship chapter here.

Improve your family's diet.

Remember frozen produce counts!

Subscribe to a simple-food newsletter like *Better Homes & Gardens* with basic five-ingredient recipes.

Sign up for a parent-child cooking class.

Reduce social stress.

Restrict social media—seriously.

THE PAST IS NOT THE FUTURE

Beware of "futurizing." This is thinking that we can extrapolate from the past to predict the future. True, our past provides a good way to learn from mistakes, but we must allow for variations. Times change and people change. For example:

■ Organizations have demonstrated increased flexibility since the pandemic. For example, prepandemic, a former employer denied my repeated requests to work remotely. Since then, it has decreased its expensive real estate footprint and allowed staff to work remotely.

- My daughter has dyscalculia, and requests for accommodations in math classes had been denied every year of college. Her last year (postpandemic), the college opened accommodations for all students to use basic function calculators. Nothing changed with my daughter's disability. Only her environment changed.

Circumstances have changed and will continue to change. While the past informs the future, the present mutates continuously.

Sixteen Secrets of Successful Single Parenting

1. No partner to help? Build a team.

2. Respite is necessary to refuel. Read the childcare chapter (chapter 3) on how to pay for it.

3. If your kid is acting out, surround them with purpose. Use third parties. Not you. Send them to summer camp, on vacation with a relative, or on a volunteer trip. A paying job is good, too. Hopefully, it is a job with physical activity and no alcohol.

4. If tasks feel overwhelming, do less.

5. Focus on one need at a time, starting with the basics of shelter and food. Work your way up from there.

6. People want to help. Have a list of your needs to hand over a task when someone offers.

7. In high cost of living areas, if your household income is less than $100,000, you need subsidies. This is due to the high proportion of income that needs to go to housing, childcare, and healthcare. See number 6 above to get help applying for subsidies.

8. Not all institutions are evil. Some actually have helpful programs.

9. Life is messy. Even when we do everything right, things happen. Your kids are human and so are their parents. Few things in life work perfectly. Keep trying.

10. Nothing gets done well without the holy trinity of nutrition, exercise, and sleep.

11. The Avengers don't live in this universe. We are the superheroes here.

12. Find friends who take you in the direction of your goals, not away. It's just as easy to pick up good habits as bad ones.

13. The phone number 211 is a national mega resource. It is staffed by volunteers from social service agencies such as the United Way.

14. Child support amounts in this country are shockingly low, if paid at all. The top 12 percent paid an average of $2,900 annually, and the median amount of all is just $900 per year. If that's you, explore options for income—a better job, more subsidies, and/or less spending.

15. To get a better solution, ask yourself: What is the goal here and what do my counterparties (employer/teachers/coparent) need?

16. You're a professional, not a fake. Parenting requires the same professionalism as your workday job.

    You show up and stay on the job. You even "perform while hurt."

    You're committed for the long haul. You're not dabbling.

    The stakes are high. It's about feeding our families.

    You're continuously looking to improve and master skills.

And finally, I've heard enough self-doubt from single parents to know it is common. You aren't a fake parent, a fraud, an imposter, or "failing your kids" because you aren't a partnered parent. Au contraire! My daughter exclaims: "You're more a parent than most. You do it all. You couldn't hand off anything, even anxiety." Thanks, child.

Two Steps Forward

THROUGH MY WORK MODERATING ONLINE COMMUNITIES since their inception, I've been witness to amazing acts of bravery and fortitude from parents. Even before becoming involved in single-parent communities, I oversaw online communities for firms like Kellogg's, Schwab, Bank of America, and Novartis. I listened to members' conversations about health, diet, money, and dreams. Over ten years I sat with them holding virtual hands over family, love, loss, and success. Through all these people, I've gained the courage to put forth the lessons from their lives and my own.

Behind every person I've never met is a tale of transformation. People getting unstuck from bad domestic situations, moving on from relationships, raising children to adults, and succeeding in different ways. What they've all had in common is living in countries where people can vote, drink clean water (mostly), and educate both their sons and daughters. With that foundation, I hope this book takes you forward to the next level of living your best life.

The pandemic interrupted a lot of plans. It disrupted lives and caused untold sorrow and illness. Nothing can make up for the lives lost.

But disruption had its upsides. We learned the social value of universal income. So many parents wrote about the federal pandemic payments giving them a floor to stand on and the ability to move closer to their goals. It put remote work, a lifeline for single parents, into the mainstream. Time-saving services, so vital to one-parent households, became the norm. Grocery delivery, online shopping, car sharing, telehealth, hotels to house the homeless, online education, and remote work are all here to stay and are moving single parents toward equal footing.

There is still much to do. The health profession needs to confront and shed its ingrained bias about single parents. Employers, while they have learned to trust employees, need to rethink job requirements. *Single parents are engines of efficiency.* Businesses need to think differently to get the best from their single-parent employees. Designing job descriptions for this particular class can only benefit everyone.

Finally, single parents need a reputation reversal. *We are models of perseverance and parenting. Not a drag on society.* We raise kids to be independent, responsible, and sociable. We, as single parents, should insist that this be recognized, celebrated, and supported.

My own story of single parenting is still unfolding. My daughter graduated from college with the STEM degree she wanted. She wants to revive species from extinction. I retired from full-time corporate work. We've made it to the other side of childhood and have adulthood to look forward to. I hope this book helps you do that, too.

Acknowledgments

Part 1 of this book emphasizes the importance of single parents assembling their team. Little did I know what a front-row seat I would get on that subject. As I turned into the homestretch in writing this book, I experienced five unrelated health events, ultimately ending with a total hip replacement. My successful journey through that year is attributed to the healthcare team.

Dr. Helen M. Hunt, my longtime primary care doctor served as my sounding board and quarterback. While I kept a spreadsheet of all the appointments, players, and treatments, Dr. Hunt cleared extraneous processes, interfaced with specialists, and kept up my morale.

Drs. Michael Muto and **Vito Pugliano**, the surgeons whose skill along with their teams at Dana Farber, Brigham & Women's, and the New England Baptist hospitals minimized the recovery times needed and humanized medicine for this layperson.

Dean A. Bonneau, PT, DPT, the physical therapist who got me back on my feet and kept me there through the rolling waves of diagnoses for one year. He unflinchingly adapted to each new challenge thrown his way.

And especially **Christopher L. Brown, CSCS, CES,** a gifted strength, conditioning, and health coach who stood by me through diagnoses, prehabs, and rehabs over the course of several years. Chris made me a practical believer in the mind/body approach to be "better than before."

Thanks also to the production team who made this book possible:

Gary Rosenberg, Designer

Julie Wittes Schlack, Developmental Editor

Natalie Silver, Copyeditor

Larissa Henoch, Illustrator

Lori Lewis, Proofreader

Lanette Sweeney, Editorial Assessment

And special thanks to my cheerleaders:

Christine Fordyce, a single parent who told me to "just write the book."

Nancy Goulet, a graphic designer who encouraged me throughout the journey

Notes

Why and How to Use This Book

there are a lot of us: "U.S. Census Table FG.5," U.S. Census ACS 2023, 2023, www2.census.gov/programs-surveys/demo/tables/families/2023/cps-2023/taba3.xls.

internal vulnerability and external stress: Zoe E. Taylor and Rand D. Conger, "Promoting Strengths and Resilience in Single-Mother Families," *Child Development* 8, no. 2 (2017): 350–358, https://srcd.onlinelibrary.wiley.com/doi/10.1111/cdev.12741; and Elizabeth Kjellstrand and Melanie Harper, "Yes, She Can: An Examination of Resiliency Factors in Middle- and Upper-Income Single Mothers," *Journal of Divorce and Remarriage* 53, no. 4 (2012): 311–327, https://www.tandfonline.com/doi/full/10.1080/10502556.2012.671677.

Part 1: Keeping Yourself Healthy and (Relatively) Sane

■ Chapter 1: The Tao of Single Parenting

social bias: Sarah L. DeJean, Christi R. McGeorge, and Thomas Stone Carlson, "Attitudes Toward Never-Married Parents: Does Gender Matter," *Journal of Feminist Family Therapy* 24 (2012): 121–124, https://www.tandfonline.com/doi/abs/10.1080/08952833.2012.648121.

"good enough mother": D. W. Winnicott, *The Child, the Family, and the Outside World* (UK: Penguin, 2021).

"you need to start building your team of people": John D. Spooner, *No One Ever Told Us That: Money and Life Lessons for Young Adults* (New York: John Wiley and Sons, 2015).

■ Chapter 2: The Art of Well-Being in the Face of Stress

a clothing rotation: Amy Dacyczyn, *The Complete Tightwad Gazette: Promoting Thrift as a Viable Alternative Lifestyle* (New York: Villard, 1998).

In fact, they are mimicking nature: P. Hunter, "Understanding Redundancy and Resilience, *EMBO Reports (Print)* 23, no. 3 (2022), https://doi.org/10.15252/embr.202254742.

good health outcomes with the length of a doctor relationship: R. Olaison, "Assessing the Longitudinal Impact of Physician-Patient Relationship on Functional Health," *Ann Fam Med*, no. 5 (September 2020): 422–429, https://doi.org/10.1370/afm.2554.

Chapter 3: Childcare

Even the most income constrained: Living Wage Calculator, livingwage.mit.edu.

Elliot-Pearson School of Child Development: Tufts Child Development Center, Tufts University, Medford, MA.

Foundation grants: Raise the Barr Foundation provides grants for BIPOC student parents. RaisetheBarr.org. Lumina Foundation makes grants directly to community colleges, and you can see their grantees on their website. Lumina Foundation, "Lumina Foundation | Working to Make Learning After High School Available to All," August 25, 2022, luminafoundation.org.

Chapter 4: Legal Help

Consumer Reports conducted a review: "LegalZoom | Nolo | Rocket Lawyer," Consumer Reports, www.consumerreports.org/cro/magazine/2012/09/legal-diy-websites-are-no-match-for-a-pro/ index.htm.

using in-kind types of support: Lenna Nepomnyaschy et al., "Nonresident Fathers and the Economic Precarity of Their Children," *Annals of the American Academy of Political and Social Science* 702, no. 1 (July 2022): 78–96, https://doi.org/10.1177/00027162221119348.

Chapter 6: The "Medicals," AKA Your Care Team

Continuity—having a long-term relationship: R. Henry Olaisen, Mark D. Schlucter, Susan A. Flocke, Kathleen A. Smyth, Siran Koroukian, and Kurt C. Stange, "Assessing the Longitudinal Impact of Physician-Patient Relationship on Functional Health," *Annals of Family Medicine* 18, no. 5 (2020): 422–429, https://pmc.ncbi.nlm.nih.gov/articles/PMC7489969/

Maintenance Medicals: "Physician Assistants and Nurse Practitioners Serve Similar Purposes in Medical Settings. Learn About Differences in Their Training and Approach to Patient Care," Mass College of Pharmacy and Health Sciences (n.d.), www.mcphs.edu/about/news/physician-assistant-vs-nurse-practitioner#:~:text=Physician%20assistants%20train%20using%20the,the%20patient%20with%20the%20disease.

same or better outcome: Kjellstrand and Harper, "Yes, She Can."

Speak Up About Insecurities: K. C. Davis, *How to Keep House While Drowning: A Gentle Approach to Cleaning and Organizing,* (New York: Simon and Schuster, 2022).

single-parent negative bias: Kjellstrand and Harper, "Yes, She Can."

Chapter 7: Therapists

"two years of 'psychological malnutrition' from the pandemic": Shoba Sreenivasan, "Psychological Nutrition for Caregivers," *Psychology Today*, March 11, 2021, www.psychologytoday.com/us/blog/emotional-nourishment/201906/psychological-nutrition-caregivers#:~:text=In%20the%20zone%20of%20psychological%20malnutrition%2C%20it%20is%20impossible%20to,fatigue%2C%20emptiness%2C%20and%20burnout.

fatherhood counseling in North Carolina: D.W. Anderson, *Daddy's Green Book* (North Carolina: Dar'ron Anderson, 2020).

Part 2.   Time: How to Make More when You Have None

▧ Chapter 8: Time Management for Single Parents

a "Miracle Worker" moment: "The Miracle Worker," Wikipedia, February 26, 2023, en.wikipedia.org/wiki/The_Miracle_Worker.

▧ Chapter 9: Creating Time

chores to work into their schedule: Tara Aronson, *Mrs. Clean Jean's Housekeeping with Kids: Family Pick Up Lines (and Household Routines) That Work with Less Work from You* (Emmaus, PA: Rodale Press, 2004).

fast getaways because I tipped: John D. Spooner, *No One Ever Told Us That: Money and Life Lessons for Young Adults* (New York: John Wiley and Sons, 2015).

description of bullet journaling: Ryder Carroll, *The Bullet Journal Method: Track Your Past, Order Your Present, Plan Your Future* (New York: Fourth Estate, 2018).

We free ourselves by planning: Tracey McBride, *Frugal Luxuries: Simple Pleasures to Enhance Your Life and Comfort Your Soul* (New York: Bantam: 1997).

With enough practice, it gets easier: James Clear, *Atomic Habits: An Easy and Proven Way to Build Good Habits & Break Bad Ones* (New York: Penguin, 2018).

a self-compassionate approach to managing your home: Davis, *How to Keep House While Drowning.*

Lose the Time Wasters: Dave Navarro, *More Time Now: A Pretty Simple Way to Invest One Hour a Week to Free Up 1000 Hours a Year* (n.d.), www.rockyourday.com.

▧ Chapter 10: What Is the Value of Your Time?

snowplow drivers to sixteen-hour shifts: Karen Anderson, "Fatigue, Few Rules Surround Snowplow Drivers in Storms," WCVB, www.wcvb.com/article/5-investigates-fatigue-few-rules-surround-snowplow-drivers-in-storms/8216959.

Bureau of Labor Statistics reports: US Census Bureau, "Explore Census Data," data.census.gov/table?q=DP02.

the "expected value" to estimate a wage equivalent: "Calculating the Value of Time: How Much Is Your Time Really Worth?," Lifehacker, December 28, 2015, lifehacker.com/calculating-the-value-of-time-how-much-is-your-time-re-1749954358.

Determine your salary: "Salary.com Homepage," Salary.com, April 2021, salary.com.

▧ Chapter 11: Home Management: Finding Efficiencies on Every Front

It Started with the Pilgrims: Nathaniel Philbrick, *Mayflower. A Story of Courage, Community, and War* (New York: Penguin Books, 2007).

"You can accomplish a lot": Gretchen Rubin, *The Happiness Project: Or, Why I Spent a Year Trying to Sing in the Morning, Clean My Closets, Fight Right, Read Aristotle, and Generally Have More Fun*, rev. ed. (New York: HarperCollins, 2015).

from an a la carte junk food line: Janet Poppendieck, *Free for All: Fixing School Food in America* (Berkeley, C.A.: Univ of California Press, 2011).

putting out the ingredients: "Mise En Place, Teach the Sous Chef, Save the Patient," ICE (blog), April 6, 2021, icenetblog.royalcollege.ca/2021/02/02/mise-en-place-teach-the-sous-chef-save-the-patient.

"Thrifty Food Plan": "Recipes and Tips for Healthy, Thrifty Meals | Food and Nutrition Service," USDA Food Plans, https://ucanr.edu/sites/default/files/2010-06/14394.pdf.

Expired Food: Lea Ceasrine, "How to Tell Whether Expired Food Is Safe to Eat," *Consumer Reports*, July 24, 2018, www.consumerreports.org/food-safety/how-to-tell-whether-expired-food-is-safe-to-eat-a1083080425.

Expired Food: Sarah Gonzalez, "Expiration Dates Lead to Lots of Food Waste, Though These Dates Vary Widely by State," NPR, July 28, 2022, www.npr.org/2022/07/28/1114335397/expiration-dates-lead-to-lots-of-food-waste-though-these-dates-vary-widely-by-st.

the seven-year maintenance rule: Penelope Wang, "How Long to Keep Tax Records and Other Documents," *Consumer Reports*, February 18, 2019, www.consumerreports.org/money/taxes/how-long-to-keep-tax-documents-a5302825423.

Part 3: Money

Chapter 12: Increasing Your Income from Wages

Single parents need more childcare hours: Brigid Schulte and Stavroula Pabst, "How Companies Can Support Single Parents," SHRM, July 8, 2021, www.shrm.org/resourcesandtools/hr-topics/employee-relations/pages/how-companies-can-support-single-parents.aspx.

"Great Exploitation": Juhohn Lee, "Why American Wages Haven't Grown Despite Increases in Productivity," CNBC, July 19, 2022, www.cnbc.com/2022/07/19/heres-how-labor-dynamism-affects-wage-growth-in-america.html#:~:text=Wages%20in%20the%20U.S.%20have,times%20as%20fast%20at%2061.8%25.

"Great Exploitation": Daniel H. Pink, *A Whole New Mind: Why Right-Brainers Will Rule the Future* (New York: Penguin, 2006).

Enter the Growth Multiplier: Indeed Editorial Team, "What Is the Multiplier Effect and How Do You Calculate It?," Indeed Career Guide, August 2022, www.indeed.com/career-advice/career-development/multiplier-effect.

improving single parents' income: Emma Johnson, *The Kickass Single Mom: Be Financially Independent, Discover Your Sexiest Self, and Raise Fabulous, Happy Children* New York: Penguin, 2017).

Read Warren Berger's book: Warren Berger, *The Book of Beautiful Questions* (New York: Bloomsbury USA, 2019), questions online in "Qcards," http://amorebeautifulquestion.com/wp-content/uploads/2019/02/Q-Cards-2019.pdf.

This requires a budget: "Gain Total Control of Your Money with YNAB," YNAB, Dec 8, 2022, www.ynab.com.

cost-of-living calculations: Living Wage Calculator, livingwage.mit.edu.

CareerOneStop centers: Massachusetts Get Hired, https://portal.masscis.intocareers.org.

"a credential in a skill they need": Jon Marcus, "More Students Are 'Stacking' Credentials en Route to a Degree," *Wired*, June 2, 2020, www.wired.com/story/students-stacking-credentials-route-degree.

◼ Chapter 13: Other Income Streams

Aiming for Financial Independence: Johnson, *The Kickass Single Mom.*

advice on spousal and child support: Suze Orman, *The Road to Wealth: The Answers You Need to More Than 2,000 Personal Finance Questions, Revised and Updated* (New York: National Geographic Books, 2010).

Solely focusing on [child support and alimony] has impacts: Nepomnyaschy et al., "Nonresident Fathers."

Massachusetts Institute of Technology 2022 Cost of Living study: Living Wage Calculator, living-wage.mit.edu.

◼ Chapter 14: Expenses: How to Spend Your Money

Ameriprise Financial published a study: Ameriprise Financial. "Retirement and Life Events Insights," Ameriprise Financial, www.ameriprise.com/financial-news-research/studies.

suggests that accepting childcare in lieu of payments: Nepomnyaschy et al., "Nonresident Fathers."

estimated my car was costing me: Jeff S. Bartlett, "The Cost of Car Ownership over Time," Consumer Reports, Apr 8, 2021, www.consumerreports.org/cars/car-maintenance/the-cost-of-car-ownership-a1854979198.

Graduation Employment Outcomes: National Center for Education Statistics, "Employment Outcomes of Bachelor's Degree Holders," 2020, nces.ed.gov/programs/coe/pdf/coe_sbc.pdf.

◼ Chapter 15: Savings

Dave Ramsey's Snowball Debt Reduction Plan: Dave Ramsey, *The Total Money Makeover: A Proven Plan for Financial Fitness* (Nashville, TN: Thomas Nelson, 2009).

message of prioritizing what's important: Vicki Robin and Joe Dominguez, *Your Money or Your Life: 9 Steps to Transforming Your Relationship with Money and Achieving Financial Independence* (New York: Penguin, 2008).

another financial celebrity: Orman, *The Road to Wealth.*

following six strategies: Bankrate, "What Will It Take to Pay Off My Credit Card?," Bankrate, https://bankrate.com/finance/credit-cards/credit-card-payoff-calculator.

try the debt snowball method: Anna Baluch, "What Is the Debt Snowball Strategy?," Bankrate, www.bankrate.com/personal-finance/debt/debt-snowball/.

How to Save for Multiple Goals: Brian Spinelli, "How to Balance Saving for Retirement and Your Kids' Education," Kiplinger.com, October 29, 2021; and "How to Save for Multiple Financial Goals," Schwab Brokerage, www.schwab.com/learn/story/how-to-save-multiple-financial-goals.

■ Chapter 16: Insurance: Protecting What's Yours

Calculating How Much Life Insurance: US Department of Agriculture. "Expenditures on Children by Families | Food and Nutrition Service," USDA, www.fns.usda.gov/cnpp/expenditures-children-families; and US Department of Agriculture, "The Cost of Raising a Child," USDA, www.usda.gov/media/blog/2017/01/13/cost-raising-child.

what a child costs to raise: Carolyn Edwards, *USDA Estimates of the Cost of Raising a Child: A Guide to Their Use and Interpretation* (UK: Forgotten Books, 2018. USDA, Washington, DC).

Part 4: Relationships with Kids, Peers, and Potential Partners

■ Chapter 17: Parenting Alone or Coparenting

interaction with noncustodial parents is more important than: Nepomnyaschy et al., "Nonresident Fathers."

seminal book on negotiation: Roger Fisher and William Ury, *Getting to Yes: Negotiating an Agreement Without Giving In* (New York: Random House, 2012).

"Don't Make Trust an Issue": Roger Fisher and Scott Brown, *Getting Together: Building a Relationship That Gets to Yes* (Boston: Houghton Mifflin Harcourt, 1988).

Don't make trust an issue: Shelly M. Ingram, "Using Technology to Find Answers to Common Child Custody Problems and Keep the Peace While Co-Parenting," ABA Family Law Section, 2021, www.americanbar.org/groups/family_law/publications/family-advocate/2021/summer/using-technology-find-answers-common-child-custody-problems-keep-peace-while-co-parenting.

"Rules of Engagement": Camilla Guldahl Cooper, *NATO Rules of Engagement on ROE, Self-Defence and the Use of Force During Armed Conflict*, n.d., https://brill.com/view/title/55119?language=en.

■ Chapter 18: Mindful Parent, Resilient Kids

It is easier to build strong children: Frederick Douglass, *My Bondage and My Freedom* (London, U.K.: Open Road Media, 2020).

What if, instead, we focus: Annie E. Casey Foundation, "Child Well-Being in Single-Parent Families," June 23, 2023, www.aecf.org/blog/child-well-being-in-single-parent-families.

islands of competence: Robert B. Brooks and Sam Goldstein, *Nurturing Resilience in Our Children: Answers to the Most Important Parenting Questions* (New York: McGraw Hill 2002).

"It is possible to commit no mistakes and still lose": *Star Trek: The Next Generation*, season 2, episode 21, "Peak Performance," www.youtube.com/watch?v=t4A-Ml8YHyM.

"Would you rather be right": Warren Berger, "Home Overview—a More Beautiful Question by Warren Berger," A More Beautiful Question by Warren Berger, March 3, 2022, https://amorebeautiful-question.com/.

■ Chapter 19: Understanding Child Development (in Brief) for the Early Years

a developmental psychologist: Howard E. Gardner, *Multiple Intelligences: The Theory in Practice, a Reader* (New York: Basic Books, 1993).

■ Chapter 20: School Age Through Young Adulthood

Single parents, this is your time: Elizabeth M. White, Mark D. DeBoer, and Rebecca J. Scharf, "Associations Between Household Chores and Childhood Self-Competency," *Journal of Developmental and Behavioral Pediatrics* 40, no. 3 (2019): 176–182, https://doi.org/10.1097/dbp.0000000000000637.

A *New York Times* article: Lisa Damour, "What Do Teenagers Want? Potted Plant Parents," *New York Times,* December 14, 2016, www.nytimes.com/2016/12/14/well/family/what-do-teenagers-want-potted-plant-parents.html?action=click&module=RelatedCoverage&pgtype=Article&ion=Footer.

Brain development undergoes a "rewiring": Mariam S. Arain et al., "Maturation of the Adolescent Brain," *Neuropsychiatric Disease and Treatment* (April 2013): 449, https://doi.org/10.2147/ndt.s39776.

Boomerang Kids: Richard Fry et al., "A Majority of Young Adults in the U.S. Live with Their Parents for the First Time Since the Great Depression," Pew Research Center, September 9, 2020, www.pewresearch.org/fact-tank/2020/09/04/a-majority-of-young-adults-in-the-u-s-live-with-their-parents-for-the-first-time-since-the-great-depression; and National Academies of Sciences, Engineering, and Medicine et al., *Families Caring for an Aging America* ([Place of publication]: National Academies Press, 2016).

discusses in detail the mental pivots: Laurence Steinberg, *You and Your Adult Child: How to Grow Together in Challenging Times* (New York: Simon and Schuster, 2023).

Treating a Grown Child: Jim Burns, *Doing Life with Your Adult Children: Keep Your Mouth Shut and the Welcome Mat Out* (Grand Rapids, MI: Zondervan, 2019).

■ Chapter 21: Parenting Through Troubling Behavior

care for "an adult with an emotional or mental health issue": Jessica Grose, "When the Parenting Never Stops," *New York Times,* February 16, 2022.

professor at the Graduate School of Social Service: Judith R. Smith, *Difficult: Mothering Challenging Adult Children Through Conflict and Change* (Lanham, MD: Rowman & Littlefield, 2022).

caregiving for adults with mental illness: National Alliance for Caregiving, *On Pins and Needles: Caregivers of Adults with Mental Illness,* February 2016, www.caregiving.org/wp-content/uploads/2020/05/NAC_Mental_Illness_Study_2016_FINAL_WEB.pdf.

■ Chapter 22: Fun: How to Laugh and Enjoy Each Other

oddball collections: "Your Online Guide to Offbeat Tourist Attractions," Roadside America, RoadsideAmerica.com.

"small but mighty": Patricia Corrigan, "Quirky Museums Across America," NextAvenue, June 10, 2022, https://www.nextavenue.org/life-coach-powerful-questions/.

tastes run sophisticated: "The Definitive Guide to the World's Hidden Wonders," Atlas Obscura, www.atlasobscura.com.

sculptures presenting nine planets: "Solar System Models," Wikipedia, en.wikipedia.org/wiki/Solar_System_model.

▨ Chapter 23: Friends, Enemies, and Peripherals

How Many Friends Is Enough?: Suzanne Degges-White, "How Many Friends Do You Really Need in Adulthood?," *Psychology Today*, August 9, 2019, www.psychologytoday.com/us/blog/lifetime-connections/201908/how-many-friends-do-you-really-need-in-adulthood.

Atlantic magazine wrote a fun article: Sheon Han, "You Can Only Maintain So Many Close Friendships," *Atlantic*, May 20, 2021, www.theatlantic.com/family/archive/2021/05/robin-dunbar-explains-circles-friendship-dunbars-number/618931.

Different Friends for Different Purposes: Shasta Nelson, *Friendships Don't Just Happen! The Guide to Creating a Meaningful Circle of Girlfriends* (Nashville, TN: Turner, 2013).

Tone is important: Warren Berger, *A More Beautiful Question*, March 3, 2022, amorebeautifulquestion.com.

Metro Boston declared a natural disaster: "March 2010 Nor'easter Boston, MA," Wikipedia, en.wikipedia.org/wiki/March_2010_nor%27easter.

▨ Chapter 24: Pests, Pervs, Annoyances, and Other Distractions

scandal of the Boston Catholic Archdiocese: Josh Singer, *Spotlight*, directed by Tom McCarthy, 2013.

Big Tobacco once used the same playbook: Naomi Nix et al., "Is This Facebook's 'Big Tobacco' Moment?," BusinessLive.com, www.businesslive.co.za/bd/life/gadgets-and-gear/2021-09-27-is-this-facebooks-big-tobacco-moment.

▨ Chapter 26: Start Living the Life You Want

"Single mothers might set goals": Kjellstrand and Harper, "Yes, She Can."

"Write down 25 things": Oliver Burkeman, *Four Thousand Weeks: Time Management for Mortals* (New York: Picador USA, 2023).

"it's hard for us to think about what we want to do": Dana Shavin, "Ask Yourself These Six Powerful Questions Today," NextAvenue.org, July 9, 2021, www.nextavenue.org/life-coach-powerful-questions/.

a grumpy old guy wrote a tongue-in-cheek book: Arnold Bennett, *How to Live on 24 Hours a Day* (Glasgow, Scotland: Moncrieff Press, 2011).

It put remote work: Pabilonia, S. W. and J. J. Redmond. 2024. "The Rise in Remote Work Since the Pandemic and Its Impact on Productivity." Bureau of Labor Statistics: Beyond the Numbers 13, no. 8. https://www.bls.gov/opub/btn/volume-13/remote-work-productivity.htm.

About the Authors

Patricia Hankin independently raised her child to adulthood and regularly contributed to an online single-parent forum with 470,000 members. After repeatedly answering the same questions, she started keeping a file of resources in response to many of those questions. It was one post that put her into action to codify that information: "What books can I read to find out about single parenting?" A light bulb went off and Pat wrote THE book—a resource guide to help deal with the most common questions and offering advice tailored to the 19 million single parents in this country.

Her long business career allows her to speak with authority on personal finance, time management, risk management, and building personal teams to support oneself. Her daughter, now a laboratory science specialist, chimes in from her experience. They live in the Boston area.

Jessica Ames, LICSW, is a well-known family engagement therapist and contributes here to the parenting topics. She received a master's degree in clinical social work from Smith College. Jessica has worked at renowned institutions—Boston Children's, Mass General Hospitals, and the Manville School at Judge Baker Children's Center. She also has a private practice in Wellesley, Massachusetts.